THE
CREDIT
REPAIR
KIT

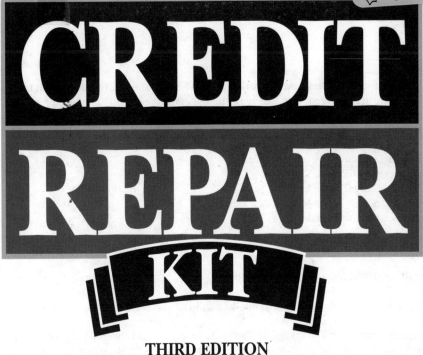

THIRD EDITION

JOHN VENTURA

Dearborn
Financial Publishing, Inc.®

This publication is designed to provide accurate and authoritative information in regard to the subject matter covered. It is sold with the understanding that the publisher is not engaged in rendering legal, accounting, or other professional service. If legal advice or other expert assistance is required, the services of a competent professional person should be sought.

Editorial Director: Cynthia A. Zigmund
Managing Editor: Jack Kiburz
Interior Design: Lucy Jenkins
Cover Design: S. Laird Jenkins Corporation
Typesetting: the dotted i

Published by Dearborn Financial Publishing, Inc.®

Printed in the United States of America

98 99 00 10 9 8 7 6 5 4 3 2

Library of Congress Cataloging-in-Publication Data
Ventura, John.
   The credit repair kit / John Ventura. — 3rd ed.
     p. c.m.
   Includes index.
   ISBN 0-7931-2746-7 (pbk.)
    1. Credit ratings—United States.   2. Credit bureaus—United
States.   3. Consumer credit—United States.   4. Consumer protection—
Law and legislation—United States.   I. Title
   HG3751.7.V46   1998
   332.7′43—dc21
                                     97-38969
                                       CIP

Dearborn books are available at special quantity discounts to use as premiums and sales promotions, or for use in corporate training programs. For more information, please call the Special Sales Manager at 800-621-9621, ext. 4384, or write to Dearborn Financial Publishing, Inc., 155 North Wacker Drive, Chicago, IL 60606-1719.

Dedication

To my beautiful daughters, Wendy and Misty, of whom I am very proud.

Contents

Preface

During the early 1990s, when the first edition of *The Credit Repair Kit* was published, the credit reporting industry was under fire from state attorneys general, the Federal Trade Commission (FTC), and consumer groups. Among the complaints: Consumer credit record problems were causing consumers to be turned down for credit, jobs, and insurance; credit bureaus were not responsive to consumers' efforts to correct the problems; and credit reporting agencies were making money selling personal information about the consumers whose records were in their databases.

Since that time, the credit reporting industry has gone through a tremendous number of changes for the better. Some of those changes have been the result of actions by state attorneys general and the FTC. Others were initiated by the credit reporting industry itself. In addition, at the end of 1996, Congress passed a sweeping piece of legislation called the Consumer Credit Reporting Reform Act of 1996. This law amends the federal Fair Credit Reporting Act (FCRA) in many important ways. The FCRA is the federal law that governs the credit reporting industry and that established the rights of consumers in dealing with credit bureaus. Some of the new amendments are good for consumers, others are not.

Despite the new legislation and all of the industry reforms we have seen over the past nearly ten years, understanding your credit report, dealing with any problems in it, and rebuilding your credit after financial difficulties still can be challenging and confusing. Therefore, my goal for this third edition of *The Credit Repair Kit* remains the same—to provide you with the knowledge and tools you need to deal successfully with credit bureaus and to rebuild your credit history, whether it was damaged because you took on too much debt, or you lost your job and could no longer pay all of your bills, or because of other circumstances. To help you, the third edition of *The Credit Repair Kit* includes the following:

- A full explanation of all your rights under the FCRA, including explanations of the 1996 amendments that are most important to you
- Updated instructions on obtaining your report from "the big three" credit bureaus—Experian (formerly TRW), Equifax, and Trans Union

- Up-to-date sample reports from the big three with easy-to-understand explanations of how to read them
- Time-saving sample letters that get results and create a paper trail that you may need later
- Addresses of government agencies and consumer groups that can help you
- A detailed explanation of the special credit-related issues that women face as well as information about how to protect your credit when you are getting a divorce

This new edition of *The Credit Repair Kit* also includes an expanded chapter on preserving the privacy of your credit record information and other personal financial information in today's high-tech world, and a brand new chapter on using credit wisely once you have rebuilt your credit history after serious money troubles.

The Credit Repair Kit is not just for the financially distressed. It's for anyone who wants to be sure that credit record misinformation or other problems will not jeopardize their chances to obtain an important loan, new job, or the insurance they need. In fact, every consumer, regardless of income, should request a copy of his or her credit report from each of the big three once a year and review it for problems.

In a culture where an estimated 50 percent of all American marriages end in divorce, this book can help prepare both men and women for the financial repercussions of a failed marriage. It explains to the female reader why it is so important for her to have a credit history in her own name separate from her husband's, and how to build one. *The Credit Repair Kit* also advises couples contemplating divorce about the things they should do before they divorce so that their credit is not damaged as a result of their change in marital status, and it tells them how to keep their postdivorce financial ties to a minimum.

I have seen many sad cases of people whose lives have been damaged by negative credit histories. Sometimes those histories were the result of credit bureau mistakes; sometimes they were due to creditors that provided a credit bureau with erroneous information about a consumer; and sometimes they were the fault of the consumers themselves—who didn't pay credit accounts on time or took on more debt than they could handle. Regardless of the reason, if you have a bad credit history, your life will be tougher than it needs to be as a result. Without good credit, you will be denied many opportunities for success and happiness.

You and you alone must take responsibility for the accuracy of your credit record and for maintaining or rebuilding a good credit history for yourself. Your wise use of credit combined with the information in this book can help you create a positive financial future for yourself and your family. Good luck!

Acknowledgments

Special thanks to all the people at Dearborn whose dedication helps make working with them such a pleasure.

CHAPTER 1

The Power of Credit Bureaus

Margaret and Joe O. were unaware that a "sleeping giant" was following them through their credit life. Not until they applied for a loan to buy their first home did they realize how important that giant was—and how much trouble it would cause them. The sleeping giant was a credit bureau.

When Margaret and Joe were refused a loan for their dream house, they came to see me about what they could do. The mortgage lender they had applied to for a loan had told them that information in their credit file was responsible for the denial of their credit application. They brought with them a copy of the credit report that reflected the negative information.

"We have worked hard to keep our credit clean," Joe said. "We just don't understand what's wrong."

After reviewing their report with them, we discovered that it contained credit information on a bad debt that Margaret and Joe didn't know anything about.

I explained Margaret and Joe's rights under the Fair Credit Reporting Act, and we sent a letter to the credit bureau disputing the bad debt.

......

After a wait that almost lost the couple their dream home, the credit bureau determined that the incorrect information actually belonged to someone with a name similar to Joe's and notified Margaret and Joe that the error in their credit record had been corrected; however, the couple had experienced a lot of anguish and worry waiting to find out if their credit record would be corrected and if they would get their home loan.

This is just one example of the role that credit reporting agencies can play in your life. It's also a good example of why it's important to request a copy of your credit record at least once a year so you can review it for problems and why you should always review your credit record before you apply for important credit. If you don't, you may find yourself in the same situation as Joe and Margaret.

The Fair Credit Reporting Act (FCRA) was passed by Congress in 1970 to regulate the credit reporting industry. It established consumers' legal rights in regard to their credit records and credit record information, and it gave them certain rights when dealing with credit reporting agencies. In late 1996, this law was amended in many important ways with the passage of the Consumer Credit Reporting Reform Act (CCRRA). Some of the amendments benefit consumers but others work to their disadvantage, benefiting the credit reporting industry and users of credit bureau information.

As you read this book, three facts will become very apparent:

1. The credit reporting industry can have a significant effect on your life.
2. Not having a positive credit history can cause you to miss out on important opportunities.
3. Despite the many changes that have occurred in the credit reporting industry since the last edition of this book was written, consumers still find inaccuracies in their credit records and still encounter problems getting those inaccuracies permanently removed.

Therefore, it's important that each of you have a basic understanding of the credit reporting industry and of your legal rights when you are dealing with credit bureaus. This chapter will help build that understanding by explaining how credit bureaus work and the roles they play in our lives.

What Are Credit Bureaus?

Credit reporting agencies or credit bureaus are part of a $1 billion industry. According to Associated Credit Bureaus, Inc., a trade association of credit bureaus and mortgage reporting companies in the United States, the industry consists of approximately 650 credit bureaus, most of which are association members. Most credit bureaus are owned by or affiliated with one of the three national companies that dominate the industry—Experian (formerly TRW), Equifax, and Trans Union—and are linked to their computer systems. These three companies are often referred to as "the big three." There are also smaller local or regional credit bureaus that have no relationship with the big three as well as large, national information brokers that purchase consumer credit information from the big three and resell that information to other businesses. These national information brokers often maintain multiple databases, consumer credit information being just one of those databases.

The vast computerized libraries maintained by credit bureaus act as credit-related information clearinghouses on most American adults. Credit bureaus sell this information to their subscribers—retailers, credit card companies, insurance companies, banks and savings and loans, credit unions, finance companies, and the like. It is estimated that the big three update almost 2 billion pieces of credit file information each month, received from thousands of businesses across the country, and generate more than 600 million consumer credit reports annually.

Information in Your Credit Record

A credit bureau maintains the information it collects on you in a credit record or file, which is actually a history of your use and management of credit.

Basic information in your credit record tells who has extended credit to you, whether you pay your bills on time, and how much you owe each of your creditors. A more complete discussion of credit record information can be found in Chapter 2.

Where Do Credit Bureaus Get Their Information?

Credit reporting agencies obtain information about you from four basic sources: *subscribers, collection agencies, public records,* and *you.* Credit bureaus update their information regularly to provide a month-to-month profile of your use of credit.

In most instances, credit bureau subscribers are companies that extend credit to consumers. They provide credit bureaus with information on the bill-paying habits of their account holders. Many credit bureaus require their subscribers to provide them with consumer account information on a monthly basis. Increasingly, creditors are using computers to relay consumer account information to credit reporting agencies, but some creditors continue to use manual methods.

Some collection agencies provide credit bureaus with information on accounts that are in collection.

Public records, the third source of credit bureau information, include bankruptcy filings, tax liens, and judgments. This information also appears in your credit record.

You are the fourth source of the data gathered and maintained by credit bureaus. When you fill out a credit application, you list identifying information, such as your name, current and former addresses, age, and Social Security number. This information becomes a part of your credit file.

Who Sees Your Credit Record?

A credit record is an extremely important document because it contains information that can affect many aspects of your life. Among other things, your credit record can influence your ability to obtain new or additional credit and the terms of that credit as well as your opportunity to have the type of job you would like, especially if you will have responsibility for money or expensive equipment.

Employers are increasing their use of credit reports because lie detector tests and other screening devices have been banned.

Credit record information may also affect your ability to get adequate insurance or to rent or buy a home or apartment. In addition, credit report information may prevent you from being granted a government security clearance or special license.

The FCRA specifies who may review your credit record and for what purposes. According to that law, access to your file is limited to the following:

- *Potential creditors.* Creditors may access consumer credit records to decide whether to extend credit, to review an account, or to collect a debt.
- *Potential insurers.* Insurers may access consumer credit records for information that will assist them in the underwriting of a personal, automobile, family, household, or medical insurance policy.
- *Employers.* Consumer credit record information is made available to employers or potential employers to help them make decisions regarding hiring, firing, reassignment, or promotion.
- *Potential investors, loan servicers, and current insurers.* These businesses can use consumer credit record data to value or assess the risks associated with an existing obligation.
- *The head of a state or local child support enforcement agency or a state or local government official authorized by the head of a child support enforcement agency.* The agency can review consumer credit record information to help it decide whether a parent must pay child support and the amount of those payments.
- *Others.* Others may review your credit record if you give them written permission to do so.

Additionally, your credit record may be reviewed if

- someone gets a court order to do so;
- the IRS subpoenas that information; or
- someone has a "legitimate business need" in connection with a business transaction you initiate. "Business transaction" includes the purchase of goods or services for your personal, family, or household use.

Insurers

Under the FCRA, insurers may review your credit record before granting you insurance. Some companies use the information in credit records to screen out high-risk applicants. Others use it to determine whether to give someone who is already insured additional coverage, to raise that person's insurance rate, or to terminate coverage altogether.

Employers

If you apply for a job with a new employer or for a promotion with your current employer, the employer can review a copy of your credit record as part of the screening process. Your current employer can also read your credit file as part of the process for deciding whether to take an adverse action against you—firing you perhaps. However, the FCRA says that before the employer can look at your credit record information, you must give it your written permission to do so.

Furthermore, before the employer can purchase your credit report, it must certify certain things in writing to the credit bureau selling it. Among other things, it must certify that it has told you in writing that it may review your credit record as part of its decision-making process and that you have a right to obtain a copy of your report.

Credit bureaus will not provide an employer certain kinds of consumer credit record information—the consumer's age, marital status, and account numbers for example.

If you do not get a job or promotion or if your current employer takes an adverse action against you as the result in whole or in part of information in your credit file, the employer must provide you with a copy of the credit report it reviewed along with information about your rights under the FCRA, including information about how to correct credit record problems. However, even if you contend that there are inaccuracies in your file, the employer still can deny you the job or promotion, or take adverse action against you. This is a good argument for the importance of reviewing your credit record on a regular basis and clearing up any problems you may find in it.

The employer must also provide you with the name, address, and telephone number of the credit reporting agency that generated the credit report. It must also give you the credit bureau's toll-free number, assuming that the agency maintains information on consumers nationwide.

Government Agencies

Any government agency may review your credit record for purposes of granting credit, hiring, or insuring. Government agencies may also review your credit file if you are being considered for a special license or a security clearance. For cases in which the law requires that your financial status or financial responsibility be reviewed, a government agency may use the information in your file to help determine your eligibility for a government benefit, including eligibility for welfare benefits. In addition, as a consequence of the 1996 amendments to the FCRA, the FBI is now allowed to access consumer credit reports in connection with an investigation.

Other than the specific purposes listed above, a government agency may access only identifying information from a credit report, such as your name, address, and the name of your employer.

Legitimate Business Need

Before the 1996 amendments to the FCRA, the law allowed anyone with a "legitimate business need" to gain access to a consumer's file. The FCRA did not define this term, which created a major loophole that credit reporting agencies used to their financial advantage. By interpreting the term *legitimate business need* broadly, the agencies turned consumer credit information into a profitable commodity. Many used the consumer information in their databases to develop new products and services not directly related to the extension of credit. Some of these products and services are reviewed later in this chapter.

During the early 1990s, consumer advocates attacked the buying and selling of consumer credit data as a violation of consumer privacy. They pointed out that when consumers provided the information in their credit files, they assumed the information would be used only to evaluate their creditworthiness. The consumer advocates also pointed out that credit bureaus are not required to remunerate consumers for the money they make buying and selling their credit record information. (The subject of credit bureaus and the buying and selling of consumer credit record information is discussed in detail in Chapter 9.)

State attorneys general and the Federal Trade Commission (FTC) responded to this criticism by taking a closer look at the buying and selling of consumer credit record information, and the FTC placed specific restrictions on the activity. In addition, under pressure from the FTC, Experian and Equifax stopped developing and selling target marketing lists derived from consumer credit record account data. Trans Union decided to fight the FTC in a lawsuit over its right to sell target marketing lists. The court's ruling on that suit is currently being appealed. If Trans Union wins, Experian and Equifax will be able to resume target marketing activities.

With the passage of the CCRRA, the term *legitimate business need* has been somewhat more narrowly defined. The law now allows anyone with a legitimate business need for a consumer's credit record information to review it in connection with a business transaction that a consumer has initiated or to determine whether the consumer continues to meet the terms of existing credit. For example, a bank card company might review an account to determine if it should initiate collection action, or a bank might use a consumer's credit record information to help it decide if it should modify a consumer's terms of credit. Prior to the CCRRA, a credit report could be provided in connection with any business transaction involving the consumer; in other words, the consumer did not have to initiate it.

What kind of impact this change in wording will actually have is up for debate. Although on the surface, for example, the change seems to prohibit credit bureaus from developing and selling target marketing lists, lawyers representing the credit industry argue otherwise. Ultimately, the issue will be resolved by the court's ruling in the Trans Union case mentioned above.

One thing, however, is for sure: the wording change now explicitly sanctions prescreening. Prescreening occurs when a credit bureau compares the information in its database of consumer credit record information against a set of criteria provided by creditors or insurers to compile a list of consumers that they can market to. They must make a firm offer to all of the consumers on the prescreened list. Creditors and insurers pay a lot of money for this service.

Related to a legitimate business need is a new provision in the law that applies to bank holding companies or to any conglomerate. The amended FCRA now provides that these kinds of businesses can obtain consumer credit record information and then share it with their affiliated companies— companies related by common ownership. In turn, those affiliated companies can share and use that information without having to comply with most of the FCRA's privacy protections and accuracy requirements. This new provision may even allow conglomerates to create their own in-house credit bureaus for the use of their affiliated companies as a way to get around most of the FCRA's consumer protection provisions. This change in the law may mean that countless companies will be beyond the FCRA when it comes to the data in your credit record.

Credit Bureau Security

To become a credit bureau subscriber, a company must meet certain qualifications—and prove that it is in fact a business. For proof, someone from the credit bureau must actually visit the business. These security measures help protect credit bureau information from being scrutinized by companies that are not intending to use it for authorized purposes.

Once accepted as a subscriber, a company gets a special code and a security number, both of which are part of the security system that credit reporting agencies must have to help prevent unauthorized access to the data in their files. Companies must provide the credit bureau with its security code and number when requesting information about your credit history.

Credit bureau security systems, however, have been known to fail. Therefore, when reading your credit report, take note of who has reviewed your file. Whenever someone asks to review your credit file, that request will show up in your credit report as an inquiry. If you don't recognize the name of the company or organization that has made an inquiry into your credit file, contact the credit reporting agency. For more information about the inquiries section of a credit report, see Chapter 2.

 HOT TIP

To help protect your credit information from getting into the wrong hands, the FCRA now requires that companies purchasing credit record information for resale tell the credit bureau the name of the end user and explain how the end user will be using the information. Credit bureaus are required to establish systems for establishing and certifying the identity of end users.

Investigative Reports

A few credit reporting agencies provide investigative reports for companies, primarily insurance companies and potential employers. Although they are not new, these reports are not familiar to most consumers. Members of Associated Credit Bureaus, Inc., rarely prepare this type of report.

Investigative reports contain subjective information about you, such as details about your lifestyle, personal habits, and character that are gathered through personal interviews with individuals who know you.

Before a company can obtain an investigative report on a consumer, it must provide the consumer with written notification of its request for a report no later than three days after the company first asks a credit bureau to begin preparing the report. It must also inform the consumer of his or her rights under FCRA provisions covering investigative reports. Furthermore, before the credit bureau can prepare the investigative report, the company must provide a written explanation of why it wants the report and certify in writing that it will not use the report information for any other purpose and that it has provided the consumer with the notifications described earlier in this paragraph. In addition, the company must certify to the credit bureau that a complete and accurate disclosure of the nature and the scope of its investigation will be mailed to the consumer upon request no later than five days after it receives the request.

 HOT TIP

Your request for a complete and accurate disclosure must be in writing.

The amendments to the FCRA further protect consumers by requiring that before a credit bureau can include in an investigative report any public record information relating to a consumer's arrest, indictment, conviction, tax lien, outstanding judgment, and the like, it must verify the accuracy of the information. Also, the FCRA now bars a credit bureau from including in the report any negative personal information about a consumer that it obtains from the consumer's friend, neighbor, or associate without first trying to corroborate the information through another source unless the person who provides the information is its best possible source.

If your application for insurance is denied as a result of information about you in an investigative report, the law requires the company that requested the report to provide you with the name, address, and phone number of the credit bureau that prepared the report as well as written notification of your right to obtain a free copy of the report and of your right to dispute information in it that you disagree with.

The Evolution of the Consumer Credit Industry and Passage of the FCRA

Credit records and credit reporting agencies were not always as important as they are today. Until the 1950s most businesses loaned money to people in their neighborhood or community. As a result, creditors usually knew something about a consumer's personal background, family, and bill-paying habits before extending credit. Companies therefore did not make extensive use of credit bureaus. However, during the 1950s and 1960s, the number of national and regional consumer-oriented businesses began growing. Consequently, consumer-creditor transactions became more impersonal and, increasingly, businesses began to rely on credit reporting agencies for the information they needed to evaluate a consumer's creditworthiness.

Congress approved the FCRA in 1970 as a response to the changes just described. The major purpose of this federal legislation is to ensure that credit-related information will be collected and used in a way that will not violate a consumer's right to privacy while guaranteeing consumers access to their own credit records.

The FCRA, which is enforced by the Federal Trade Commission, states that its purpose is "to require that consumer reporting agencies adopt reasonable procedures for meeting the needs of commerce for consumer credit, personnel, insurance, and other information in a manner which is fair and equitable to the consumer, with regard to confidentiality, accuracy, relevancy, and proper utilization of such information."

Figure 1.1 summarizes consumer rights under the FCRA. The complete text of the FCRA, including the CCRRA amendments, is located in Appendix A, and detailed discussions of the consumer rights provided by the FCRA may be found throughout this book.

FIGURE 1.1 Summary of Consumers' Rights under the Fair Credit Reporting Act

The FCRA grants you a number of important rights, including the following:

- The right to know what your credit record says about you

- The right to be told by a credit bureau the nature, substance, and sources of the information it collects about you (A credit bureau does not, however, have to tell you the sources of the information it used to prepare an investigative report about you.)

- The right to know the name and address of the credit bureau responsible for preparing a credit report used to deny you credit, insurance, or employment, or to increase the cost of your insurance or credit

- The right to a free copy of your credit report if you are denied credit and the denial is due in whole or in part to information in your credit record (Requests for a free copy must be made within 60 days of your receipt of a notification of denial.)

- The right to have a credit bureau subscriber or a user of credit bureau information show you a copy of your credit report if it took an adverse action against you as a result in whole or in part to information in that report (Prior to the recent FCRA amendments, you did not have this right.)

- The right to obtain a free copy of your credit report if you are unemployed and intend to apply for employment within the next 60 days, if you are on welfare, if you believe that you are the victim of credit fraud, or if you have been told by a collection agency that it has reported or may report negative information about you to the credit bureau it is affiliated with

- The right to have an employer provide you with a free copy of your credit report before turning you down for a job or promotion, or firing you as the result in whole or in part of information in your credit file

- The right to review your credit report in person at the credit bureau by phone or by mail

- The right to take someone with you to review your file if you visit a credit bureau in person

- The right to have a credit bureau investigate information in your credit report that you believe is inaccurate or out-of-date (If the credit bureau deems your request "frivolous or irrelevant," the law states that the credit bureau need not investigate.)

FIGURE 1.1 Summary of Consumers' Rights under the FCRA (Continued)

- The right to have inaccurate information in your credit record corrected and outdated information deleted if a credit bureau investigation finds the information to be in error

- The right to have information deleted if the credit bureau cannot verify it through its investigation within 30 days of receiving your investigation request

- The right to know the name, address, and phone number of anyone who has seen your credit record over the past two years for employment purposes and the right to know who has reviewed your credit record information for any other purpose over the past year

- The right to have a credit bureau notify employers who reviewed your credit record over the past two years, or anyone else who looked at it over the past six months, of any corrections or deletions made to your credit file (You must specifically request that the credit bureau do this and provide the names of the companies and individuals you want notified, and you may have to pay a fee.)

- The right to have a brief written explanatory statement added to your credit file regarding information in your credit record that you have disputed but been unable to change or get deleted (Whenever a creditor, employer, insurer, and the like tells the credit bureau that it wants to review your file, the written statement must be included with the rest of the information in your credit file.)

- The right to have most negative credit-related information deleted from your credit record after seven years

- The right to have a bankruptcy deleted after ten years

- The right to sue a credit bureau in either state or federal court if it willfully or negligently violates the law (If you are successful in your lawsuit, you may collect attorney fees and court costs as well.)

- The right to be notified by a company that it has requested an investigative report on you

- The right to request from a company pursuing an investigative report more information about the nature and the scope of the investigation

FIGURE 1.1 Summary of Consumers' Rights under the FCRA (Continued)

The FCRA does *not* require that

- a business or individual do business with you;

- an employer hire you or promote you;

- any federal agency intervene on your behalf; or

- a credit bureau add to your file information on accounts that it does not ordinarily report on. (Some credit bureaus will do this for a fee.)

The FCRA does not apply to applications for commercial credit or business insurance. And although most information in a consumer's credit file cannot be reported after seven years, according to the FCRA, the following are exceptions:

- Bankruptcies can be reported for ten years, but each of the big three reports successfully completed Chapter 13 bankruptcies for seven years after the date of filing, not ten years.

- There are no time limitations on reporting information when you apply for a job with an annual salary of $75,000 or more if the employer requests a credit report as part of the application process.

- There are no time limitations on reporting information when you apply for $150,000 or more in credit, or for life insurance with a face value of $150,000 or more.

- Information concerning a lawsuit or judgment against you can be reported for seven years.

Influence of Technology on the Credit Reporting Industry

Over the years the consumer credit reporting industry has expanded and evolved; during the 1980s, in particular, it experienced dramatic changes. Technological advances only dreamed about at the time the FCRA was written literally transformed the face of the industry. It went from using paper-based credit files to computerized databases, and it became easier for credit bureaus to collect and access consumer data so that creditors can now gain immediate online access to a credit bureau's databases.

Computer technology also facilitated the development of many of the new specialized products and services that the larger credit bureaus market to their subscribers and others. Many of these new products and services help creditors evaluate, analyze, and monitor consumer accounts, highlighting those that are at a high risk for delinquency, default, and the like. Some products and services help create more effective direct mailing lists or better marketing databases for businesses.

Most consumers are unaware of these additional products and services because they are marketed to businesses, not to consumers. A review of some of these products and services follows.

Credit Bureau Products and Services for Subscribers

Not all credit bureaus offer each of the products and services described in this section nor is this section intended to provide a comprehensive review of all of the products and services marketed to subscribers by credit bureaus. However, the following list illustrates the many ways that firms can generate additional income by using consumer credit information:

- *Fraud detection databases.* To help creditors detect fraudulent credit applications, credit reporting agencies have developed computerized systems that allow identifying information from a credit application to be compared with the agency's fraud file. When a match is found, the creditor is notified of the possibility for fraud.
- *Automated cross-directories.* Credit reporting agencies can help creditors locate missing or delinquent consumers by offering them direct online access to the names and addresses of hundreds of thousands of consumers all over the country.
- *Collections.* Many credit reporting agencies offer collection services to their subscribers.
- *Risk scoring.* Credit reporting agencies can provide creditors with risk scores on consumers that are based on a statistical evaluation of information in credit files. These scores rate how well a consumer is likely to manage additional or new credit. Some creditors rely more on these ratings than they do on the actual content of a consumer's file when evaluating that consumer's creditworthiness.
- *Account monitoring.* Credit bureaus can help creditors minimize the number of consumer accounts that are in default or delinquent by monitoring the payment histories and credit use patterns of the account holders. They can also let creditors know when they add

new derogatory information to an account holder's credit file, when an account holder moves, changes jobs, and so on and can even monitor the performance of account holders with other lenders.

- *Weekly compilations of information from courthouse records.* Such information, including federal tax liens, civil judgments, bankruptcies, and defaulted mortgages, is not necessarily used by creditors to help them make decisions about the extension of credit but rather to help them pinpoint those accounts that may end up delinquent and/or in collections.

- *Location finding.* Some credit bureaus help creditors, landlords, collection agencies, and others track down "missing" consumers.

- *Delinquency/bankruptcy predictors.* Credit reporting agencies are able to combine the information in their files with risk evaluation measures to identify consumers likely to become delinquent or to file for bankruptcy.

- *Prescreening.* Over the years, prescreening has come under fire from consumer advocates and privacy watchdog groups, which object to the big profits that precreening generates for credit reporting agencies and feel that it violates the privacy of consumers. Despite the criticism, the recent FCRA amendments actually liberalize the rules governing prescreening by broadening its permitted uses. Now, credit bureaus can create prescreened lists for insurers, not just for creditors. In addition, the definition of what constitutes a "firm offer" has been weakened. On the other hand, the FCRA now requires all credit bureaus in the business of prescreening to offer consumers the opportunity to "opt out" of receiving prescreened offers. The bureaus are also required to establish and maintain a notification system, including a toll-free number, that consumers can use to opt out for a period of two years. (See Chapter 9 for an additional discussion of prescreening.)

- *Database enhancement.* Some credit bureaus extract very specific, limited information from their consumer files to help companies improve their marketing databases. By carefully defining exactly what information it provides, a credit reporting agency can circumvent the restriction placed on prescreening by the FTC.

Criticism of Credit Reporting Agencies

During the late 1980s and early 1990s, the credit reporting industry came under considerable criticism from consumer watchdog groups, policy makers, state attorneys general, and the media. Reasons for this criticism included:

- High rates of error and inaccuracy in consumers' credit records (although to be fair, some of these problems were the result of credit grantors providing inaccurate information to credit bureaus)
- Mingling of credit record information in the credit files of people with similar names
- Consumers' difficulty correcting problems in their records
- Invasion of consumers' privacy through the collection, storage, and resale of massive amounts of sensitive and highly personal consumer information without the consumers' knowledge

During this time, consumers became increasingly aware of the potential threats that the credit reporting industry posed to their privacy. They also realized that they needed help dealing with the industry. As a result, attorneys general in several states as well as the FTC became more aggressive, taking legal action against one or more of the big three in some instances. Some of the important reforms that resulted have changed the way credit reporting agencies relate to consumers and the way the industry does business. The industry also initiated some of its own changes. Finally, after numerous false starts Congress addressed some important weaknesses in the FCRA by passing the CCRRA. Although the CCRRA is not a panacea, it is a helpful next step in ensuring that the sensitive consumer data maintained in credit bureau files is adequately protected.

 HOT TIP

It is illegal for information providers to knowingly supply erroneous information to credit reporting agencies.

Penalties for Violation of Your Rights under the FCRA

If your FCRA rights are violated, your legal options are as follows:

- If a credit bureau or a user of credit bureau information willfully fails to comply with the FCRA, you can sue in civil court for willful noncompliance. You can sue for the greater of actual damages or statutory damages of not less than $100 and not more than $1,000 plus attorney fees and punitive damages. If an individual obtains a copy of your credit report under false pretenses, you can sue for a minimum of $1,000, attorney fees, and punitive damages.
- If you sue a credit bureau for negligent noncompliance, you can sue for actual damages plus attorney fees.

The FCRA also provides that anyone who gains access to information in your credit file under false pretenses is subject to fines under Title 18 of the U.S. Code or imprisonment for up to two years. Similar penalties apply to an employee or an officer of a credit bureau who provides such information to an unauthorized individual.

CHAPTER 2

Credit Report Basics

Constance M. was referred to me by a friend. An intelligent, successful woman who had reached a senior management position in an insurance company, Constance had no financial problems. She was following up on some good advice she had received about the importance of reviewing her credit file at least once a year. Sitting across from me, Constance removed a file from her briefcase neatly marked "Credit Report."

This was the first time Constance had ever seen her credit report, and she wanted to make sure that she understood all of it. We went through each item in her report.

As we did so, Constance was relieved to discover that her report was problem-free. I told her that she was lucky—I had worked with many consumers who had found problems in their credit records. I also explained to Constance that each of the major credit reporting agencies may keep a file on her and that the credit-related information in each file may be different. Disconcerted to learn this, Constance left my office prepared to obtain a copy of her credit report from all of the major credit reporting agencies.

This chapter provides the information and the tools that you need to determine the status of your credit files. If you have a good credit history, checking your credit record once a year is a wise preventive measure. If you have had credit problems in the past, however, the first step in the credit rebuilding process involves reviewing your credit history regularly. Before applying for an important loan, it's also a good idea to review your credit file to make sure that it doesn't contain any problems that could cause a delay in the loan approval process or could cause your application to be denied. It is also advisable to review your file if you are applying for insurance or a new job.

Some of the more subtle—but very important—ways that credit record information can affect your life will be explained in this chapter. Such information underscores the importance of regularly monitoring what credit reporting agencies are saying about you.

Which Credit Bureaus Maintain a Record on You?

To gain a comprehensive picture of yourself as a credit managing consumer, it's a good idea to request a copy of your credit report from each of the big three credit reporting agencies. You may also need to get copies of your credit record from regional and local credit reporting agencies in your area that are not affiliated with one of the nationals, although the number of independent credit bureaus is declining.

Credit bureaus, as mentioned in Chapter 1, obtain much of their information from the businesses and organizations that subscribe to their services. Because different companies subscribe to the services of different credit reporting agencies, each credit bureau may have slightly different information about a consumer. For example, Company A may report to Experian and Equifax, whereas Company B reports to Trans Union and Company C reports only to Experian. However, most large credit grantors now report data to each of the big three. In addition, although each of the big three credit reporting agencies are separate businesses that compete with one another for the same subscriber base, they have begun sharing some of their consumer credit information. Therefore, all of the major credit bureaus increasingly have the same information about you in their computer files, which also means that an error in the files of one of the big three is likely to appear in the files of the others.

To locate the credit reporting agencies in your area, look in your local yellow pages under "credit reporting agencies" or "credit bureaus." If you live in a small town or rural community, go to an available library and use the yellow pages for the city nearest you. If you see a listing for any of the major credit reporting agencies, jot down an address and telephone number for each. Do the same for any local or regional credit bureaus you may find listed.

Then call each of the credit bureaus you've identified to find out if any of them maintain a file on you.

If you don't see a local listing for any of the big three in the yellow pages, you can order a copy of your report from their national office. Instructions on how and where to order are in the next section.

Requesting a Copy of Your Credit Report

There are a number of ways to request a copy of your credit report from one of the big three. You can

- send the credit bureau a request letter;
- order by phone using the credit bureau's automated credit report request system and paying for your report with a Visa, MasterCard, or American Express card; or
- order an online copy of your credit report if you have access to the Internet.

Each of these options is discussed in more detail later in this chapter.

The information about ordering a credit report in this chapter is subject to change. To avoid delays in processing your credit report requests from Equifax, Experian, and Trans Union, it's always best to call their national consumer assistance office for up-to-date instructions (their numbers follow later in this chapter) or to visit their Web sites as shown below:

- Experian—http://www.experian.com/personal.html
- Equifax—http://www.equifax.com/
- Trans Union—http://www.tuc.com/

These Web sites offer a lot of helpful information and advice about credit and your credit report.

Writing a Letter to Request a Copy of Your Credit Report

When you write a letter to obtain a copy of your credit report, you must include very specific information. Print your full name, including your middle name, and be sure to include "Jr.," "Sr.," "III," and so forth when applicable. Also include your date of birth, Social Security number, current address and former address if you've not been at your current address for at least five years, and the name of your current employer. Include your spouse's name if you're married and your daytime and evening phone numbers with area codes. Send along a copy of a billing statement from a major national bankcard, a utility bill, your driver's license—any document that reflects your current name and address—to help the credit reporting agency verify for security purposes that you are in fact the person requesting the copy of your credit report. Finally, be sure to sign your letter so the credit bureau has your signature on file; it too is needed for security purposes.

If you are writing to a credit bureau because you have been denied credit, insurance, or employment within the past 60 days because of information about you that the bureau is maintaining, you will not have to pay anything for a copy of your credit record. However, be sure that you include with the letter you send a copy of the denial letter you received from the creditor, insurer, or employer that reviewed your credit file. If, on the other hand, you are writing to the credit bureau because you want to know what is in your credit record and to review it for errors, be sure to enclose a check or money order for the appropriate amount.

Once a credit bureau receives your request letter, it should respond within three business days. For a sample credit report request letter, see Figure 2.1.

Where to Send Your Letter When You Are Requesting a Copy of Your Credit Report from One of the Big Three

Instructions for ordering a copy of your credit report from one of the big three will vary depending on why you are ordering it: You have been denied credit, employment, or insurance because of information in your credit record or in an investigative report, or you want to review your report to make sure it contains no errors or omissions. Special ordering instructions may apply for residents of certain states. You can learn if your state is one of them and what the special instructions are by calling the phone numbers listed below.

Send your request letter to:

Experian
National Consumer Assistance Center
PO Box 949
Allen, TX 75013-0949
800-682-7654

FIGURE 2.1 Sample Credit Report Request Letter

Date
Address of Credit Bureau

Dear Sir or Madam:
    I am writing to request a copy of my credit report.
    My complete name is:
    My Social Security number is:
    My date of birth is:
    My spouse's complete name *(if applicable)* is:
    My spouse's Social Security number is:
    My current address *(do not use a PO Box number):*
    My previous address(es) over the past five years are:
    My employer is:
    My daytime phone number is: ( )
    My evening phone number is: ( )
    To pay for the cost of the report, I have enclosed a check *(or money order)* in the amount of $.
    Please send the report to me at the following address:
    Thank you for your cooperation. If you have any questions, you may contact me at: *(area code/telephone number).*

Sincerely,
Signature

Trans Union
Consumer Disclosure Center
PO Box 390
Springfield, PA 19064-0390
610-690-4909

Equifax
Information Service Center
PO Box 740241
Atlanta, GA 30374-0241
800-685-1111

Purchasing a Copy of Your Credit Report from One of the Big Three through Its Automated Interactive Dialing System

To order a copy of your credit report using an interactive dialing system, you will need a Touch-Tone phone and a MasterCard, Visa, or American Express card.

The numbers to call are:

Experian
888-EXPERIAN (888-397-3742)

Trans Union
316-636-6100

Equifax
770-612-3200

You can't use these phone numbers for a free copy of your credit report because you've been denied credit, employment, or insurance.

Online Ordering

Currently, Equifax is the only one of the big three that will allow you to obtain an online copy of your credit report. To order online, go to its Web site at http://www.equifax.com/.

Experian and Trans Union may allow online ordering at some point in the future. To find out when they do, simply visit their Web sites on a periodic basis. Experian's is http://www.experian.com/personal.html and Trans Union's is http://www.tuc.com/.

If You've Been Denied Credit, Employment, or Insurance

If you're ordering a copy of your credit report because you have been denied credit, employment, or insurance as a result in whole or in part to information about you in your credit record or in an investigative report, under the FCRA you are entitled to receive a free copy of either report from the credit bureau that prepared it. The company that denied you credit, employment, or insurance must give you the name and address of the credit bureau that provided the negative information. To get your free report, you must request it within 60 days of your denial.

Put your request in writing following the instructions outlined in the previous section of this chapter entitled "Writing a Letter to Request a Copy of Your Credit Report." Don't forget to include a copy of your denial letter and send everything to the address of the appropriate credit bureau. Addresses of the big three bureaus were provided earlier in this chapter.

The Cost of Your Report

At the time this edition of *The Credit Repair Kit* was being researched, the cost of a credit report in most states was $8 with some states adding a sales tax. However, a number of states cap the cost of a credit report at less than $8 and some also require that state residents be allowed to obtain one or more free copies of their credit report each year. These states include, but are not limited to, the following:

Colorado	One free copy a year; $8.00 for each additional copy
Connecticut	$5.30 for the first copy each year; $7.95 for subsequent reports in the same year (dollar figures include 6% state tax)
Georgia	Two free credit reports a year; $8.00 for each additional copy
Maine	$2.00 for each copy
Maryland	One free report each year and $5.25 for each additional report
Massachusetts	One free copy each year and $8.00 for each additional copy
Vermont	One free report a year; $7.50 for each additional report

To be sure that you pay the appropriate amount for your credit report, call the consumer information or credit practices office of your state attorney

---

 HOT TIP

You are entitled to one free copy of your credit report each year if you are unemployed and intend to apply for work within 60 days, if you are on welfare, if you feel you have been the victim of credit fraud, or if a collection agency tells you that it has reported, or may report, negative information about you to a particular credit bureau.

general to confirm its cost before ordering. Don't rely on the cost information that the consumer assistance lines of the big three provide as their information is not always complete and up-to-date.

What's in a Credit Report?

All credit reports include the same basic types of information: an identification number, identifying data, credit history, inquiries, and public record information. Each credit reporting agency, however, uses a different format for presenting this information.

Several years ago, each of the big three made an effort to simplify its credit reports so that consumers would find them easier to understand. The Experian credit report is the easiest to decipher because it dispenses with all codes and symbols, using a narrative format instead to present consumer account information. Trans Union has removed some of the codes and symbols that make credit reports so confusing and has added explanatory text as well. The Equifax credit report still needs improvement because it continues to rely primarily on codes and symbols. To help you understand your credit report, explanations of the formats used by each of the big three are provided in Chapter 3.

If you don't understand some of the information in your credit report, call the credit bureau that generated it for explanations. The FCRA requires the credit bureau that generated your report to have personnel available who can help you. Your report should include either a toll-free number to call or the address and phone number of an affiliated bureau.

Identifying Data

The identifying information in your credit report usually includes the following:

- Name, including any nicknames you may have used and whether you are a junior, a senior, a III, a IV, and so on
- Current and previous addresses
- Birthdate
- Spouse's name
- Current and previous employers
- Social Security number

This information generally comes from credit and loan applications that you have filled out.

Credit History

The heart of any credit report is the payment history on accounts that were reported to the credit reporting agency. Despite the slightly different credit report formats used by each credit bureau, most reports reflect the following types of account information:

- Name of the creditor and account/loan number
- Nature of the account/loan (i.e., whether it is joint or individual)
- Type of account/loan—revolving, installment, student loan, mortgage
- Date account was opened or loan was established
- Credit limit on account/loan amount
- Current balance on account/loan (*Note:* The dollar amount shown in this section of a consumer's report reflects the account balance at the time the information was obtained. It will not reflect what has been paid on the account or charged on the account since that time.)
- Monthly payment amount
- Account payment history, including the number of late payments and whether an account has been referred to collections or has been closed by the consumer or the creditor (*Note:* Just as with the item above, this part of a consumer's credit report reflects what was history at the time the account information was reported and will not reflect subsequent account activities.)
- Date information on the account/loan was last reported
- Number of months for which information has been reported
- Amount of credit that has been extended to a consumer
- Whether the consumer is disputing information related to an account

Inquiries

The inquiries section of a credit report indicates those creditors and others who have checked your credit file for any reason. Some of the inquiries listed will be preceded by such abbreviations as *PRM, AM,* and *AR.* PRM indicates that the inquiry was made for *promotional* purposes—your credit file was reviewed or screened for a preapproved credit offer. AM stands for *account monitoring* and AR for *account review,* both of which mean that one of your creditors reviewed the information in your file, perhaps to determine whether your line of credit should be increased or your credit card canceled. The only inquiries that are reported to businesses when they review the information in your credit file are those that result from your application for new or additional credit.

HOT TIP

The amended FCRA requires that credit bureaus list the full name, not an abbreviation, of anyone who reviews your credit report for any reason. Furthermore, you now have the right to ask a credit bureau to provide you with the address and phone number of the businesses and individuals who show up on your report as having made inquiries.

The FCRA does not specify the maximum amount of time that an inquiry can and/or should remain on a credit report, but it does indicate the minimum amount of time that an inquiry should stay there. That minimum is two years for employment purposes and six months for all other purposes.

Although the inquiries section of a credit report may seem relatively unimportant, it can have a significant bearing on your ability to get credit because lenders consider the number of credit-related inquiries in your file to be an indicator of how much credit you are trying to obtain. If lenders see a lot of inquiries, they may assume that you are applying for too much credit and will not be a responsible user of credit, and they are therefore likely to deny your credit request.

HOT TIP

Every time you apply for a credit card, a mortgage loan, a loan from a car financing company, or some other type of credit, your credit record is likely to reflect an additional inquiry. To minimize the number of inquiries in your file, apply only for the credit you most need or want.

The FCRA does not provide consumers any rights with regard to inquiries. Regardless, it is always a good idea to challenge any inquiries that you do not recognize as the credit reporting agency may be willing to investigate them for you.

Public Record Information

The information in this section of a credit report refers to credit-related events that are a matter of public record, such as bankruptcies, foreclosures, judgments, and tax liens. The public information section may also make note of convictions. In an effort to reduce the number of parents who are falling behind or totally ignoring their child support payments, state or local agencies that enforce child support agreements are beginning to report child support delinquencies to credit bureaus.

What Your Credit Report Says about You

After you receive a copy of your credit report, you'll probably be surprised to discover what is and isn't in the report and that it may be quite incomplete.

Your credit record is not a truly comprehensive portrait of you as a consumer for a number of reasons. First, as mentioned earlier in this chapter, all credit reporting agencies do not necessarily get their consumer credit information from the same subscribers. Therefore, no credit bureau will have a comprehensive history of your use of credit.

Second, not every creditor maintains an ongoing subscriber relationship with every credit reporting agency and thus does not regularly report consumer account information to every credit bureau. In fact, some creditors may only provide credit record information to a credit bureau when a consumer account is in collection or in default. Auto dealers, mortgage companies, small department stores and local retailers, utility companies, and medical providers all tend to work this way. Figure 2.2 summarizes reporting patterns of key subscribers.

For the above reasons, when you review your credit record, you may find that it does not reflect significant account information but that information you would rate as relatively unimportant is in your credit file. For example, unless you have ever been 90 days late or more on your mortgage

FIGURE 2.2 Regularly Reported Consumer Account Data

Consumer account data are reported regularly for the following accounts:

- Bankcards

- Large retailers such as Sears and J. C. Penney

- American Express and other travel and entertainment cards

- Airline charge cards

- Federally guaranteed student loans

In most cases, consumer data on the following accounts are not reported to credit bureaus unless the account is past due, in collection, or results in a lawsuit or a judgment against the consumer:

- Utility bills

- Oil and gas cards (some oil and gas companies report regularly)

- Medical bills

- Rent

- Mortgages that are at least 90 days past due

- Auto dealer loans

- Credit union loans (some credit unions report regularly)

- Accounts with smaller department stores and local retailers

payment, your payment history on that loan will probably not be reflected in your credit history. Yet for most consumers a mortgage is the single largest financial commitment they make! On the other hand, the fact that you may have been a couple of days late with a small monthly bankcard payment *will* most likely appear in your report.

CHAPTER 3

How to Read Credit Reports from the Big Three

Mike R. came to see me about rebuilding his credit. Following my advice, he got a copy of his credit report from each of the big three credit bureaus. He was going to review them for misinformation or for information he disputed.

Several weeks after our first meeting, Mike showed up in my office. He had gotten his credit reports but had questions about some of the information.

Mike and I sat down and looked over each of his credit reports. He was amazed to learn how much information each report contained. As I explained what some of the abbreviations and symbols in the reports meant and discussed which accounts presented the biggest problems for him, we also noted two items that we thought were incorrect and might cause Mike problems in the future if he didn't get them removed from his record.

In this chapter I will review the credit report formats of each of the big three credit reporting agencies and explain how to read them. I will also review the format of the credit report produced by CREDCO, Inc., which consolidates credit information from each of the big three into a single report. If after reading this chapter you are confused about how to interpret anything in your credit report, call the appropriate credit bureau for help using the number listed on your credit report, or call the consumer assistance numbers provided in the previous chapter. As already mentioned, the FCRA requires credit bureaus to have personnel available to help consumers make sense of their reports.

Systems for Reporting Consumer Information

Although the types of information found in the credit reports of the big three are basically the same, as reported in Chapter 2, the presentation of that information varies from company to company.

Traditionally, two basic systems for reporting a consumer's account payment history have been *method of payment* (MOP) and *historical method of payment* (HOP).

MOP classifies all accounts as *revolving (R), installment (I),* or *open-end (O)* loans and then uses a number code to note the timeliness of payments on each account.

HOP focuses on the frequency with which a consumer has been late with an account payment, how late the payments have been, and the like.

Credit reporting agencies typically combine elements of both MOP and HOP, although Experian uses a consumer-friendly narrative format for credit reporting.

The Equifax Credit Report

Figure 3.1 is a sample of an Equifax credit report with its detailed explanation of each section and how to read its codes and abbreviations. The Equifax report also comes with a research request form to use if you find a problem with anything in your report.

The Equifax address to which you should direct correspondence about credit record corrections, omissions, or other queries is listed in the upper right-hand corner of the report. Below that address is the consumer identification section, including your name and current address, Social Security number, and date of birth.

FIGURE 3.1 Sample Equifax Credit Report

Note: This is a copy of an actual credit file. Identifying information (i.e., name, address, Social Security number, date of birth, account numbers, etc.) has been removed to protect consumer's identity.

Please address all future
correspondence to this address ▶

```
CSC AUSTIN
652 NORTH SAM HOUSTON PKWY E STE 133
BOX 674402
HOUSTON, TX 77267
```

```
DATE  05/21/97
SOCIAL SECURITY NUMBER
DATE OF BIRTH
```

CREDIT HISTORY

Company Name	Account Number	Whose Acct.	Date Opened	Months Reviewed	Date Of Last Activity	High Credit	Terms	Balance	Past Due	Status	Date Reported
AMERICAN EXPRESS TRA		I	04/75	01	05/97	311		311		O1	05/97
BLOOMINGDALES NY/FAC CHARGE		I	01/74	99	06/93	153		0		R1	05/97
NORWEST MORTGAGE REAL ESTATE MORTGAGE CONVENTIONAL MORTGAGE		J	03/81		04/97	31K	365	23K		I1	04/97
AMERICAN EXPRESS /OP AMOUNT IN H/C COLUMN IS CREDIT LIMIT		I	12/89	01	04/97	6000		1114		R1	04/97
FROST NATIONAL BANK		J	08/94	31	04/97	5000	163	621		I1	04/97
FROST NATIONAL BANK		J	04/94	35	04/97	14K	137	13K		I1	04/97
CHASE NA CREDIT CARD AMOUNT IN H/C COLUMN IS CREDIT LIMIT		I	04/84	78	01/97	600	20	48		R1	03/97
ASSOCIATES FIN CREDI PAID ACCOUNT/ZERO BALANCE CLOSED ACCOUNT		I	04/84	08	09/96	2200		0		R1	03/97
ASSOCIATES FIN CREDI PAID ACCOUNT/ZERO BALANCE CLOSED ACCOUNT		I	04/84	85	03/97	2200		0		R1	03/97
WACHOVIA BANK CARD S CREDIT CARD AMOUNT IN H/C COLUMN IS CREDIT LIMIT		J	05/96	05	03/97	3000		879		R1	03/97
NEIMAN MARCUS		I	04/88	99	03/97	180		0		R1	04/97
CHEVRON USA CREDIT CARD		J	09/66	99	02/97	406		50		R1	02/97
NORWEST BANK TEXAS PAID ACCOUNT/ZERO BALANCE REAL ESTATE MORTGAGE		S	03/81	46	01/97	31K	352	0		I1	01/97
WELLS FARGO		I	04/84	99	05/94	3000		0		R1	04/95
>>> PRIOR PAYING HISTORY - 30(04)60(01)90+(00) 06/91-R2,05/91-R3,02/91-R2 <<< CLOSED ACCOUNT CREDIT CARD											
FROST NATIONAL BANK		J	07/93	15	11/93	25K	231	0		I1	11/94
BANK OF AMERICA		I	11/83	71	03/93	6000		0		R1	03/93
NORWEST BANK TEXAS CLOSED ACCOUNT REAL ESTATE MORTGAGE		J	03/81	35	01/93	31K	347	0		I1	01/93
SEARS AMOUNT IN H/C COLUMN IS CREDIT LIMIT		I	09/81	25	03/92	3240		0		R1	03/92

```
**********  ADDITIONAL INFORMATION  **********

FORMER/OTHER ADDRESS

FORMER/OTHER ADDRESS

LAST REPORTED EMPL -

FORMER EMPLOYMENT -

FORMER EMPLOYMENT -
VERIFIED 07/81

**********  COMPANIES THAT REQUESTED YOUR CREDIT HISTORY  **********

05/21/97 EQUIFAX - DISCLOSURE        04/25/97 FIRST AMERICAN CREDC
04/22/97 AR  AMERICAN EXPRESS        04/17/97 PRM SPIEGEL
04/11/97 AR  AMERICAN EXPRESS        04/09/97 PRM SPIEGEL
03/10/97 VERBAL COPY                 03/07/97 PRM SPIEGEL
02/28/97 FROST BANK LENDING          02/07/97 PRM DISCOVER CARD
01/16/97 PRM SPIEGEL                 01/07/97 PRM CHEVY CHASE FSB
12/26/96 PRM DISCOVER CARD           12/21/96 AR  CHEVRON USA
12/19/96 PRM SPIEGEL                 12/16/96 AR  AMERICAN EXPRESS
```

A15   PAGE 1 OF 2

FIGURE 3.1 Sample Equifax Credit Report (Continued)

Please address all future
correspondence to this address ➧

CSC AUSTIN
852 NORTH SAM HOUSTON PKWY E STE 133
BOX 674402
HOUSTON, TX 77287

DATE 05/21/97
SOCIAL SECURITY NUMBER

CREDIT HISTORY

| Company Name | Account Number | Whose Acct. | Date Opened | Months Re-viewed | Date Of Last Activity | High Credit | Terms | Items as of Date Reported | | | Date Reported |
								Balance	Past Due	Status	
12/04/96 PRM SPIEGEL			11/19/96 PRM DISCOVER CARD								
11/09/96 PRM SPIEGEL			11/02/96 AR WACHOVIA BANK CARD S								
10/24/96 PRM SPIEGEL			10/15/96 PRM SPIEGEL								
10/12/96 AR ASSOCIATES FIN CREDI			10/12/96 PRM AT&T WIRELESS								
09/18/96 PRM FIRST NORTH AMERICAN			08/28/96 PRM SPIEGEL								
08/24/96 WACHOVIA BANK CARD S			08/08/96 PRM SPIEGEL								
08/01/96 PRM SPIEGEL			07/22/96 PRM SPIEGEL								
09/07/95 CONFIDENTIAL CR- CRE			08/09/95 EQUIFAX - DISCLOSURE								

A15-RESTART 00066

COMPLETE PAGE 2 OF 2

Source: Reprinted by permission of Equifax, Inc.

Credit History

Proceeding down the page, you find a section with a large block of information clearly labeled *Credit History*, the heart of your credit report that includes a list of both open and closed accounts being reported to Equifax. Under this major heading is a series of subheadings. Moving from left to right, the first subheading is *Company Name*, under which are listed the creditors who report to Equifax, with an account number for each creditor listed to the right.

To the right of the account numbers is a series of narrow columns, each with a heading, that contain specific information for each of the accounts listed on the credit report. A brief explanation of these columns follows.

Whose Account

Equifax uses nine different letter codes to indicate who is responsible for an account and the type of participation you have with each account. For example, on the sample credit report four letter codes appear: *I* (individual), *J* (joint), *S* (shared), and *U* (undesignated).

Explanations for all of the letter codes are provided in the material that Equifax sends along with each consumer credit report.

Date Opened

Date Opened indicates the month and year you opened the account with the credit grantor.

Months Reviewed and Date of Last Activity

Months Reviewed refers to the number of months of account payment history reported to Equifax by a creditor. On the sample report those numbers range from 1 month to 99 months.

Date of Last Activity is the last date for which there was any activity on your account. That activity could include the last time you made an account payment or the last time you charged something to the account.

High Credit and Terms

High Credit indicates either the maximum amount you have ever charged to an account or your credit limit on an account.

Terms indicates the number of installment payments for a revolving account—signified by a number—or the monthly payment for an installment account—signified by an *M*.

Items as of Date Reported

This subheading contains three columns of information. *Balance* refers to the amount you owe on an account at the time that it is reported to Equifax by your creditor. The *Past Due* column reflects any amount past due at the time the account information was reported.

Two kinds of information are represented by the letter/number codes found in the *Status* column of the Equifax report. The letter part of each code indicates the type of account being reported. *O* refers to an open account, one in which the entire balance is due each month. *R* refers to a revolving account; payment will depend on your account balance. *I* signifies an installment account, one with a fixed number of payments.

The number part of the code provides information about the timeliness of your payments to a particular creditor. For example, *1* indicates that you have made your account payments as agreed and that your account is in good standing; *2* means that the account is 30 days or more past due; *7* signifies that regular payments are being made under a wage earner plan (Chapter 13 bankruptcy) or similar arrangement. There are six other numbers, each of which is defined on the printed explanatory information that comes with your credit report.

Date Reported

The date the account was last reported to the credit bureau is indicated in the far right column of the credit history section.

Other Account Information

For some accounts listed in the credit history section, your Equifax credit report may reflect prior paying history data. For example, on the sample credit report this information is provided for the Wells Fargo credit account.

Prior paying history information tells how frequently you were either 30, 60, or 90 days past due making payments on an account during the number of months of account information provided by a creditor. For example, in the case of the Wells Fargo account on the sample report, the consumer was 30 days late four times—30 (04)—and 60 days late one time—60 (01). This section of the report also provides the date when the two most recent payment delinquencies occurred as well as the date of the most serious delinquency. On the sample credit report the dates of the consumer's most recent late payments to Wells Fargo were June 1991 and May 1991, and the date that the account was most seriously delinquent was February 1991.

Other data that might appear in this section of your Equifax report include whether you or a creditor closed one of your accounts and details on an account that was transferred or sold.

Collection Accounts

This section of the Equifax report notes any accounts that have been turned over to a collection agency. It follows immediately after the basic credit history section of your report.

The sample credit report shows no collection accounts. When collection accounts are listed, the following information is provided for each account:

- The date the collection was reported
- The date the account was assigned to a collection agency and the name and phone number of the collection agency
- The creditor who turned the account over to a collection agency
- The dollar amount in collection
- The status of the collection effort—if any money has been paid by the consumer to the collection agency, the amount paid will be indicated on the report
- The date of the last activity on the account
- The type of account (i.e., individual, joint, etc., and the account number)

Courthouse Records

This section of the Equifax report presents public record information pulled from local, state, and federal court records. This could include information on liens filed against your property, details on any bankruptcies you may have filed, and information about any judgments an individual or business may have won against you as a result of a lawsuit.

Lien information will include the date the lien was filed and where it was filed, the lien's identifying number, the amount of the lien, and whether it was released.

Bankruptcy-related information will include the date the bankruptcy was filed, the name of the federal district court it was filed in, the case number, the dollar amounts of your assets and liabilities, and whether your bankruptcy had been discharged at the time the report was issued.

Judgment information will include the date the judgment was filed, the case number or other identifying number, the names of the defendant and the plaintiff, the amount of the judgment, whether the judgment was satisfied or paid and, if so, the date it was satisfied.

The sample report reflects no courthouse record information.

Additional Information

This section of your Equifax credit report provides additional creditor-reported identification information. Typically, it will include your previous addresses and basic information about your current and former job positions—the name and location of your employer, your job title, and the dates of your employment.

Companies That Requested Your Credit History

At the end of the Equifax report is a list of the businesses that requested a copy of your credit report over the past 24 months and the date of each request. This is the inquiries section of the report.

A letter code will precede some requesters' names. Possible codes include *PRM, AM,* and *AR.* As explained in Chapter 2, PRM stands for promotional and means that a creditor or insurer obtained your name and address from Equifax so that it could offer you credit or insurance. AM or AR appears when one of your creditors makes a periodic review of your Equifax report.

The Trans Union Credit Report

Figure 3.2 is a sample Trans Union credit report. Of the big three agencies, it is the most difficult to understand.

FIGURE 3.2 Sample Trans Union Credit Report

Note: This is a copy of an actual credit file. Identifying information (i.e., name, address, Social Security number, date of birth, account numbers, etc.) has been removed to protect consumer's identity.

TRANS UNION NETWORK MEMBER   **SARMA**

OPER NO.	BATCH NO	OPT	RPT TYPE	DATE MAILED
	28	36		
TRADE CLEARED		EMPLOYMENT VERIFIED		INCOME VERIFIED

FOR	MARKET SUB	IN FILE SINCE	DATE	TIME OF ISSUE
(I) ZSN5250	15 CT	9/86	03/13/97	11:25CT

REPORT ON   SSN   BIRTH DATE 5/49

CURRENT ADDRESS   DATE REPORTED 5/94R   TELEPHONE

FORMER ADDRESS   SPOUSE'S NAME / SSN

                                                    9/86R

CURRENT EMPLOYER AND ADDRESS   POSITION / INCOME   EMPL. DATE   DATE REPORTED

FORMER EMPLOYER AND ADDRESS

SPOUSE'S EMPLOYER AND ADDRESS

HAWK-ALERTSEE END RPT

SUBSCRIBER NAME	SUBSCRIBER CODE	DATE OPENED	HIGH CREDIT	DATE VERIFIED	PRESENT STATUS BALANCE OWING	AMOUNT PAST DUE	PAYMENT PATTERN 1-12 MONTHS	TYPE ACCOUNT $ MOP
ACCOUNT NUMBER		TERMS	CREDIT LIMIT	DATE CLOSED	MAXIMUM DELINQUENCY DATE	AMOUNT MOP	13-24 MONTHS	
ECOA	COLLATERAL			REMARKS	TYPE LOAN		HISTORICAL STATUS NO OF MON 30-59 60-89 90+	

```
TRADES
WELL FARG VS B 908N663  4/84  $3000  4/95A    $0    $0  1X1X1X111111 R01
                              $3000  7/93C  5/91 $128 03 1X11X1111111
I                            *ACCOUNT CLOSED  /CREDIT CARD  38  3  1  0

WACH BKCRD    B 3763001   9/96  $3000  2/97A $1051   $0  11111          R01
                          MIN26
I                                          /CREDIT CARD   5  0  0  0

FROST NTL BK B 588M001   8/94  $5000  2/97A  $935   $0  111X11111111 I01
                          36M163                        111X11111111
C UNSECURED                                             30V 0  0  0

FROST NTL BK B 588M001   4/94 $14.4K 2/97A $12.7K   $0  111X11111111 I01
                         180M137                        111X11111111
C LOT 3 A AMENDED PLAT L 2  3                           34V 0  0  0

AE OPTIMA    N 656N003  12/89 $1162  2/97A $1162    $0  111111X11111 R01
                              $6000                     XX111111X111
I                                          /CREDIT CARD  48  0  0  0

AMERICAN EXP N 656N001   4/75  $186  2/97A  $186    $0  111X1111111X D01
                                                       1X1111111111
I                                          /CREDIT CARD  48  0  0  0
```

COPYRIGHT 1993. TRANS UNION CORPORATION

PAGE 1   CONT

FORM 2000 11/95   CREDIT REPORTING ON-LINE NETWORK UTILITY SYSTEM

FIGURE 3.2 Sample Trans Union Credit Report (Continued)

TRANS UNION
NETWORK MEMBER

SARMA

OPER NO.	BATCH NO. 28	DPT 36	RPT TYPE	DATE MAILED
TRADE CLEARED	EMPLOYMENT VERIFIED		INCOME VERIFIED	

FOR (I) ZSN5250	MARKET SUB	IN FILE SINCE 9/86	DATE 03/13/97	TIME OF ISSUE 11:25CT

REPORT ON	SSN	BIRTH DATE
		TELEPHONE

CURRENT ADDRESS	DATE REPORTED 5/94R	SPOUSE'S NAME / SSN
FORMER ADDRESS		

CURRENT EMPLOYER AND ADDRESS	POSITION / INCOME	EMPL. DATE	DATE REPORTED
FORMER EMPLOYER AND ADDRESS			
SPOUSE'S EMPLOYER AND ADDRESS			

SUBSCRIBER NAME	SUBSCRIBER CODE	DATE OPENED	HIGH CREDIT	DATE VERIFIED	BALANCE OWING	AMOUNT PAST DUE	1-12 MONTHS	TYPE ACCOUNT & MOP
ACCOUNT NUMBER		TERMS	CREDIT LIMIT	DATE CLOSED	DATE	AMOUNT	MOP 13-24 MONTHS	
ECOA	COLLATERAL			REMARKS	TYPE LOAN		NO. OF MON. 30-59 60-89 90+	

```
FRANKLIN SAV B 414M001   3/81 $30.5K  1/97A    $0     $0   X11111111111 I01
                 360M352            1/97C               X11111111111
P                          *CLOSED/CONVENTIONAL REAL EST  48  0   0   0

CHEVRON      O 103T001    9/66  $406  1/97A    $50    $0   11111X11111X R01
                                                          X11111111111
U                                           /CREDIT CARD   48  0   0   0

CHASE NA     B 402D017    4/84        12/96A   $10    $0   111111111111 R01
                 MIN10    $600                            111X1X111111
I                                           /CREDIT CARD   48  0   0   0

ANBCC        B 282E001    4/84         1/97A    $0     $0   111111111111 R01
                          $2200        9/96C              12  0   0   0
I                          *CLOSED          /CREDIT CARD

ANBCC        B 282E001    4/84 $1935   1/97A    $0     $0   111111111111 R01
                          $2200        8/96C              1111111111
I                          *CLOSED          /CREDIT CARD   48  0   0   0

PHILLIPS 66  O 858V001   12/87   $16   2/97A    $0     $0   111111111111 R01
                                       4/96P              1111111111
I                                           /CREDIT CARD   24  0   0   0


             COPYRIGHT 1993. TRANS UNION CORPORATION


                              PAGE 2              CONT
```

FIGURE 3.2 Sample Trans Union Credit Report (Continued)

TRANS UNION NETWORK MEMBER	SARMA	OPER NO.	BATCH NO. 28	DPT 36	RPT TYPE	DATE MAILED
		TRADE CLEARED		EMPLOYMENT VERIFIED		INCOME VERIFIED

FOR (I) ZSN5250		MARKET SUB	IN FILE SINCE 9/86	DATE 03/13/97	TIME OF ISSUE 11:25CT
REPORT ON		SSN		BIRTH DATE	
					TELEPHONE
CURRENT ADDRESS			DATE REPORTED 5/94R	SPOUSE'S NAME / SSN	
FORMER ADDRESS					
CURRENT EMPLOYER AND ADDRESS			POSITION / INCOME	EMPL DATE	DATE REPORTED
FORMER EMPLOYER AND ADDRESS					
SPOUSE'S EMPLOYER AND ADDRESS					

SUBSCRIBER NAME	SUBSCRIBER CODE	DATE OPENED	HIGH CREDIT	DATE VERIFIED	BALANCE OWING	AMOUNT PAST DUE	PAYMENT PATTERN 1-12 MONTHS	TYPE ACCOUNT & MOP
ACCOUNT NUMBER		TERMS	CREDIT LIMIT	DATE CLOSED	MAXIMUM DELINQUENCY DATE AMOUNT MOP		13-24 MONTHS	
ECOA COLLATERAL				REMARKS	TYPE LOAN		HISTORICAL STATUS NO. OF MON. 30-59 60-89 90+	

```
NEIMAN MARCU  D 2816001   4/88  $180   3/97A   $0      $0    11XXXXXXXXXX  R01
                                 $200  11/95P                 XXX111XXX111
 I                                                              48   0   0   0

FROST NTL BK  B 588M001    7/93 $25.0K 11/94A   $0      $0    XX1               I01
                180M231                 12/93C
 C B   M LIEN    1101 CHARLOTTE                               16V  0   0   0

BLOMINGDALES  D 989D002    1/74  $153   2/97A   $0      $0    1111XXXXXXX   R01
                                 $500   6/93P                 111
 I                                                              37   0   0   0

BK OF AMER    B 163P016   11/83          3/93A   $0      $0    X1111111111   R01
                                $6000   3/93P                 111111111111
 I                                                              34   0   0   0

CITIBANK MC   B 64DB002    7/83 $2300   3/92A           $0    111111111111  R01
                                $2300                         1111X11111
 I                             *ACCOUNT CLOSED BY CONSUMER     22   0   0   0

SEARS         D 6256416    9/81 $1300   3/92A   $0      $0    111111111111  R01
                                $3200   2/92P                 11111111
 I                                                              21   0   0   0
```

COPYRIGHT 1993. TRANS UNION CORPORATION

PAGE 3　　　　　　　　　　　CONT

FIGURE 3.2 Sample Trans Union Credit Report (Continued)

TRANS UNION
NETWORK MEMBER

SARMA

OPER NO.	BATCH NO.	DPT	RPT TYPE	DATE MAILED
	28	36		
TRADE CLEARED		EMPLOYMENT VERIFIED		INCOME VERIFIED

FOR
(I) ZSN5250

MARKET SUB	IN FILE SINCE	DATE	TIME OF ISSUE
	9/86	03/13/97	11:25CT

REPORT ON

SSN

BIRTH DATE

TELEPHONE

CURRENT ADDRESS

DATE REPORTED
5/94R

SPOUSE'S NAME / SSN

FORMER ADDRESS

CURRENT EMPLOYER AND ADDRESS

POSITION / INCOME

EMPL. DATE

DATE REPORTED

FORMER EMPLOYER AND ADDRESS

SPOUSE'S EMPLOYER AND ADDRESS

SUBSCRIBER NAME	SUBSCRIBER CODE	DATE OPENED	HIGH CREDIT	DATE VERIFIED	PRESENT STATUS		PAYMENT PATTERN	TYPE ACCOUNT & MOP
					BALANCE OWING	AMOUNT PAST DUE	1-12 MONTHS	
ACCOUNT NUMBER		TERMS	CREDIT LIMIT	DATE CLOSED	MAXIMUM DELINQUENCY		13-24 MONTHS	
ECOA	COLLATERAL			REMARKS	DATE	AMOUNT	MOP	HISTORICAL STATUS
					TYPE LOAN		NO. OF MON. 30-59 60-89 90 +	

```
COOLIDGE BK   B 583T043  10/76        $0  10/91A              $0   11                C01
  I                                                                2    0   0   0

COOLIDGE BK   B 588T036  10/76        $0   4/91A              $0   11111XXX111       C01
                                      $0
  I                             *CLOSED                            11   0   0   0

FROST BROS    D 931P001   11/83    $396   9/90A    $0         $0                     R01
                                          4/90P
  I

FST OMNI BK   B 3568012    7/80   $1211   5/91A    $0         $0                     R01
                                  $1000   1/90P
  I

FIB BKCRD     B 9287001    4/84           2/90A    $0         $0                     R01
                                  $1900   1/90P
  I                             *TRANSFER

COMMERICAL    F 7212624    7/86   $6951   7/89A    $0         $0                     I01
                             36M          7/89P
  I                                               /NOTE LOAN
```

COPYRIGHT 1993, TRANS UNION CORPORATION
PAGE 4   CUNT

FORM 2000 11/95   CREDIT REPORTING ON-LINE NETWORK UTILITY SYSTEM

FIGURE 3.2 Sample Trans Union Credit Report (Continued)

TRANS UNION
NETWORK MEMBER

SARMA

OPER NO.	BATCH NO.	DPT	RPT TYPE	DATE MAILED
	28	36		

TRADE CLEARED	EMPLOYMENT VERIFIED	INCOME VERIFIED

FOR						
(I) ZSN5250						

	MARKET SUB	IN FILE SINCE	DATE	TIME OF ISSUE
		9/86	03/13/97 11:25CT

REPORT ON	SSN	BIRTH DATE

		TELEPHONE

CURRENT ADDRESS	DATE REPORTED	
	5/94R	SPOUSE'S NAME / SSN

FORMER ADDRESS

CURRENT EMPLOYER AND ADDRESS — POSITION / INCOME — EMPL. DATE — DATE REPORTED

FORMER EMPLOYER AND ADDRESS

SPOUSE'S EMPLOYER AND ADDRESS

SUBSCRIBER NAME	SUBSCRIBER CODE	DATE OPENED	HIGH CREDIT	DATE VERIFIED	PRESENT STATUS		PAYMENT PATTERN	TYPE ACCOUNT & MOP
					BALANCE OWING	AMOUNT PAST DUE	1-12 MONTHS	
ACCOUNT NUMBER		TERMS	CREDIT LIMIT	DATE CLOSED	MAXIMUM DELINQUENCY		13-24 MONTHS	
ECOA	COLLATERAL			REMARKS	DATE	AMOUNT	MOP	HISTORICAL STATUS
				TYPE LOAN			NO. OF MON. 30-59 60-89 90 +	

```
INQR  4
    DATE     ECOA SUBCODE          SUBNAME          TYPE AMT
    3/13/97    I   ZSN5250          CONSUM DISCL

    2/28/97    C   BSN0006122       FROST BK-CON

    9/7/95     I   ZSD8256090(CAL)  CONFID CREDT

    8/15/95    I   ZPA5251(NYC)     CONSUM DISCL

PRMO  7
    DATE     ECOA SUBCODE          SUBNAME          TYPE
    1/97       I   B369E021         NATIONS BK       P

    12/96      I   B701N012         PROVIDIAN        P

    11/96      I   B369E049                          P

    11/96      I   B701N012         PROVIDIAN        P

    11/96      I   B3763001         WACH BKCRD       P

    10/96      I   B701N012         PROVIDIAN        P

    9/96       I   B701N012         PROVIDIAN        P

              COPYRIGHT 1993. TRANS UNION CORPORATION


                        PAGE 5                    CONT
```

FIGURE 3.2 Sample Trans Union Credit Report (Continued)

SUBSCRIBER NAME	SUBSCRIBER CODE	DATE OPENED	HIGH CREDIT	DATE VERIFIED	BALANCE OWING	AMOUNT PAST DUE	1-12 MONTHS	TYPE ACCOUNT & MOP
ACCOUNT NUMBER		TERMS	CREDIT LIMIT	DATE CLOSED	MAXIMUM DELINQUENCY		13-24 MONTHS	
ECOA	COLLATERAL			REMARKS	TYPE LOAN		HISTORICAL STATUS NO. OF MON. 30-59 60-89 90 +	

```
***HAWK-ALERT:CLEAR FOR ALL SEARCHES PERFORMED***

**END OF CREDIT REPORT**

REPORT SERVICED BY:
SARMA CENTRAL TEXAS
1801 BROADWAY
SAN ANTONIO. TX. 78215
512-459-7876


*** LOOK ***
SUBNAME            SUBCODE            TELEPHONE

WELL FARG VS       B908N663           (800) 642-4720
POB 4051           CONCORD            CA. 94524

WACH BKCRD         B3763001           (800) 241-7990
PO BOX 4635        ATLANTA            GA. 30302

FROST NTL BK       B588M001           (210) 220-4471
POB 1600           SAN ANTONIO        TX. 78296

AE OPTIMA          N656N003           (954) 503-3787
POB 7871           FT LAUDERDALE      FL. 33329
```

COPYRIGHT 1993. TRANS UNION CORPORATION

PAGE 6   CONT

FORM 2000 11/95   CREDIT REPORTING ON-LINE NETWORK UTILITY SYSTEM

FIGURE 3.2 Sample Trans Union Credit Report (Continued)

TRANS UNION NETWORK MEMBER	**SARMA**	OPER NO. BATCH NO. DPT RPT TYPE **28 86** DATE MAILED	
		TRADE CLEARED EMPLOYMENT VERIFIED INCOME VERIFIED	

FOR
  (I) ZSN5250

REPORT ON	MARKET SUB	IN FILE SINCE 9/86	DATE 03/13/97	TIME OF ISSUE 11:25CT

SSN   BIRTH DATE

CURRENT ADDRESS   DATE REPORTED   5/94R   TELEPHONE

FORMER ADDRESS   SPOUSE'S NAME / SSN

CURRENT EMPLOYER AND ADDRESS   POSITION / INCOME   EMPL DATE   DATE REPORTED

FORMER EMPLOYER AND ADDRESS

SPOUSE'S EMPLOYER AND ADDRESS

SUBSCRIBER NAME	SUBSCRIBER CODE	DATE OPENED	HIGH CREDIT	DATE VERIFIED	PRESENT STATUS BALANCE OWING	AMOUNT PAST DUE	PAYMENT PATTERN 1-12 MONTHS	TYPE ACCOUNT & MOP
ACCOUNT NUMBER		TERMS	CREDIT LIMIT	DATE CLOSED	MAXIMUM DELINQUENCY DATE AMOUNT MOP		13-24 MONTHS	
ECOA COLLATERAL				REMARKS TYPE LOAN			HISTORICAL STATUS NO. OF MON. 30-59 60-89 90+	

```
AMERICAN EXP      N656N001      (954) 503-3787
P O BOX 7871      FT LAUDERDALE  FL. 33329

FRANKLIN SAV      B414M001      (512) 477-5000
111 CONGRESS      AUSTIN        TX. 78701

CHEVRON           O103T001      (510) 602-7020
POB 5010          CONCORD       CA. 94524

CHASE NA          B402D017      (800) 356-5555
100 DUFFY AVE     HICKSVILLE    NY. 11801

ANBCC             B282E001      (800) 533-5600
P O BOX 15687     WILMINGTON    DE. 19850

PHILLIPS 66       0858V001
POB 30            BARTLESVILLE  OK. 74004

NEIMAN MARCU      D2816001      (800) 753-0407
1201 ELM ST       DALLAS        TX. 75270

BLOMINGDALES      D989D002      (800) 950-0339
9111 DUKE BLVD    MASON         OH. 45040


          COPYRIGHT 1993. TRANS UNION CORPORATION



                        PAGE 7              CONT
```

FORM 2000 11/95   CREDIT REPORTING ON-LINE NETWORK UTILITY SYSTEM

FIGURE 3.2 Sample Trans Union Credit Report (Continued)

SUBSCRIBER NAME	SUBSCRIBER CODE	DATE OPENED	HIGH CREDIT	DATE VERIFIED	PRESENT STATUS		PAYMENT PATTERN	TYPE ACCOUNT & MOP
					BALANCE OWING	AMOUNT PAST DUE	1-12 MONTHS	
ACCOUNT NUMBER		TERMS	CREDIT LIMIT	DATE CLOSED	MAXIMUM DELINQUENCY		13-24 MONTHS	
ECOA	COLLATERAL			REMARKS	DATE	AMOUNT	MOP	
				TYPE LOAN	HISTORICAL STATUS			
					NO. OF MON.	30-59	60-89	90 +

BK OF AMER   B163P016   (800) 423-3811
101 S MARENGO   PASADENA   CA. 91101

CITIBANK MC   B64DB002   (800) 843-0777
POB 6241   SIOUX FALLS SD. 57117

SEARS   D6256416
4241 WOODCOCK DR SAN ANTONIO TX. 78228

COOLIDGE BK   B583T043   (617) 736-9125
200 PROSPECT ST   WALTHAM   MA. 02254

COOLIDGE BK   B583T036   (617) 926-7098
75 ARLINGTON ST   BOSTON   MA. 02116

FROST BROS   D931P001
POB 691045   SAN ANTONIO TX. 78269

FST OMNI BK   B3568012   (800) 338-1141
499 MITCHELL ST   MILLSBORO   DE. 19966

FIB BKCRD   B9287001   (800) 955-5050
POB 9700   SIMI VALLEY CA. 93097

COPYRIGHT 1993. TRANS UNION CORPORATION

PAGE 8   CONT

FORM 2000 11/95   CREDIT REPORTING ON-LINE NETWORK UTILITY SYSTEM

FIGURE 3.2 Sample Trans Union Credit Report (Continued)

TRANS UNION NETWORK MEMBER	**SARMA**		

OPER NO.	BATCH NO.	DPT	RPT TYPE	DATE MAILED
	28	36		
TRADE CLEARED	EMPLOYMENT VERIFIED		INCOME VERIFIED	

FOR	MARKET SUB	IN FILE SINCE	DATE	TIME OF ISSUE
(I) ZSN5250		9/86	03/13/97	11:25CT

REPORT ON	SSN	BIRTH DATE	
			TELEPHONE
CURRENT ADDRESS	DATE REPORTED		
	5/94R	SPOUSE'S NAME / SSN	
FORMER ADDRESS			

CURRENT EMPLOYER AND ADDRESS	POSITION / INCOME	EMPL. DATE	DATE REPORTED
FORMER EMPLOYER AND ADDRESS			
SPOUSE'S EMPLOYER AND ADDRESS			

SUBSCRIBER NAME	SUBSCRIBER CODE	DATE OPENED	HIGH CREDIT	DATE VERIFIED	PRESENT STATUS		PAYMENT PATTERN	TYPE ACCOUNT & MOP
					BALANCE OWING	AMOUNT PAST DUE	1-12 MONTHS	
ACCOUNT NUMBER		TERMS	CREDIT LIMIT	DATE CLOSED	MAXIMUM DELINQUENCY		13-24 MONTHS	
ECOA	COLLATERAL			REMARKS	DATE AMOUNT MOP		HISTORICAL STATUS	
					TYPE LOAN		NO. OF MON. 30-59 60-89 90 +	

```
COMMERICAL              F7212624        (512) 467-6878
5775 AIRPORT            AUSTIN          TX. 78752


FROST BK-CON            BSN0006122      (210) 220-4205
P.O. BOX 1600           SAN ANTONIO     TX. 78296

CONFID CREDT            ZSD8256090      (800) 443-9342
9444 BALBOA AVE         SAN DIEGO       CA. 92123

CONSUM DISCL            ZPA5251
1211 CHESTNUT ST.       PHILA           PA. 19107


NATIONS BK              B369E021        (800) 462-6257
POB 831400-7 NAK        DALLAS          TX. 75283

PROVIDIAN               B701N012
POB 9007                PLEASANTON      CA. 94566

WACH BKCRD              B3763001        (800) 241-7990
PO BOX 4635             ATLANTA         GA. 30302

*** END OF LOOK ***

            COPYRIGHT 1993. TRANS UNION CORPORATION

                            PAGE 9              LAST
```

FORM 2000 11/95   CREDIT REPORTING ON-LINE NETWORK UTILITY SYSTEM

Source: Reprinted by permission of Trans Union.

The Trans Union report comes with an investigation request form that serves the same purpose as the Equifax research request form. Use this form to dispute information in your credit report.

Identifying Information

Your name, Social Security number, current address and any former addresses reported, your birth date, and your phone number will all appear close to the top of your Trans Union credit report. Information on your current and former employers may also appear here, although there is no such information on the sample report.

Credit History

Your history with creditors reporting to Trans Union follows the identifying information.

Account information is presented under a series of headings. To the far left under these headings is the name of the creditor reporting to Trans Union and below that, your account number. The series of numbers and letters to the immediate right of each creditor's name represents a creditor's subscriber code; you do not need to be concerned with those codes.

Below your account number is a letter indicating whose reponsibility it is to pay on the account. Trans Union uses nine different letters. Reading the sample credit report, you will note that most of the accounts are designated as *I*, or individual accounts. On this same line there may also be information regarding any collateral that was used to secure the credit. For example, on the sample credit report, you'll note that the Frost Bank loan for $14,400 was secured with a piece of real estate, "lot 3 A amended plat."

On the same line as the creditor's name but to the right is the date the account was opened, the most ever owed on the account, and the date that the credit information on the account was reported to Trans Union. Following that date is a letter *(C, F, P, A,* or *V)*, which designates whether the account was closed, written off, paid off, or whatever. Below that block of information is the credit limit for the account and the date the account was closed, if applicable. Looking at the Wells Fargo account on the sample credit report, you will see that the account credit limit was $3,000 and that the account was closed in 7/93.

If you continue reading to the right, the block of information labeled *Present Status* shows the account balance as of the date the account information was verified by Trans Union or the account was closed, and any past due amount as of the same date. Below that information is delinquency information on the account: the date of the maximum delinquency, the dollar amount of that delinquency, and how the account was being paid at the time of the delinquency.

Finally, below the delinquency information may be information describing the kind of credit the account represents—for example, credit card, real estate loan, or automobile, boat, or personal loan.

The next large block of information to the right—*Payment Pattern*—provides detailed payment history information for each account in your report. Up to 24 months' worth of information is provided. Read the symbols in this section from left to right. The most current information is to the far left of the top line. You will see either a number or *X*s as you read. A *1* means that your account payment that month was on time; *2* through *8* indicate different degrees of lateness; *X* means that no information was provided by the creditor for that particular month. An explanation appears on the reverse side of the very last page of your Trans Union credit report explaining what each number means. The explanations will be under this heading: *MOP Current Manner of Payment.*

The final block of information to the far right of the Trans Union report indicates the account type and current method of payment (MOP). Type of account includes revolving, open, installment, mortgage, and so on. Current method of payment reflects the timeliness of the payments you make on an account. Most of the accounts on the sample credit report are revolving *(R)* and are paid within 30 days *(01).*

The very bottom line of information for each acccount presents miscellaneous additional remarks about the account—that account information is being disputed, for example. There are no miscellaneous additional remarks in the sample credit report.

Inquiries

This information follows the credit history section of the Trans Union report. Like the reports of the other credit reporting agencies, the inquiries section shows who has made an inquiry regarding your credit report and the date of each inquiry. The designation *Consum Discl* in the sample report indicates that the consumer requested a copy of his or her own report.

Following the inquiries is a list of the companies to whom Trans Union provided the consumer's name and address, so the companies could offer the consumer credit or insurance, and the dates the information was provided. The sample report shows that Trans Union provided such information six times from 9/96 to 1/97.

Public Record

The public record section of the Trans Union report presents the usual information on any applicable liens, bankruptcies, or judgments.

Address to Contact

The words *End of Credit Report* designate the final page of the Trans Union report. Immediately following these words is the address and phone number of the credit bureau affiliated with Trans Union that generated the report. On the sample report it is Sarma Central Texas in San Antonio. Contact the office listed here if you have any questions about the information in your Trans Union report.

The Experian Credit Report

A sample of Experian's credit report is shown in Figure 3.3. This report's straightforward narrative format makes it extremely easy to read. The report comes with a reinvestigation request form for consumers who find problems in their credit reports.

Consumer ID Number

Experian gives each consumer an ID number that's at the top of the first page of the sample report. Use this number if you have to call or write Experian about information in your credit report.

Credit History

Like the credit reports of Trans Union and Equifax, Experian's begins with your credit history.

FIGURE 3.3 Sample Experian Credit Report

Note: This is a copy of an actual credit file. Identifying information (i.e., name, address, Social Security number, date of birth, account numbers, etc.) has been removed to protect consumer's identity.

experían

This is your consumer identification number. Please refer to this number when you call or write us.

ID #

HOW TO READ THIS REPORT:

EXPERIAN IS THE INDEPENDENT COMPANY FORMED FROM TRW'S INFORMATION SERVICES BUSINESSES.

AN EXPLANATORY ENCLOSURE ACCOMPANIES THIS REPORT. IT DESCRIBES YOUR CREDIT RIGHTS AND OTHER HELPFUL INFORMATION. IF THE ENCLOSURE IS MISSING, OR YOU HAVE QUESTIONS ABOUT THIS REPORT, PLEASE CONTACT THE OFFICE LISTED ON THE LAST PAGE.

AS PART OF OUR FRAUD-PREVENTION PROGRAM, ACCOUNT NUMBERS MAY NOT FULLY DISPLAY ON THIS REPORT.

YOUR CREDIT HISTORY:

THIS INFORMATION COMES FROM PUBLIC RECORDS OR ORGANIZATIONS THAT HAVE GRANTED CREDIT TO YOU. AN ASTERISK BY AN ACCOUNT INDICATES THAT THIS ITEM MAY REQUIRE FURTHER REVIEW BY A PROSPECTIVE CREDITOR WHEN CHECKING YOUR CREDIT HISTORY. IF YOU BELIEVE ANY OF THE INFORMATION IS INCORRECT, PLEASE LET US KNOW.

ACCOUNT	DESCRIPTION
1 AMERICAN EXPRESS OPTIMA P O BOX 7871/SROC FORT LAUDERDALE FL 33329 BANKING ACCT #	THIS CREDIT CARD ACCOUNT WAS OPENED 12/01/89 AND HAS REVOLVING REPAYMENT TERMS. YOU HAVE CONTRACTUAL RESPONSIBILITY FOR THIS ACCOUNT AND ARE PRIMARILY RESPONSIBLE FOR ITS PAYMENT. CREDIT LIMIT: $6,000. HIGH BALANCE: $1,590.

AS OF 12/01/89, THIS OPEN ACCOUNT IS CURRENT AND ALL PAYMENTS ARE BEING MADE ON TIME. BALANCE $1,114 ON 04/24/97. MONTHS REVIEWED: 90.

2 AMERICAN EXPRESS CO P O BOX 7871 SROC FORT LAUDERDALE FL 33329 NATL CREDIT CARDS ACCT #	THIS CREDIT CARD ACCOUNT WAS OPENED 04/01/75 AND HAS REVOLVING REPAYMENT TERMS. YOU HAVE CONTRACTUAL RESPONSIBILITY FOR THIS ACCOUNT AND ARE PRIMARILY RESPONSIBLE FOR ITS PAYMENT. HIGH BALANCE: $637.

AS OF 06/01/77, THIS OPEN ACCOUNT IS CURRENT AND ALL PAYMENTS ARE BEING MADE ON TIME. BALANCE $311 ON 05/05/97. MONTHS REVIEWED: 99.

CONSUMER CREDIT REPORT (CDI) P-91611597   05/19/97 00:22:00   Page 1

FIGURE 3.3 Sample Experian Credit Report (Continued)

```
        ACCOUNT                    DESCRIPTION

3    ANBCC                  THIS CREDIT CARD ACCOUNT WAS OPENED 04/01/84 AND HAS
     4550 NEW LINDEN HILL ROA   REVOLVING REPAYMENT TERMS. YOU HAVE CONTRACTUAL
     WILMINGTON DE 19808     RESPONSIBILITY FOR THIS ACCOUNT AND ARE PRIMARILY
     BANKING                RESPONSIBLE FOR ITS PAYMENT. CREDIT LIMIT: $2,200.
     ACCT #

AS OF 11/01/96, THIS ACCOUNT IS PAID. PREVIOUSLY WAS CURRENT AND ALL PAYMENTS WERE MADE ON
TIME. MONTHS REVIEWED: 16.
** CREDIT LINE CLOSED/CONSUMER REQUEST/REPORTED BY SUBSCRIBER **

4    ANBCC                  THIS CREDIT CARD ACCOUNT WAS OPENED 04/01/84 AND HAS
     4550 NEW LINDEN HILL ROA   REVOLVING REPAYMENT TERMS. YOU HAVE CONTRACTUAL
     WILMINGTON DE 19808     RESPONSIBILITY FOR THIS ACCOUNT AND ARE PRIMARILY
     BANKING                RESPONSIBLE FOR ITS PAYMENT. CREDIT LIMIT: $2,200. HIGH
     ACCT #                 BALANCE: $252.

AS OF 09/01/96, THIS ACCOUNT IS PAID. PREVIOUSLY WAS CURRENT AND ALL PAYMENTS WERE MADE ON
TIME. MONTHS REVIEWED: 99.
** CREDIT LINE CLOSED/GRANTOR REQUEST/REPORTED BY SUBSCRIBER **

5    ANN TAYLOR             THIS CHARGE ACCOUNT WAS OPENED 09/03/87 AND HAS
     P O BOX 1304           REVOLVING REPAYMENT TERMS. YOU HAVE CONTRACTUAL
     NEW HAVEN CT 06505     RESPONSIBILITY FOR THIS ACCOUNT AND ARE PRIMARILY
     UNDEFINED FIRM TYPE    RESPONSIBLE FOR ITS PAYMENT. CREDIT LIMIT: $700.
     ACCT #

AS OF 09/01/87, THIS OPEN ACCOUNT IS CURRENT AND ALL PAYMENTS ARE BEING MADE ON TIME.
BALANCE $0 ON 04/27/97. MONTHS REVIEWED: 99.

6    BANK OF AMERICA        THIS CREDIT CARD ACCOUNT WAS OPENED 11/09/83 AND HAS
     1825 EAST BUCKEYE ROAD REVOLVING REPAYMENT TERMS. YOU HAVE CONTRACTUAL
     PHOENIX AZ 85034       RESPONSIBILITY FOR THIS ACCOUNT AND ARE PRIMARILY
     BANKING                RESPONSIBLE FOR ITS PAYMENT. CREDIT LIMIT: $6,000. HIGH
     ACCT #                 BALANCE: $1,667.

AS OF 04/01/93, THIS ACCOUNT IS PAID. PREVIOUSLY WAS CURRENT AND ALL PAYMENTS WERE MADE ON
TIME. MONTHS REVIEWED: 99.

7    BLOOMINGDALE*S         THIS CHARGE ACCOUNT WAS OPENED IN 1974 AND HAS
     9111 DUKE DRIVE        REVOLVING REPAYMENT TERMS. YOU HAVE CONTRACTUAL
     MASON OH 45040         RESPONSIBILITY FOR THIS ACCOUNT AND ARE PRIMARILY
     UNDEFINED FIRM TYPE    RESPONSIBLE FOR ITS PAYMENT. CREDIT LIMIT: $501. HIGH
     ACCT #                 BALANCE: $153.

AS OF 06/01/77, THIS OPEN ACCOUNT IS CURRENT AND ALL PAYMENTS ARE BEING MADE ON TIME. LAST
PAYMENT REPORTED TO EXPERIAN: 06/28/93. BALANCE $0 ON 05/07/97. MONTHS REVIEWED: 99.


CONSUMER CREDIT REPORT (CDI) P-91611597        05/19/97 00:22:00        Page   2
```

FIGURE 3.3 Sample Experian Credit Report (Continued)

experían

This is your consumer identification
number. Please refer to this number
when you call or write us.

ID #

_____
_____

ACCOUNT	DESCRIPTION

8   CHASE NA
     100 DUFFY AVENUE
     HICKSVILLE NY 11801
     BANKING
     ACCT #

THIS CREDIT CARD ACCOUNT WAS OPENED 04/28/84 AND HAS
REVOLVING REPAYMENT TERMS. YOU HAVE CONTRACTUAL
RESPONSIBILITY FOR THIS ACCOUNT AND ARE PRIMARILY
RESPONSIBLE FOR ITS PAYMENT. CREDIT LIMIT: $600. HIGH
BALANCE: $696.

AS OF 05/01/84, THIS OPEN ACCOUNT IS CURRENT AND ALL PAYMENTS ARE BEING MADE ON TIME.
SCHEDULED MONTHLY PAYMENT: $10. LAST PAYMENT REPORTED TO EXPERIAN: 01/17/97. BALANCE $10
ON 02/10/97. MONTHS REVIEWED: 99.

9   * CHEVRON U S A
     P O BOX 5010
     CONCORD CA 94524
     OIL COMPANIES
     ACCT #

THIS CREDIT CARD ACCOUNT WAS OPENED 09/01/66 AND HAS
REVOLVING REPAYMENT TERMS. YOUR ASSOCIATION WITH THIS
ACCOUNT IS UNSPECIFIED. HIGH BALANCE: $406.

AS OF 05/01/92, THIS OPEN ACCOUNT IS CURRENT AND PAYMENTS ARE BEING MADE ON TIME BUT WAS
DELINQUENT 60 DAYS. ORIGINAL DELINQUENCY DATE 04/30/92. BALANCE $20 ON 04/30/97. MONTHS
REVIEWED: 99.
TIMES LATE: 30=0, 60=1, 90+=0

10   CITIBANK MASTERCHARGE
     PO BOX 6500
     SIOUX FALLS SD 57117
     BANKING
     ACCT #

THIS CREDIT CARD ACCOUNT WAS OPENED 07/01/83 AND HAS
REVOLVING REPAYMENT TERMS. YOU HAVE CONTRACTUAL
RESPONSIBILITY FOR THIS ACCOUNT AND ARE PRIMARILY
RESPONSIBLE FOR ITS PAYMENT.

AS OF 07/01/83, THIS CLOSED ACCOUNT IS CURRENT AND ALL PAYMENTS ARE BEING MADE ON TIME.
LAST PAYMENT REPORTED TO EXPERIAN: 04/06/92. BALANCE $0 ON 04/30/96. MONTHS REVIEWED: 99.
** CREDIT LINE CLOSED/CONSUMER REQUEST/REPORTED BY SUBSCRIBER **

11   FCNB/SPIEGL/EBAUR/NWPT
     9300 S W GEMINI DR
     BEAVERTON OR 97008
     BANKING
     ACCT #

THIS CHARGE ACCOUNT WAS OPENED 04/15/84 AND HAS
REVOLVING REPAYMENT TERMS. YOU HAVE CONTRACTUAL
RESPONSIBILITY FOR THIS ACCOUNT AND ARE PRIMARILY
RESPONSIBLE FOR ITS PAYMENT. CREDIT LIMIT: $400.

AS OF 05/01/84, THIS OPEN ACCOUNT IS CURRENT AND ALL PAYMENTS ARE BEING MADE ON TIME. LAST
PAYMENT REPORTED TO EXPERIAN: 05/30/87. BALANCE $0 ON 04/30/97. MONTHS REVIEWED: 99.

CONSUMER CREDIT REPORT (CDI) P-91611597   05/19/97 00:22:00   Page   3

FIGURE 3.3 Sample Experian Credit Report (Continued)

```
        ACCOUNT                         DESCRIPTION

  12    FIRST OMNI BANK          THIS CREDIT CARD ACCOUNT WAS OPENED 07/25/80 AND HAS
        P O BOX 825              REVOLVING REPAYMENT TERMS. YOU HAVE CONTRACTUAL
        MILLSBORO DE 19966       RESPONSIBILITY FOR THIS ACCOUNT AND ARE PRIMARILY
        BANKING                  RESPONSIBLE FOR ITS PAYMENT. CREDIT LIMIT: $1,000. HIGH
        ACCT #                   BALANCE: $1,211.

  AS OF 05/01/91, THIS ACCOUNT IS PAID. PREVIOUSLY WAS CURRENT AND ALL PAYMENTS WERE MADE ON
  TIME. BALANCE $0 ON 05/05/91. MONTHS REVIEWED: 99.

  13    FROST NATIONAL BANK      THIS EXTENSION OF CREDIT, REVIEW OR OTHER PERMISSIBLE
        PO BOX 1600              PURPOSE WAS OPENED 04/07/94 AND HAS 180 MONTH REPAYMENT
        SAN ANTONIO TX 78296     TERMS. YOU ARE OBLIGATED TO REPAY THIS JOINT ACCOUNT.
        BANKING                  ORIGINAL AMOUNT: $14,436.
        ACCT #

  AS OF 04/01/94, THIS OPEN ACCOUNT IS CURRENT AND ALL PAYMENTS ARE BEING MADE ON TIME.
  SCHEDULED MONTHLY PAYMENT: $137. LAST PAYMENT REPORTED TO EXPERIAN: 04/06/97. BALANCE
  $12,603 ON 04/27/97. MONTHS REVIEWED: 37.

  14    FROST NATIONAL BANK      THIS EXTENSION OF CREDIT, REVIEW OR OTHER PERMISSIBLE
        PO BOX 1600              PURPOSE WAS OPENED 08/19/94 AND HAS 36 MONTH REPAYMENT
        SAN ANTONIO TX 78296     TERMS. YOU ARE OBLIGATED TO REPAY THIS JOINT ACCOUNT.
        BANKING                  ORIGINAL AMOUNT: $5,000.
        ACCT #

  AS OF 08/01/94, THIS OPEN ACCOUNT IS CURRENT AND ALL PAYMENTS ARE BEING MADE ON TIME.
  SCHEDULED MONTHLY PAYMENT: $163. LAST PAYMENT REPORTED TO EXPERIAN: 04/14/97. BALANCE $621
  ON 04/27/97. MONTHS REVIEWED: 33.

  15    FROST NATIONAL BANK      THIS EXTENSION OF CREDIT, REVIEW OR OTHER PERMISSIBLE
        PO BOX 1600              PURPOSE WAS OPENED 07/16/93 AND HAS 180 MONTH REPAYMENT
        SAN ANTONIO TX 78296     TERMS. YOU ARE OBLIGATED TO REPAY THIS JOINT ACCOUNT.
        BANKING                  ORIGINAL AMOUNT: $25,000.
        ACCT #

  AS OF 11/01/93, THIS ACCOUNT IS PAID. PREVIOUSLY WAS CURRENT AND ALL PAYMENTS WERE MADE ON
  TIME. BALANCE $0 ON 11/25/93. MONTHS REVIEWED: 5.

  16    LORD & TAYLOR            THIS CHARGE ACCOUNT WAS OPENED 06/01/72 AND HAS
        424 5TH AVENUE           REVOLVING REPAYMENT TERMS. YOU HAVE CONTRACTUAL
        NEW YORK NY 10018        RESPONSIBILITY FOR THIS ACCOUNT AND ARE PRIMARILY
        UNDEFINED FIRM TYPE      RESPONSIBLE FOR ITS PAYMENT. CREDIT LIMIT: $400. HIGH
        ACCT #                   BALANCE: $502.

  AS OF 06/01/95, THIS ACCOUNT IS PAID. PREVIOUSLY WAS CURRENT AND ALL PAYMENTS WERE MADE ON
  TIME. BALANCE $0 ON 06/05/95. MONTHS REVIEWED: 99.




  CONSUMER CREDIT REPORT (CDI) P-91611597         05/19/97 00:22:00         Page    4
```

FIGURE 3.3 Sample Experian Credit Report (Continued)

experían

This is your consumer identification
number. Please refer to this number
when you call or write us.

    ID #

ACCOUNT   DESCRIPTION

17   NEIMAN MARCUS   THIS CHARGE ACCOUNT WAS OPENED 04/01/88 AND HAS
     P.O. BOX 729080   REVOLVING REPAYMENT TERMS. YOU HAVE CONTRACTUAL
     DALLAS TX 75372   RESPONSIBILITY FOR THIS ACCOUNT AND ARE PRIMARILY
     DEPARTMENT STORES   RESPONSIBLE FOR ITS PAYMENT. HIGH BALANCE: $180.
     ACCT #

AS OF 04/01/88, THIS OPEN ACCOUNT IS CURRENT AND ALL PAYMENTS ARE BEING MADE ON TIME. LAST
PAYMENT REPORTED TO EXPERIAN: 11/16/95. BALANCE $0 ON 04/30/97. MONTHS REVIEWED: 99.

18   NORWEST BANK,TX   THIS CONVENTIONAL REAL ESTATE MORTGAGE WAS OPENED
     ONE O CONNER PLAZA   03/18/81 AND HAS 30 YEAR REPAYMENT TERMS. YOU HAVE USE
     VICTORIA TX 77902   OF THIS ACCOUNT. ORIGINAL AMOUNT: $30,500.
     FINANCE
     ACCT #

AS OF 1997, THIS ACCOUNT IS PAID. PREVIOUSLY WAS CURRENT AND ALL PAYMENTS WERE MADE ON
TIME. MONTHS REVIEWED: 99.

19   NORWEST BANK,TX   THIS CONVENTIONAL REAL ESTATE MORTGAGE WAS OPENED
     ONE O CONNER PLAZA   03/18/81 AND HAS 30 YEAR REPAYMENT TERMS. YOU ARE
     VICTORIA TX 77902   OBLIGATED TO REPAY THIS JOINT ACCOUNT. ORIGINAL AMOUNT:
     FINANCE $30,500.
     ACCT #

AS OF 03/01/81, THIS OPEN ACCOUNT IS CURRENT AND ALL PAYMENTS ARE BEING MADE ON TIME.
SCHEDULED MONTHLY PAYMENT: $417. LAST PAYMENT REPORTED TO EXPERIAN: 12/01/95. BALANCE
$25,553 ON 12/21/95. MONTHS REVIEWED: 99.

20   PHILLIPS PETROLEUM CO   THIS CREDIT CARD ACCOUNT WAS OPENED 12/23/87 AND HAS
     PO BOX 77   REVOLVING REPAYMENT TERMS. YOU HAVE CONTRACTUAL
     BARTLESVILLE OK 74004   RESPONSIBILITY FOR THIS ACCOUNT AND ARE PRIMARILY
     NATL CREDIT CARDS   RESPONSIBLE FOR ITS PAYMENT. HIGH BALANCE: $16.
     ACCT #

AS OF 1988, THIS OPEN ACCOUNT IS CURRENT AND ALL PAYMENTS ARE BEING MADE ON TIME. LAST
PAYMENT REPORTED TO EXPERIAN: 04/29/96. BALANCE $0 ON 05/03/97. MONTHS REVIEWED: 99.

FIGURE 3.3 Sample Experian Credit Report (Continued)

```
        ACCOUNT                           DESCRIPTION

21    SEARS ROEBUCK & CO          THIS CHARGE ACCOUNT WAS OPENED 09/01/81 AND HAS
      PO BOX 5000                 REVOLVING REPAYMENT TERMS. YOU HAVE CONTRACTUAL
      RANCHO CUCAMONGA CA 91729   RESPONSIBILITY FOR THIS ACCOUNT AND ARE PRIMARILY
      DEPARTMENT STORES           RESPONSIBLE FOR ITS PAYMENT. CREDIT LIMIT: $3,240.
      ACCT #

AS OF 09/01/81, THIS OPEN ACCOUNT IS CURRENT AND ALL PAYMENTS ARE BEING MADE ON TIME.
BALANCE $0 ON 04/13/97. MONTHS REVIEWED: 99.

22    WACHOVIA BANKCARD SVCS      THIS CREDIT CARD ACCOUNT WAS OPENED 09/05/96 AND HAS
      3565 PIEDMONT RD            REVOLVING REPAYMENT TERMS. YOU ARE OBLIGATED TO REPAY
      ATLANTA GA 30305            THIS JOINT ACCOUNT. CREDIT LIMIT: $3,000. HIGH BALANCE:
      BANKING                     $1,192.
      ACCT #

AS OF 09/01/96, THIS OPEN ACCOUNT IS CURRENT AND ALL PAYMENTS ARE BEING MADE ON TIME.
SCHEDULED MONTHLY PAYMENT: $26. LAST PAYMENT REPORTED TO EXPERIAN: 03/05/97. BALANCE $879
ON 03/31/97. MONTHS REVIEWED: 7.

23    WELLS FARGO BANK            THIS CREDIT CARD ACCOUNT WAS OPENED 04/01/84 AND HAS
      P O BOX 29476               REVOLVING REPAYMENT TERMS. YOU HAVE CONTRACTUAL
      PHOENIX AZ 85038            RESPONSIBILITY FOR THIS ACCOUNT AND ARE PRIMARILY
      BANKING                     RESPONSIBLE FOR ITS PAYMENT. CREDIT LIMIT: $3,000. HIGH
      ACCT #                      BALANCE: $871.

AS OF 04/01/94, THIS CLOSED ACCOUNT IS CURRENT AND PAYMENTS ARE BEING MADE ON TIME BUT WAS
DELINQUENT 60 DAYS. ORIGINAL DELINQUENCY DATE 07/31/91. BALANCE $0 ON 04/30/96. MONTHS
REVIEWED: 99.
TIMES LATE: 30=0, 60=1, 90+=0
** CREDIT LINE CLOSED/REPORTED BY SUBSCRIBER **
```

YOUR CREDIT HISTORY WAS REVIEWED BY:

```
THE FOLLOWING INQUIRIES ARE REPORTED TO THOSE WHO ASK TO REVIEW YOUR CREDIT HISTORY

        INQUIRY                           DESCRIPTION

24    CREDCO OF OREGON INC        04/25/97 INQUIRY MADE FOR REAL ESTATE LOAN. THE INQUIRY
      4550 SW MACADAM #200        WAS MADE ON BEHALF OF NORWEST MTG 8024 AUS.
      PORTLAND OR 97201
      FINANCE

25    CREDCO/CONFIDENTIAL CRED    09/07/95 INQUIRY MADE FOR A MORTGAGE REPORT. THE
      9444 BALBOA AVENUE SUITE    INQUIRY WAS MADE ON BEHALF OF CONFIDENTIAL CREDIT.
      SAN DIEGO CA 92123
      PERSONAL SERVICES




CONSUMER CREDIT REPORT (CDI) P-91611597          05/19/97 00:22:00          Page   6
```

FIGURE 3.3 Sample Experian Credit Report (Continued)

experían

This is your consumer identification number. Please refer to this number when you call or write us.

ID #

_____

_____

INQUIRY	DESCRIPTION
26 FROST NATIONAL BANK PO BOX 1600 SAN ANTONIO TX 78296 BANKING	05/01/97 INQUIRY MADE FOR EXTENSION OF CREDIT, REVIEW OR OTHER PERMISSIBLE PURPOSE..

THE FOLLOWING INQUIRIES ARE NOT REPORTED TO THOSE WHO ASK TO REVIEW YOUR CREDIT
HISTORY. THEY ARE INCLUDED SO THAT YOU HAVE A COMPLETE LIST OF INQUIRIES.

INQUIRY	DESCRIPTION
27 AMEX ACCOUNT REVIEW P O BOX 7871 FORT LAUDERDALE FL 33329 NATL CREDIT CARDS	10/30/96 INQUIRY MADE FOR PURPOSES OF ACCOUNT REVIEW.
28 ATT UNIVERSAL CARD 8775 BAYPINE ROAD JACKSONVILLE FL 32256 BANKING	01/24/97 INQUIRY MADE FOR PRESCREEN PROGRAM. YOUR FILE WAS MATCHED AGAINST THIS CREDITOR'S CRITERIA TO DEVELOP A LIST OF NAMES FOR A CREDIT OFFER OR SERVICE.
29 BANKBOSTON N A 9910 EAST 42ND STREET TULSA OK 74146 BANKING	03/07/97 INQUIRY MADE FOR PRESCREEN PROGRAM. YOUR FILE WAS MATCHED AGAINST THIS CREDITOR'S CRITERIA TO DEVELOP A LIST OF NAMES FOR A CREDIT OFFER OR SERVICE.
30 EXPERIAN P O BOX 949 ALLEN TX 75013 UNDEFINED FIRM TYPE #8107876196921674	08/10/95 INQUIRY MADE FOR FREE CREDIT REPORT.
31 PROVIDIAN BANCORP 2301 CAMINO RAMON SAN RAMON CA 94583 BANKING	05/10/96 INQUIRY MADE FOR PRESCREEN PROGRAM. YOUR FILE WAS MATCHED AGAINST THIS CREDITOR'S CRITERIA TO DEVELOP A LIST OF NAMES FOR A CREDIT OFFER OR SERVICE.
32 PROVIDIAN BANCORP 2301 CAMINO RAMON SAN RAMON CA 94583 BANKING	06/06/96 INQUIRY MADE FOR PRESCREEN PROGRAM. YOUR FILE WAS MATCHED AGAINST THIS CREDITOR'S CRITERIA TO DEVELOP A LIST OF NAMES FOR A CREDIT OFFER OR SERVICE.

CONSUMER CREDIT REPORT (CDI) P-91611597   05/19/97 00:22:00   Page   7

FIGURE 3.3 Sample Experian Credit Report (Continued)

```
         INQUIRY                        DESCRIPTION

33    PROVIDIAN BANCORP          07/03/96 INQUIRY MADE FOR PRESCREEN PROGRAM.  YOUR FILE
      2301 CAMINO RAMON          WAS MATCHED AGAINST THIS CREDITOR'S CRITERIA TO
      SAN RAMON CA 94583         DEVELOP A LIST OF NAMES FOR A CREDIT OFFER OR SERVICE.
      BANKING

34    PROVIDIAN BANCORP          10/29/96 INQUIRY MADE FOR PRESCREEN PROGRAM.  YOUR FILE
      2301 CAMINO RAMON          WAS MATCHED AGAINST THIS CREDITOR'S CRITERIA TO
      SAN RAMON CA 94583         DEVELOP A LIST OF NAMES FOR A CREDIT OFFER OR SERVICE.
      BANKING

35    PROVIDIAN BANCORP          11/22/96 INQUIRY MADE FOR PRESCREEN PROGRAM.  YOUR FILE
      2301 CAMINO RAMON          WAS MATCHED AGAINST THIS CREDITOR'S CRITERIA TO
      SAN RAMON CA 94583         DEVELOP A LIST OF NAMES FOR A CREDIT OFFER OR SERVICE.
      BANKING

36    PROVIDIAN BANCORP          01/17/97 INQUIRY MADE FOR PRESCREEN PROGRAM.  YOUR FILE
      2301 CAMINO RAMON          WAS MATCHED AGAINST THIS CREDITOR'S CRITERIA TO
      SAN RAMON CA 94583         DEVELOP A LIST OF NAMES FOR A CREDIT OFFER OR SERVICE.
      BANKING

37    PROVIDIAN BANCORP          03/13/97 INQUIRY MADE FOR PRESCREEN PROGRAM.  YOUR FILE
      2301 CAMINO RAMON          WAS MATCHED AGAINST THIS CREDITOR'S CRITERIA TO
      SAN RAMON CA 94583         DEVELOP A LIST OF NAMES FOR A CREDIT OFFER OR SERVICE.
      BANKING

38    PROVIDIAN BANCORP          04/10/97 INQUIRY MADE FOR PRESCREEN PROGRAM.  YOUR FILE
      2301 CAMINO RAMON          WAS MATCHED AGAINST THIS CREDITOR'S CRITERIA TO
      SAN RAMON CA 94583         DEVELOP A LIST OF NAMES FOR A CREDIT OFFER OR SERVICE.
      BANKING

39    SIGNET BANK                01/17/97 INQUIRY MADE FOR PRESCREEN PROGRAM.  YOUR FILE
      101 GATEWAY PARKWAY        WAS MATCHED AGAINST THIS CREDITOR'S CRITERIA TO
      RICHMOND VA 23235          DEVELOP A LIST OF NAMES FOR A CREDIT OFFER OR SERVICE.
      BANKING

40    TEXACO CRED CRD BK PRESC   05/23/96 INQUIRY MADE FOR PRESCREEN PROGRAM.  YOUR FILE
      P O BOX 2000               WAS MATCHED AGAINST THIS CREDITOR'S CRITERIA TO
      BELLAIRE TX 77402          DEVELOP A LIST OF NAMES FOR A CREDIT OFFER OR SERVICE.
      OIL COMPANIES

41    VICTORIAS SECRET           10/21/96 INQUIRY MADE FOR PRESCREEN PROGRAM.  YOUR FILE
      4590 E BROAD               WAS MATCHED AGAINST THIS CREDITOR'S CRITERIA TO
      COLUMBUS OH 43213          DEVELOP A LIST OF NAMES FOR A CREDIT OFFER OR SERVICE.
      CLOTHING




CONSUMER CREDIT REPORT (CDI) P-91611597        05/19/97 00:22:00        Page   8
```

FIGURE 3.3 Sample Experian Credit Report (Continued)

experían

ID #

PLEASE HELP US HELP YOU:

AT EXPERIAN WE KNOW HOW IMPORTANT YOUR GOOD CREDIT IS TO YOU. IT IS EQUALLY IMPORTANT TO
US THAT OUR INFORMATION BE ACCURATE AND UP TO DATE. LISTED BELOW IS THE INFOMATION YOU
GAVE US WHEN YOU ASKED FOR THIS REPORT. IF THE INFORMATION IS NOT CORRECT OR YOU DID NOT
SUPPLY US WITH YOUR FULL NAME, ADDRESS FOR THE PAST 5 YEARS, SOCIAL SECURITY NUMBER AND
YEAR OF BIRTH, THIS REPORT MAY NOT BE COMPLETE. IF THIS INFORMATION IS INCOMPLETE OR NOT
ACCURATE, PLEASE LET US KNOW.

YOUR NAME: SOCIAL SECURITY #:
                                                    DATE OF BIRTH:
ADDRESS: SPOUSE:

IDENTIFICATION INFORMATION:

THE FOLLOWING ADDITIONAL INFORMATION HAS BEEN PROVIDED TO US BY ORGANIZATIONS THAT REPORT
INFORMATION TO US.

SOCIAL SECURITY #:

DRIVERS LICENSE #:
                LAST REPORTED   10/96

ADDRESSES:
                            GEOGRAPHICAL CODE=453-1200-3
THIS SINGLE FAMILY DWELLING ADDRESS WAS FIRST REPORTED 1990 AND LAST REPORTED 2/97 BY
UPDATE. LAST REPORTED BY FROST NATIONAL BANK. ADDRESS REPORTED 3 TIMES.

                            GEOGRAPHICAL CODE=453-1305-4
THIS SINGLE FAMILY DWELLING ADDRESS WAS FIRST REPORTED 9/90 AND LAST REPORTED 11/92 BY
UPDATE. LAST REPORTED BY LORD & TAYLOR.

                            GEOGRAPHICAL CODE=339-90247-4
THIS SINGLE FAMILY DWELLING ADDRESS WAS FIRST REPORTED 10/87 BY UPDATE.

                            GEOGRAPHICAL CODE=453-1200-3
THIS SINGLE FAMILY DWELLING ADDRESS WAS FIRST REPORTED 5/97 BY INQUIRY. LAST REPORTED BY
FROST NATIONAL BANK.

CONSUMER CREDIT REPORT (CDI) P-91611597   05/19/97 00:22:00   Page   9

FIGURE 3.3 Sample Experian Credit Report (Continued)

```
        EMPLOYERS:

        REPORTED MORE THAN 10 YEARS AGO BY INQUIRY.

        OTHER  :           DATE OF BIRTH:
                           NAME:

                           SPOUSE  NAME:

        FROM 2/97 THE NUMBER OF INQUIRIES WITH THIS SOCIAL SECURITY # = 2
        ADDRESS REPORTED 1 TIMES.
        SOCIAL SECURITY NUMBER YOU GAVE WAS ISSUED: 1963 - 1965
        INQUIRY ADDRESS IDENTIFIED AS NON-RESIDENTIAL
        ONFILE ADDRESS IDENTIFIED AS NON-RESIDENTIAL
        CKPT: BUSINESS ON FACS+ FILE/



        CONSUMER CREDIT REPORT (CDI) P-91611597        05/19/97 00:22:00       Page  10
```

Source: Reprinted by permission of Experian.

Credit history information is presented under two headings, *Account* and *Description.* The accounts under the first heading are listed in alphabetical order and include an address and account number for each. The descriptive information is to the right of the account name, address, and number. It includes the date the account was opened, its terms of payment, who has contractual responsibility for paying the account, the account's credit limit, and its high balance.

If the account is a bank loan, the descriptive information includes the date the loan was taken out, the terms of the loan (number of years to pay it off), who has responsibility for the loan payments, and the original amount of the loan.

Other Account-Related Information

Below the account and description information are several lines of information summarizing each account's payment history, including whether account payments are current; whether all payments have been made on time; the scheduled monthly payment; the first time the account was reported to Experian; the balance due on the account as of a certain date; and the number of months of account information Experian reviewed. Also shown in this section of the report are notations as to whether an account was closed by the consumer or by the creditor.

Public Record Information

Experian, alone among the big three, presents public record information in the credit history section of its report. In fact, any public record items in your credit file will be listed before any of your credit accounts. There is no public record information in the sample report.

Inquiries

The inquiries section of the Experian credit report, *Your Credit History Was Reviewed By:,* follows the credit history section. It lists the name and address of companies that asked to review your credit history, the date of the request, and the reason for the request. Experian is the only one of the big three that provides such detailed information regarding inquiries.

Identification Information

The last part of the Experian credit report presents your personal identification information. This section begins by listing your name, address, Social Security number, date of birth, and the name of your spouse—information that you provided TRW when requesting a copy of your credit report. Then it presents additional identifying information about you provided by Experian's subscribers. That information includes your driver's license number, current and former addresses, and employer information.

CREDCO's Confidential Credit Report

The CREDCO report entitled *Confidential Credit* combines the consumer credit information found in each of the big three's files to create one comprehensive credit report.

By eliminating the need to contact three different companies and pay numerous fees, CREDCO's product makes it easier for you to find out what's in your credit files. You'll pay a premium for this convenience, however. The report costs $26.00 plus $4.95 for handling and shipping for a total cost of $30.95, which is more than the combined cost of ordering a credit report from each of the big three.

To obtain a copy of your CREDCO report, call 800-443-9342 for an application or order form. Fill it out and return it to CREDCO with your payment. You can expect to receive your report within five to seven business days. If you pay for your report with a credit card, you can fax your credit report application to 619-637-3728. If you need your report ASAP, you can take advantage of the company's express overnight service by paying $49.95. If the company receives your application by noon Pacific time, you'll receive your report the next day. If you use CREDCO's express service, you must pay with a credit card.

The CREDCO report comes with an easy-to-understand explanation of how to read it and three credit report dispute forms—one for each of the big three. The company also maintains a consumer assistance line that can be reached by calling 800-443-9342.

How to Read Your Confidential Credit Report

Figure 3.4 shows a sample confidential credit report. CREDCO's report format is relatively easy to understand; however, because it retains some of

FIGURE 3.4 Sample Confidential Credit Report

Note: This is a copy of an actual credit file. Identifying information (i.e., name, address, Social Security number, date of birth, account numbers, etc.) has been removed to protect consumer's identity.

CONFIDENTIAL CREDIT

```
REPORT DATE: 05/27/97                              Reference Number :
                                                   Membership Number:
--------------------------------------------       -------------------------------------------
NAME(S):                                           Social Security Nbr:            AGE:
                                                   -------------------------------------------
CURR ADDR:
FRMR ADDR:
--------------------------------------------
```

```
REPORT SUMMARY:
-----------------------------------------------------------------------------------------------
Oldest Account    09/66| Real Estate Bal   $23,097| Current Accts.      27|  Public    Collection
-----------------------------------------------------------------------------------------------
Credit Accounts      28| Installment Bal   $13,224| Revolving Credit Avail. 85%| Records   Accounts
-----------------------------------------------------------------------------------------------
Closed Accts.        12| Revolving Bal      $2,324| Was Delq/Derog       2| EFX   0        0
-----------------------------------------------------------------------------------------------
Inquiries            10| Total R/E Pmt        $365| Now Delq/Derog       0| TRW   0        0
-----------------------------------------------------------------------------------------------
Inqs/6 mos            7| Total Other Pmt      $346| Past Due Amt        $0| TUC   0        0
-----------------------------------------------------------------------------------------------
```

```
=================================== DEROGATORY ITEMS ==========================================

Account Name/Number/Type of Account
Credit Bureau Date  High/ Mthly  Account  Last  Account Past   Last  Past Due  Hist
(Id) Bur Code Open  Limit Pymt   Balance  Rptd  Status  Due Amt Delnq 30 60 90+ Date  Historical Acct Status
-----------------------------------------------------------------------------------------------

CHEVRON U S A /          REVOLVING
(01) EFX   U  09-66      406   N/A    50   02-97  CURRENT              00 00 00  02-97  11111111111111111111111
(02) TRW   U  10-YR      400   N/A    20   04-97  CURRENT              00 01 00  04-97  111111111111-1111111111
(03) TUC   U  09-66      406   N/A    20   04-97  CURRENT              00 00 00  04-97  11111111-111

WELLS FARGO BANK /       REVOLVING
(01) EFX   I  04-84     3000   N/A CLOSED 04-95  CURRENT        06-91  04 01 00  04-95  1--------------------
(02) TRW   I  10-YR     3000   N/A CLOSED 04-96  CURRENT               00 01 00  08-91  111111111111111111111111
(03) TUC   I  04-84     3000   N/A CLOSED 04-95  CURRENT        05-91  03 01 00  07-93  1-1-1-111111------------
     COMMENTS: EFX: CLOSED. TRW: CREDIT LINE CLOSED. TUC: CREDIT
              LINE CLOSED.

=================================== END DEROGATORY ITEMS ======================================


Account Name/Number/Type of Account
Credit Bureau Date  High/ Mthly  Account  Last  Account Past   Last  Past Due  Hist
(Id) Bur Code Open  Limit Pymt   Balance  Rptd  Status  Due Amt Delnq 30 60 90+ Date  Historical Acct Status
-----------------------------------------------------------------------------------------------

AE OPTIMA /3 REVOLVING
(01) EFX   I  12-89     6000   N/A   1114  04-97  CURRENT              00 00 00  04-97  1
(02) TRW   I  12-89     6000   N/A   1114  04-97  CURRENT              00 00 00  04-97  1111111111111111111111
(03) TUC   I  12-89     1114   N/A   1114  04-97  CURRENT              00 00 00  04-97  11111111-111

AMERICAN EXPRESS CO /3 30 DAY ACCOUNT
(01) EFX   I  04-75      311   N/A    311  05-97  CURRENT              00 00 00  05-97  1
(02) TRW   I  10-YR      600   N/A    311  05-97  CURRENT              00 00 00  05-97  1111111111111111111111
(03) TUC   I  04-75      311   N/A    311  05-97  CURRENT              00 00 00  05-97  111111-11111

ANB CC /                 REVOLVING
(01) EFX   I  04-84     2200   N/A CLOSED 04-97  CURRENT              00 00 00  04-97  1111111111111111111111111
(02) TRW   I  10-YR     2200   N/A CLOSED 09-96  CURRENT              00 00 00  09-96  1111111111111111
(03) TUC   I  04-84     2200   N/A CLOSED 03-97  UNRATED              00 00 00  09-96  -11111111111
     COMMENTS: EFX: CLOSED. TRW: CLOSED BY CREDITOR. TUC: CLOSED.
```

Continued on page Two

FIGURE 3.4 Sample Confidential Credit Report (Continued)

CONFIDENTIAL CREDIT

Page Two

Reference number :
Membership number:

```
Account Name/Number/Type of Account
Credit Bureau Date  High/   Mthly Account  Last Account Past    Last  Past Due Hist
(Id) Bur Code Open   Limit   Pymt  Balance  Rptd Status  Due Amt Delnq 30 60 90+ Date  Historical Acct Status
-------------------------------------------------------------------------------------------------------------

ANBCC /          REVOLVING
(02) TRW  I 10-YR  2200   N/A  CLOSED  11-96 CURRENT              00 00 00  11-96 1111111111111111
     COMMENTS: TRW: CLOSED BY CONSUMER.

ANBCC /          REVOLVING
(03) TUC  I 04-84  1935   N/A  CLOSED  03-97 UNRATED              00 00 00  08-96 -11111111111
     COMMENTS: TUC: CLOSED.

ANN TAYLOR /     REVOLVING
(02) TRW  I 09-87  700    N/A  -0-     04-97 CURRENT              00 00 00  04-97 111111-11--11-1111111111

BK OF AMER /     REVOLVING
(01) EFX  I 11-83  6000   N/A  -0-     03-93 CURRENT              00 00 00  03-93 1111111111111111111111111
(02) TRW  I 10-YR  6000   N/A  CLOSED  04-93 CURRENT              00 00 00  04-93 1
(03) TUC  I 11-83  6000   N/A  -0-     03-93 CURRENT              00 00 00  03-93 11111111111

BLOOMINGDALE S /     REVOLVING
(01) EFX  I 01-74  153    N/A  -0-     05-97 CURRENT              00 00 00  05-97 111111111111111111111111
(02) TRW  I 10-YR  500    N/A  -0-     05-97 CURRENT              00 00 00  05-97 111111111111111111111111
(03) TUC  I 01-74  153    N/A  -0-     04-97 CURRENT              00 00 00  04-97 111111111111111111111111
     COMMENTS: EFX: CHARGE.

CHASE NA /       REVOLVING
(01) EFX  I 04-84  600    20   48      03-97 CURRENT              00 00 00  03-97 111111111111111111111111
(02) TRW  I 10-YR  600    10   10      02-97 CURRENT              00 00 00  02-97 11111111111111111111-1111

CITIBANK MASTERCARD /      REVOLVING
(02) TRW  I 10-YR  N/A    N/A  N/A CLOSED 04-96 CURRENT           00 00 00  05-92 1111111111111111111111111
(03) TUC  I 07-83  2300   N/A  N/A     03-92 UNRATED              00 00 00  03-92 -11111111111
     COMMENTS: TRW: CLOSED BY CONSUMER. TUC: CREDIT LINE CLOSED.

COMMERICAL /          INSTALLMENT
(03) TUC  I 07-86  6951   N/A  -0-     07-89 CURRENT              00 00 00  07-89 1

COOLIDGE BK /         CREDIT LINE
(03) TUC  I 10-76  -0-    N/A  N/A     10-91 CURRENT              00 00 00  10-91 111111-1111---1
     COMMENTS: TUC: CLOSED.

FCNB/SPIEGL/EBAUR/NWPT /      REVOLVING
(02) TRW  I 10-YR  400    N/A  -0-     04-97 CURRENT              00 00 00  04-97 1111111111111111111111111

FIB BKCRD /           REVOLVING
(03) TUC  I 04-84  1900   N/A  CLOSED  02-90 CURRENT              00 00 00  02-90 1
     COMMENTS: TUC: ACCOUNT TRANSFERRED.

FIRST OMNI BANK /     REVOLVING
(02) TRW  I 10-YR  1000   N/A  CLOSED  05-91 CURRENT              00 00 00  05-91 1
(03) TUC  I 07-80  1211   N/A  -0-     05-91 CURRENT              00 00 00  05-91 1111111111111111

FROST BROS /          REVOLVING
(03) TUC  I 11-83  396    N/A  -0-     09-90 CURRENT              00 00 00  09-90 11111
```

Continued on page Three

FIGURE 3.4 Sample Confidential Credit Report (Continued)

CONFIDENTIAL CREDIT

Page Three

Reference number :
Membership number:

```
Account Name/Number/Type of Account
Credit Bureau Date   High/  Mthly  Account  Last  Account  Past   Last   Past Due  Hist
(Id) Bur Code  Open  Limit  Pymt   Balance  Rptd  Status   Due Amt Delnq  30 60 90+ Date  Historical Acct Status
----------------------------------------------------------------------------------------------------------------

FROST NATIONAL BANK /          INSTALLMENT
(01) EFX   J  08-94  5000   163    621     04-97  CURRENT                  00 00 00  04-97  111111111111111111111111
(02) TRW   J  08-94  5000   163    621     04-97  CURRENT                  00 00 00  04-97  111111111111111111111111
(03) TUC   J  08-94  5000   163    621     04-97  CURRENT                  00 00 00  04-97  11111-111111

FROST NATIONAL BANK /          INSTALLMENT
(01) EFX   J  07-93  25000  231    -0-     11-94  CURRENT                  00 00 00  11-94  111111111111111
(02) TRW   J  07-93  25000  N/A    CLOSED  11-93  CURRENT                  00 00 00  11-93  1
(03) TUC   J  07-93  25000  231    CLOSED  11-94  CURRENT                  00 00 00  12-93  1-1

FROST NATIONAL BANK /          INSTALLMENT
(01) EFX   J  04-94  14000  137    13000   04-97  CURRENT                  00 00 00  04-97  11111111111111111111111111
(02) TRW   J  04-94  14400  137    12603   04-97  CURRENT                  00 00 00  04-97  11111111111111111111111111
(03) TUC   J  04-94  14436  137    12603   04-97  CURRENT                  00 00 00  04-97  11111-111111

LORD & TAYLOR /     REVOLVING
(02) TRW   I  10-YR  400    N/A    CLOSED  06-95  CURRENT                  00 00 00  06-95  11-1111111111111111111111

NEIMAN MARCUS /     REVOLVING
(01) EFX   I  04-88  180    N/A    -0-     04-97  CURRENT                  00 00 00  04-97  111111111111111111111111
(02) TRW   I  04-88  100    N/A    -0-     04-97  CURRENT                  00 00 00  04-97  111111111111111111111111
(03) TUC   I  04-88  180    N/A    -0-     05-97  CURRENT                  00 00 00  05-97  1111111111111111111

NORWEST /     REAL ESTATE
(01) EFX   J  03-81  31000  347    CLOSED  01-93  CURRENT                  00 00 00  01-93  111111111111111111111111111
     COMMENTS: EFX: CLOSED. EFX: REAL ESTATE MORTGAGE.

NORWEST BANK /     REAL ESTATE
(01) EFX   S  03-81  31000  352    -0-     01-97  CURRENT                  00 00 00  01-97  111111111111111111111111111
(02) TRW   S  19-81  30500  417    CLOSED  01-97  CURRENT                  00 00 00  19-97  111111111111111111111111111
(03) TUC   S  03-81  30500  352    CLOSED  01-97  UNRATED                  00 00 00  01-97  -11111111111
     COMMENTS: EFX: REAL ESTATE MORTGAGE. TUC: CLOSED.

NORWEST MTGE /     REAL ESTATE
(01) EFX   J  03-81  31000  365    23000   04-97  CURRENT                  00 00 00  04-97  1
(03) TUC   J  03-81  30500  365    23097   04-97  CURRENT                  00 00 00  04-97  11
     COMMENTS: EFX: REAL ESTATE MORTGAGE.

SEARS /     REVOLVING
(01) EFX   I  09-81  3240   N/A    -0-     03-92  CURRENT                  00 00 00  03-92  1111111111111111111111111
(02) TRW   I  10-YR  3200   N/A    -0-     05-97  CURRENT                  00 00 00  05-97  1111111111111111111111
(03) TUC   I  09-81  1300   N/A    -0-     03-92  CURRENT                  00 00 00  03-92  1111111111111

WACHOVIA BANKCARD SVCS /     REVOLVING
(01) EFX   J  09-96  3000   N/A    831     04-97  CURRENT                  00 00 00  04-97  111111
(02) TRW   J  09-96  3000   26     831     05-97  CURRENT                  00 00 00  05-97  11-11111
(03) TUC   J  09-96  3000   26     879     04-97  CURRENT                  00 00 00  04-97  1-11111

RECENT INQUIRIES INTO YOUR CREDIT FILE

(Id) Bur   Date   Abbreviated Company Name:
---------------------------------------------
(03) TUC 05-05-97  NATIONSBANK
(02) TRW 05-01-97  FROST NATIONAL BANK
```

Continued on page Four

FIGURE 3.4 Sample Confidential Credit Report (Continued)

CONFIDENTIAL CREDIT

Page Four

Reference number :
Membership number:

RECENT INQUIRIES INTO YOUR CREDIT FILE

(Id) Bur   Date   Abbreviated Company Name:

```
(01) EFX 04-25-97  CREDCO
(03) TUC 04-25-97  CREDCO
(02) TRW 04-25-97  CREDCO OF OREGON INC
(01) EFX 02-28-97  FROST BK L
(03) TUC 02-28-97  FROST BK-CON
(01) EFX 08-24-96  WACH BKCRD
(02) TRW 09-07-95  CREDCO/CONFID CREDIT
(03) TUC 09-07-95  CONFID CREDT
```

CURRENT NAMES AND ADDRESSES ASSOCIATED WITH YOUR CREDIT HISTORY

(Id) Bur Names and Current Addresses:

```
(01) EFX
(02) TRW
(03) TUC
```

PREVIOUS ADDRESSES ASSOCIATED WITH YOUR CREDIT HISTORY

(Id) Bur As of Previous Addresses:

```
(01) EFX 08-94
(01) EFX 04-91
(02) TRW 09-90
(03) TUC 09-86
(02) TRW 10-87
```

OTHER INFORMATION ASSOCIATED WITH YOUR CREDIT HISTORY

(Id) Bur Type   Content:

```
(01) EFX  EMPLOYMENT    EMPLOYER:
(01) EFX  EMPLOYMENT    OCCUPATION:
                        EMPLOYER:
(01) EFX  EMPLOYMENT    OCCUPATION:
                        EMPLOYER:
(02) TRW  EMPLOYMENT    EMPLOYER:
(03) TUC  EMPLOYMENT    EMPLOYER:
(02) TRW  ALIAS NOTICE
(02) TRW  ALIAS NOTICE
```

CONSUMER REFERRAL INFORMATION

Bur   Credit Bureau Name, Address and Phone Numbers:

```
EFX - EQUIFAX INFORMATION SVCS, PHONE: (800) 378-2732
      P.O. BOX 740256, ATLANTA, GA 30374
```

Continued on page Five

FIGURE 3.4 Sample Confidential Credit Report (Continued)

CONFIDENTIAL CREDIT

Page Five

Reference number :
Membership number:

CONSUMER REFERRAL INFORMATION

Bur   Credit Bureau Name, Address and Phone Numbers:

TRW - TRW CREDIT DATA, PHONE: (800) 422-4879
      P.O. BOX 2106, ALLEN, TX 75002

TUC - TRANS UNION CORPORATION, PHONE: (800) 916-8800
      P.O. BOX 390, SPRINGFIELD, PA 19064

On behalf of CONFIDENTIAL CREDIT - NEW TX this report is furnished at your request. This credit
report is issued to permissible users as defined by the Fair Credit Reporting Act (Public Law
91-508) and is done in the strictest of confidence. Good faith effort has been made to obtain
information from sources deemed as reliable, but the accuracy of this information is not
guaranteed. (First American CREDCO, 9444 Balboa Avenue, Suite 500 X3 Dept., San Diego,
CA 92123.)

Copyright Notice 1991 CREDCO Inc.

Source: ©1991 CREDCO, Inc. Reprinted with permission.

---

the codes and symbols used by Equifax and Trans Union but does not provide an explanation, it is not as useful as it might be.

The report is organized into three basic sections: identifying information, report summary, and detailed account information. It also includes a reference number for each consumer.

Reference Number

Located on each page of the CREDCO report in the upper right-hand corner is the *Reference Number,* which you should mention whenever you contact the company about something in your report.

Identifying Information

This section provides your name, current address, former address, Social Security number, and age. Additional identifying information is located at the end of the CREDCO report.

Report Summary

A unique feature of CREDCO's report, the *Report Summary* is an overview of the account information provided in the following section of the report. Reading from top to bottom and from left to right, starting with the oldest account and ending with the block of information that summarizes the public record and collection accounts information found in the credit files maintained by each of the big three—EFX (Equifax), TRW (at the time the third edition of this book was written, CREDCO had not revised its credit report format to reflect TRW's change to Experian), and TUC (Trans Union).

Credit History

This section of CREDCO's report is organized into columns that should be read from left to right. Under each creditor/account listing are up to three lines of information—one line of account-related data for each of the credit bureaus reporting information on the account. The report always presents the account information in the following order: EFX, TRW, and TUC.

Account Name/Number/Type of Account

The *Account Name/Number/Type of Account* section of the report straightforwardly provides the name of each creditor, a number for each account, and a definition of the type of account. For example, the sample report shows that the first American Express account listed is a revolving account and the second is a 30-day account.

Date Open

The *Date Open* column reports the date when you opened an account. The sample report shows that according to both Equifax and Trans Union, the consumer opened a 30-day American Express account on 4/75. TRW reports that the account was opened "10-YR" or 10 years prior to the date that the account history was reported by TRW. This is an example of a small shortcoming in the report as there is nothing in CREDCO's report or the explanatory material to explain what the abbreviation means. However, CREDCO's toll-free customer service office will provide an answer if you call.

High/Limit

Information in the *High/Limit* column indicates your credit limit on an account or the most you have ever charged on an account.

Mthly Pymt

This column of information reflects the amount of your monthly payments on a revolving or installment account. *NA* means that the information was not available or does not apply.

Account Balance

This is the amount you owe on an account as of the date the information was reported to CREDCO. For example, the sample report shows all three credit bureaus reporting a balance of $311 on the consumer's American Express card (30-day account).

Last Rptd

Information in the *Last Rptd* column reflects the last date that a creditor updated the account information in your file. That date is not necessarily the last date that you made a payment on the account.

Account Status

Account Status indicates whether, as of the date the information was reported, your account was current, delinquent, in collection, and so on. All of the accounts on the sample report are current or unrated (not reported that month).

Past Due Amt, Last Delnq, and Past Due 30/60/90

Should an account be past due, that information will show up in the *Past Due Amt* column. Next to that is *Last Delnq,* a column that shows the last date on which an account was past due, followed by a series of three columns indicating the number of times an account was past due—30 days, 60 days, 90 days, and so on.

Historical (Date) and Account Status

This section of the report uses number codes to provide a month-by-month payment history of up to 24 months for each account listed. A *1* means the account is current; a *2* means that it is 30 days late; a *5* means that it is 120 days late, and so on. A complete explanation of the number codes comes with each report.

Other Information Provided in the Confidential Credit Report

The confidential credit report provides four additional types of information at the end of each credit report—recent inquiries (the credit bureau to which the inquiry was made, the date of the inquiry, and the company making the inquiry), public record information, and current names and addresses as well as previous addresses and other information associated with your credit history, such as your employment history. The names, addresses, and telephone numbers of the big three are also included.

CHAPTER 4

Correcting Credit Report Problems

Years ago, when Robert and Sylvia were newlyweds, they went through rough times and had trouble paying their bills. They received many credit card offers and quickly succumbed to the allure of easy credit. Robert and Sylvia wanted so many things, and charging was an easy way to get them.

About a year into their marriage, Robert's employer announced that all employees would have to take a pay cut. With too much credit card debt and a lower monthly income, Robert and Sylvia again experienced difficulty paying their bills. Soon they were in serious financial trouble.

Eventually, with the help of Consumer Credit Counseling Service (CCCS), Robert and Sylvia recovered from their money problems and paid off their debts. CCCS is a national nonprofit organization with local chapters around the country that helps consumers in financial difficulty.

During the bad times, Robert and Sylvia's credit histories were seriously damaged, but they wanted to rebuild their credit so that they could eventually buy a home. As part of the rebuilding process, they requested copies of their credit report from each of the big three credit bureaus so they could identify and correct any problems in their credit files. Not long into the process, however, they became frustrated because inaccurate information that they were able to get deleted from their credit reports kept reappearing. One month their credit records would be free of the misinformation; the next month some of the information would reappear.

Robert and Sylvia's problems are not unusual. Many consumers ruin their credit by taking on more debt than they can handle. As a result, they face the challenge of correcting any problems in their credit records and rebuilding their credit so that in the future they will be able to borrow money at reasonable terms—a process that can take years. Like Robert and Sylvia, many of these consumers learn that addressing credit record problems sometimes requires patience and perseverance. In this chapter you will learn how to correct credit record errors and inaccuracies and how to deal with credit record omissions. You will also learn about changes in the Fair Credit Reporting Act (FCRA) that are supposed to make it easier for consumers to make sure that credit record errors they thought had been removed from their credit files do not reappear later.

Credit Record Problems

No firm number exists to show the percentage of credit files that have problems. During the early 1990s, estimates ran as high as 50 percent but given industry efforts to reduce that rate, the percentage is probably lower today. In addition, some of the amendments to the FCRA are intended to further reduce the incidence of credit record problems. Realistically, however,

 HOT TIP

One way you can help reduce the potential for error in your credit file is to use exactly the same name every time you fill out a credit application. For example, if you have a middle name, use it consistently or not at all; and always specify if you are a junior or a senior.

given that the industry collects more than 2 billion pieces of credit-related information each month and generates more than 600 million credit reports on close to 200 million consumers every year, there are bound to be errors in some credit files. Credit bureaus do make mistakes. Also, sometimes creditors and other information providers give credit bureaus incorrect information. Therefore, to protect yourself, read your credit report very carefully!

As you read it, be on the alert for the credit record problems summarized in Figure 4.1.

FIGURE 4.1 Common Credit Record Errors

Common credit record errors include the following:

- Information is commingled. Your credit record includes credit information for someone with a name similar or identical to yours.

- The name of a former spouse appears on your credit record.

- Your name is misspelled, your address is wrong, or your Social Security number is incorrect.

- Duplicate accounts show up.

- Account information is inaccurate or incomplete. For example, information for an account shows that you were delinquent for several months a year ago, but it fails to show that you caught up and have paid on time for the past nine months. Other problems could include incorrect account balances and reporting paid-off or closed accounts as open.

- Outdated information is included. In most cases, a credit reporting agency is legally permitted to maintain and report negative account information about a consumer for seven years and bankruptcies for ten years.

- Account information does not relate to you.

- Unauthorized inquiries are listed.

- There is a failure to show that a tax lien has been released.

If you discover these or other problems, correct them as soon as possible to minimize any possible damage to your credit record. Regardless of which credit reporting agency you are dealing with, the process for correcting errors is always the same under the terms of the FCRA.

Correcting Problems in Your Credit Record

If you find information in your credit record that you believe is inaccurate, complete the special investigation request form that will come with your report. Follow all of the form's instructions for filling it out.

You may also want to attach a letter to your completed form, dated and signed by you, along with copies of any documentation you have that helps prove the error in your report. The documentation might include copies of canceled checks, receipts, account statements, or previous correspondence between you and the creditor involved. Or if the lien the IRS placed on your property has been released because you paid off your back taxes but your credit record still shows the lien, enclose a copy of the document that released the lien.

Attaching a letter to the investigation request form is a good idea if you don't think that the credit bureau's form gives you adequate space to explain why you think there is an error in your report.

Keep a copy of your completed investigation request form, letter, and backup documentation to provide you with a record of what you said and when you said it. Also, the date on the letter will let you know when you should have heard back from the credit bureau. The FCRA says that after you've contacted a credit bureau about a problem in your credit record, it must respond to you within 30 days of receiving your investigation request form. If you haven't heard from the credit bureau within this time, give it a call.

The third reason for sending a letter along is that if legal action becomes necessary, copies of what you sent to the credit bureau will help create a

 HOT TIP

Experian allows consumers to call it about credit record problems by dialing a number listed on the company's investigation form. Be aware, however, that although using the number will expedite Experian's investigation, you won't have a written record of your communication with Experian and you will still have to mail any backup documentation you want to be sure it reviews.

written record of exactly what steps you took and information you provided in order to clear up the problem.

Once you have completed the investigation request form, mail it, your letter, and copies of any documentation you may have to the address on the form. Send it by certified mail with a request for a return receipt. When you get the signed receipt back, file it with the rest of your credit record information.

HOT TIP

In some parts of the country you may not get an investigation request form when you receive your credit report. Instead, you'll be given a phone number to call. When you call that number, you'll get instructions on how to initiate an investigation into your problem.

What to Include in Your Letter

When you write your letter, be as succinct as possible. Explain clearly what is wrong with your credit report and attach a copy of the report to your letter. Highlight or circle each of the problems you want corrected. See Figure 4.2 for a sample letter.

Include in your letter, in addition to the above, the same identification information you must include in a credit report request letter—your full name, current addresses for the past five years, Social Security number, and so forth. For a complete review of the required information, return to Chapter 2. If you are contacting Experian about a credit record problem, include in your letter the ID number that appears at the top of your credit report.

Recordkeeping

Set up a simple recordkeeping system to help monitor the status of your dealings with a credit bureau and/or creditor and to help organize materials related to the credit record problem.

Make copies of all correspondence related to the problem that you send and receive, and keep them in a folder. If you have a telephone conversation

FIGURE 4.2 Letter to a Credit Bureau Regarding a Credit Record Problem

Date

Name & Address of Credit Bureau

Dear Sir or Madam:

I recently reviewed a copy of the credit file your company is maintaining on me. In doing so, I identified the following problem(s): *(Clearly describe each problem using as few words as possible.)*

I have enclosed the following documentation to support my claim: *(Itemize the documentation you are enclosing.)*

I would like you to investigate this problem as quickly as possible, correct it, and provide me with a corrected copy of my credit report. Please send my copy to: *(your complete mailing address)*

Also, please send a corrected credit report to anyone who has reviewed my credit history over the past six months for credit purposes. *(You may also request that a corrected credit report be sent to anyone who has reviewed it for employment purposes over the past two years.)* Please send me written confirmation that this request has been honored.

If you need to reach me by phone, call *(area code/telephone number)*. Thank you for your prompt attention to this request.

Sincerely,

Signature

Full Name _____
Identification Number *(if you are contacting Experian)* _____
Social Security Number _____
Birthdate _____

FIGURE 4.2 Letter to a Credit Bureau Regarding a Credit Record Problem (Continued)

Spouse's Name _____

Current Address _____

_____

Previous Addresses for the Past Five Years

_____

_____

_____

_____

_____

about the problem, keep a record of that discussion, including the date and time of the call as well as to whom you spoke and what was said.

Other things to keep in your recordkeeping system include receipts related to any costs you may have incurred trying to resolve the credit record problem, account statements, and your credit report. In addition, if you have to take time off from work to do something related to the credit record problem, make a note of the date, the purpose of the errand, and the amount of time you took off.

Good recordkeeping not only helps you monitor what is happening with a credit bureau's investigation into your complaint; it also creates a written record that may be useful if you have to pursue legal action against a credit bureau or file a formal complaint with the Federal Trade Commission (FTC).

Frivolous or Irrelevant Investigations

If a credit bureau determines that your request for an investigation is frivolous or irrelevant, it can refuse to conduct one. However, it must tell you in writing about its decision and provide you the reasons why it thinks your request is frivolous or irrelevant. The credit bureau must also give you information about what you must provide it if an investigation is to occur.

The Credit Bureau's Response

The amended FCRA now provides that within five business days of receiving your investigation request, the credit bureau must contact the provider of the information you are disputing and ask it to check its accuracy. The information provider must respond by certifying to the credit bureau that the information is either correct or incorrect.

 HOT TIP

If an information provider fails to conduct a proper investigation after being contacted by a credit bureau about the accuracy of certain information in your credit file, you have a right to sue it.

Although the credit bureau must complete its investigation within 30 days of receiving your investigation request, if you provide the credit bureau with new information relevant to the investigation during the 30-day time period, the credit bureau can extend its investigation for up to 15 days. This provision does not apply if the credit bureau has already determined that the information you are disputing is inaccurate or incomplete.

Informing You of the Outcome of an Investigation

Within five business days of completing its investigation, the credit bureau must send you written notice of its findings. If it has determined that the information you are disputing is in error or if the veracity of that information cannot be verified, the information must be deleted immediately from your credit record or your credit record must be modified immediately. However, if the credit bureau later receives proof that the information you disputed is accurate, it can reinsert the information into your credit file.

When you receive the credit bureau's written notice of its findings, you should also receive

- a notice that the investigation has been completed;
- a revised copy of your credit report if any changes were made to it;
- a notice that upon request the credit bureau will provide you with a description of the procedure it used to determine the accuracy and completeness of your credit file, including the name, address, and

phone number, if "reasonably available," of the information providers it contacted during its investigation;

- a notice that you have the right to add a written statement to your credit report if you disagree with the results of the credit bureau's investigation; and

- a notice that if the information you disputed was inaccurate or couldn't be verified, you can ask the credit bureau to notify any employer who may have reviewed your credit record within the past two years or anyone else who reviewed it within the previous six months. (It is 12 months for residents of Maryland, New York, and Vermont.) You must indicate specifically who should be notified, and you may be charged for these reports.

 HOT TIP

If you ask a credit bureau to send a corrected copy of your report to certain creditors, employers, and so on, be sure you ask for written confirmation that the reports were actually sent.

After you receive your corrected report, wait a couple of months and then request another copy of the report. That way you can be sure that the problem you thought had been corrected has not reappeared because of a computer glitch or human error.

 HOT TIP

Associated Credit Bureaus (ACB) maintains an automated system that allows any credit record corrections to be automatically shared with all of its members. This means that if you contact an ACB member about a credit record problem and the problem is corrected or deleted, the credit files any other ACB members are maintaining on you will be changed as well.

The amended FCRA requires the credit reporting industry to establish an automated system that credit grantors can use to report consumer credit account changes, including corrections, deletions, and the like, that you initiated. The system will simultaneously alert all of the major credit bureaus of the changes, not just the big three. This means you won't have to do all of the notifying yourself.

Dealing with Inaccurate or Outdated Information That Reappears in Your Credit Record

As this chapter has already indicated, consumers often discover that the credit record information they thought had been corrected or deleted later reappears in their credit files. Sometimes this is because the credit bureau subsequently receives proof from the provider of the information the consumer was disputing that the information was in fact accurate. Other times it is due to credit bureau error.

To help address this problem, the FCRA now requires credit reporting agencies to maintain "reasonable procedures designed to prevent the reappearance of deleted information." Because the law does not define "reasonable procedures," however, the actual impact of this new provision remains to be seen. On the other hand, the revised law also says that before deleted information can be reinserted into your credit file, the provider of the information must certify in writing to the credit bureau that the information is indeed complete and accurate. Furthermore, the credit bureau must notify you in writing, within five business days, that the information has been reinserted; provide you the name, address, and phone number, if "reasonably available," of the information provider; and explain your right to add a statement to your credit file about the disputed information.

When a Credit Bureau's Investigation Does Not Correct a Credit Record Problem

It's possible that a credit bureau's investigation will find that the information you are disputing is correct. If this happens, you have several options. One option is to locate new or additional documentation that helps support your case. Make copies of any such documentation, write the credit reporting agency, and staple everything together. Be sure to make a copy of the letter for your files and send the materials by certified mail with a request for a return receipt.

Another option is to contact the provider of the information you are disputing and ask that it correct the problem. Prepare a letter similar to the one you mailed to the credit bureau and include with it copies of your backup information. In your letter, ask that the creditor send a correction to all of the credit bureaus it reports to as well as to you. Also, ask that the information provider direct those credit bureaus to correct your credit file. See Figure 4.3 for a sample letter.

To make certain that the information provider follows your instructions, ask to be sent a copy of the letter(s) that it sends to each credit bureau.

A third option for resolving a credit record problem is to call your state attorney general's office of consumer affairs to see if it can help you. Many states have their own credit reporting laws.

Written Statements

If a credit bureau notifies you that the information you are disputing is correct, it must tell you about your fourth option—preparing a written statement of no more than 100 words for your credit file. Use the statement to explain why you believe the information in your credit file is in error. By law your statement must become a permanent part of your credit file and must be provided to anyone who reviews your credit record.

 HOT TIP

If you need help writing your statement, the FCRA requires that credit reporting agencies make a staff person available to assist you.

Limitations of a Written Statement

Adding a written statement to your credit file when you cannot get a credit record problem corrected is always a good idea. However, you should be aware that for a number of reasons, the statement may have a limited

FIGURE 4.3 Letter to a Creditor Regarding a Credit Record Problem

Date

Name & Address of Creditor

Dear Sir or Madam: *(Direct your letter to the credit manager.)*

Recently, I requested a copy of my credit report from *(name of credit bureau)*. In reviewing the report, I discovered a problem(s) relating to the account I have with you. My account number is _____. *(Provide account number.)*

The problem(s) is: *(Describe the problem(s) as clearly and succinctly as possible.)* I have enclosed documentation that supports my case.

I would appreciate your checking into this problem and advising me of your findings. If you determine that you have not been reporting accurate, complete information on my account to the credit bureaus you work with, please provide the correct information to those credit bureaus and direct them to make the appropriate change(s) in the files that they are maintaining on me.

In addition, I would like to receive a copy of whatever you send the credit bureaus in response to this letter. Please send that correspondence to me at *(your complete mailing address)*.

If you need to reach me by phone, call *(area code/telephone number)*.

Thank you for your prompt attention to this request.

Sincerely,

Signature

impact. First, there is no guarantee that whoever reviews your credit record will actually read your written statement.

Second, because a growing number of credit applications are being read by computer, your written statement may not actually be read by the person who ultimately makes the final decision whether to give you the credit you want.

Third, an increasing number of creditors now use the big three's automated credit rating systems rather than reviewing a consumer's entire file. Once again, the person making the credit decision will not see your written statement because his or her decision will be based on ratings derived from your credit record information, not on a complete review of all the information actually in that record.

For these reasons, when you apply for credit it is always a good idea to let the creditor know that your file includes a written statement and that you would like the creditor to read it. Also consider providing potential creditors (and anyone else you know who will be reviewing your credit record) a copy of your statement as it appears in your file. This advice applies too when you have applied for insurance or employment and you know that your credit record information will be included in the decision-making process.

Other Actions for Consumers to Take

If you take all of the steps this chapter has already outlined to resolve a problem in your credit record and it still remains, you may want to consider a few additional options. They include filing a formal complaint, using mediation, and taking legal action. You may also want to contact the organizations listed in Figure 4.4.

Formal Complaints

If you have a problem with a credit bureau, it's a good idea to file a formal complaint against the company with the FTC. Its Washington address is: Federal Trade Commission, Credit Practices Division, Washington, DC 20580. You can also contact your regional FTC office; the address and phone number of FTC's regional offices are located in Appendix B.

FIGURE 4.4 Helpful Organizations

The following organizations are willing to help consumers who take all of the standard steps for correcting a credit record problem and have no success:

National Foundation for Consumer Credit
Consumer Credit Counseling Service (CCCS)
8611 2nd Ave., Ste. 100
Silver Spring, MD 20910
800-388-2227
(This number automatically gives you the phone number for the CCCS office nearest you.)

Bankcard Holders of America
524 Branch Dr.
Salem, VA 24153
540-389-5445

Public Interest Research Group
218 D St., S.E.
Washington, DC 20003
202-546-9707

The FTC receives formal complaints from consumers regarding a wide variety of problems, but an estimated one-third of all the complaints it receives are about credit bureaus. Not long ago, credit bureau complaints topped the FTC's list. Although the FTC will not take action against a credit bureau just because you file a complaint about it, it *will* take action if it receives enough complaints about a credit bureau.

In your letter of complaint to the FTC, explain your credit record problem and provide a chronological account of everything you have done to try to resolve the problem and the results of your efforts. Include copies of all correspondence and any documentation you may have that supports your side of the dispute. For a sample letter, see Figure 4.5.

FIGURE 4.5 Letter to the Federal Trade Commission

Date

Federal Trade Commission
Bureau of Credit Practices
Washington, DC 20580

Dear Sir or Madam:

I am writing to register a complaint about *(name of company)*, located at *(address of company)*. A description of my problem with this company follows.

(Succinctly describe the problem you have been trying to resolve and how the problem has affected your ability to get credit, employment, insurance, or other. Include a chronology of events that illustrates how long you have been working to resolve the problem, the various steps you have taken, and people you have spoken with. Detail the response of company representatives, and when possible include the names and titles of the persons you have spoken with.)

While I understand that you do not take action on behalf of an individual consumer, I want you to be aware of the troubles I have been experiencing with *(name of company)*. I hope that if you receive enough complaints, you will do what you can to make sure that this company cannot harm other consumers as it has harmed me.

Sincerely,

Signature

You should also file a complaint with your local better business bureau and your state attorney general's office of consumer affairs. These offices can advise you of your legal rights according to any state laws that may apply to your situation, and they may put your information in their own consumer complaint files.

Mediation

Mediation is a dispute resolution process that has become increasingly popular. You may be able to use it to help you solve the problem you are having with a credit reporting agency or with a creditor who provided information to a credit bureau, particularly if the company is a local business.

As a rule, mediation is much less expensive than taking legal action, not to mention being less stressful and time-consuming. However, you will not be able to use mediation unless all of the parties involved in your dispute agree to participate.

The goal of mediation is to help everyone involved in a problem work together to identify a solution all can accept. A trained mediator will facilitate the mediation session.

Many communities have dispute resolution or mediation centers. To find out if there is a dispute resolution center in your area, call your local, county, or state bar association, or look in your telephone book under "Mediation or Dispute Resolution Services." Some attorneys also provide mediation services as part of their law practice at considerably lower fees than their fees for legal services. Your local, county, or state bar association should be able to provide you with the names of these attorneys.

Legal Options

The FCRA gives you the option of taking legal action if you are unable to resolve a credit record problem by stating that you may sue a credit reporting agency or the creditor—whoever is at fault—for both actual and punitive damages. If you win your lawsuit, you may also be able to collect attorney fees and court costs. To win your case, however, you will have to prove willful or negligent noncompliance on the part of the credit bureau or creditor, and that can be very difficult to do.

Because some states have their own credit reporting laws, be sure to contact your state's office of consumer affairs or the attorney general's office to find out if your state has such laws and to determine if you should use your state's laws rather than the FCRA as the basis of your lawsuit, although in some very specific instances the amended FCRA now preempts state laws.

If you are considering a lawsuit, it's best to consult with an attorney who has experience filing FCRA-related lawsuits. The attorney may be willing to take your case on a contingency basis—that is, the attorney is paid by taking a percentage of any money you may win from your lawsuit. If you lose your case, you won't have to pay the attorney anything other than legal fees and expenses incurred on your behalf.

Following are suggestions for how to find a good attorney:

- Ask trusted friends, family members, or coworkers if they have ever worked with an attorney and if they were happy with the attorney's services. If any interest you, get their names and phone numbers.
- Call your local, county, or state bar association for names of attorneys who can help you.
- Look for lawyers who are in the process of establishing their practices; they may charge less than more established attorneys.
- Call each attorney to find out if any of them offer an initial free consultation session; you may be able to get all the legal advice you need during this session. Also find out how much each lawyer charges on an hourly basis. That way, if none of them will provide a free initial consultation, you'll know which ones charge the least.

If you are going to pay for legal advice, schedule an hour's appointment with the attorney you select.

At the start of your initial meeting, tell the attorney that you want the meeting to last only one hour and that during that hour you'd like to get the following information:

- An assessment of your legal position and how strong a case you have
- An overview of your options
- The lawyer's recommendation for the best option to pursue and how to go about it
- An estimate of how much you can expect to pay for the attorney's services
- How the attorney wants to be paid

If you are told that your chances of winning are slim to none, don't pursue legal action, although you may want to get a second opinion. If you're told that you have a strong case, weigh carefully the costs and the benefits of legal action before you decide to hire the attorney.

When talking money with a lawyer, find out if he or she would be willing to take your case on a contingency basis.

Negative but Accurate Account Information

According to the FCRA, most negative information can be reported for up to seven years. Bankruptcies can be reported for ten years although all members of Associated Credit Bureaus, including the big three, will report a Chapter 13 bankruptcy for only seven years after the date that you filed, assuming you successfully completed your bankruptcy.

If you find that there is negative but accurate information in your credit file, you can add a 100-word written statement to your credit file if you feel that the information requires an explanation. For example, you may want to explain that your credit record was blemished because you unexpectedly lost your job in a downsizing or because your child became seriously ill and all your financial resources went toward paying for your child's medical care. Your written statement should also include an explanation of what you are doing to get your finances back on track. Don't forget, however, that some of the businesses and individuals who may use your credit record information to help them make a decision about you may actually review your credit risk scores, not actually review your credit file, and will therefore never see your written statement.

To counter this problem, it's a good idea to provide a copy of your statement to anyone who you know will be using information in your credit record to make a decision about you.

Negotiating with a Taxing Entity

If your credit record has been damaged because you have an outstanding tax debt and a taxing entity has placed a lien on your property, the sooner you can get caught up on your taxes and get the lien removed the better. If you can't pay your tax debt in full, you can still deal with your unpaid taxes, depending on to whom you owe the money. If you owe back income taxes to the IRS or to your state income taxing authority, you may be able to negotiate a deal whereby the taxing authority accepts less than the total amount you owe, removes the lien from your property, and begins reporting to credit bureaus that the lien has been removed. This is called *an offer in compromise.*

If you owe back property taxes, the taxing authority will not accept less than the amount you owe. However, you may be able to negotiate a payment plan that would allow you to get rid of your tax debt over time by making installment payments. The taxing authority may agree to remove its lien once you have begun making your installment payments or have paid off a certain amount of the taxes you owe. If it won't agree to do that, at least by making your installment payments you'll be working toward the time when your tax debt is paid in full and the lien on your property can be removed.

To initiate negotiations, contact the appropriate taxing authority, explain what you want to do, find out whom you need to talk with and the paperwork you need to complete, and so forth. If the first person you speak with is unwilling to work with you, go to the next level of decision making within the organizational structure of the taxing authority. And remember, you're working with a bureaucracy so decisions may come slowly.

One final note on negotiating with the IRS: If you decide to seek an offer in compromise, you may want to get the assistance of a lawyer or a CPA familiar with IRS or state/local tax negotiations and the tax code. These people know whether your tax liability is likely to be compromised, how best to approach the negotiations, and which laws and forms apply.

The IRS

If the IRS has placed a lien on your property, it is important that you know about Form 656, Offers in Compromise. The Internal Revenue Code states that the IRS can work with you to negotiate a compromise on payment of your tax liability, assuming that the liability is not part of a lawsuit, as long as one or both of the following criteria are met: First, there must be doubt as to whether you actually owe what the IRS says you owe; and, second, there must be a question whether the IRS will ever be able to collect the full amount of your tax debt, including penalties and interest. It is up to you to prove that you are not liable for all or part of your tax debt. Evidence of that might include canceled checks, copies of tax forms, correspondence, signed agreements, and so on. If you are able to prove doubt about your tax liability, the amount by which your tax debt will be reduced will depend on the agency's assessment of just how much doubt exists.

To determine how much of your tax debt you can afford to pay, if anything, the IRS will use a set of standard guidelines to value all your assets and your current and future earnings potential. It will also make sure that you are up-to-date on all your other IRS income tax obligations. If you are not, a compromise is unlikely.

If you and the IRS are able to negotiate a compromise, you may have to pay a percentage of your future earnings to the agency.

Handling Omissions

As discussed in Chapter 2, not all creditors report account information to credit bureaus, and some do so only under special circumstances. If, in reviewing your credit report, you notice that an account with a good payment history is missing from your file, and if you feel that your chances of getting future credit would be improved if that account information were a part of your credit history, you can try to add it to your file if you think that it will help create a more complete picture of your ability to manage credit. However, credit bureaus are not obligated to do so and if they do agree to add the information, they may charge you a fee.

 HOT TIP

You may want to add missing account information to your credit record if you are denied credit because there is not enough information in your credit file or because you do not have a credit record at all.

Adding Information

If you find important omissions in your credit record, contact the credit bureau in writing. Specify exactly what you would like to have included in your file, and provide the name, address, and telephone number of the applicable creditor together with your account number. In addition, enclose any relevant documentation that helps substantiate your payment history. Figure 4.6 shows a sample letter. Be sure that you provide all of the identifying information specified in Figure 4.1.

FIGURE 4.6 Letter to Add Information to Your Credit Record

Date

Address

Dear Sir or Madam:

In reviewing the credit file you maintain on me, I noted that my credit record does not include certain information that I feel is important to a complete portrait of me as a credit-using consumer. Therefore, I request that you add the following account information to my credit file:

(Include a copy of your credit report, and specify the account information you would like added to it. Note relevant account numbers, and provide the complete name(s) and address(es) of applicable creditor(s).)

If you need additional information from me, you can reach me at *(area code/ telephone number and mailing address).* Please let me know if there will be a fee involved.

Thank you for your assistance.

Sincerely,

Signature

Full Name _____
Identification Number *(if you are contacting Experian)* _____
Social Security Number _____
Birthdate _____
Spouse's Name _____
Current Address _____
_____
Previous Addresses for the Past Five Years

_____
_____
_____
_____
_____

The following is a list of the types of information you may want to add to your credit file to create a more complete picture of yourself as a credit manager:

- Details on loans for which you have a good history
- Active accounts with good payment histories that are not mentioned
- Information related to your mortgage, especially if you have paid it in full
- Settlements on tax liens, judgments, or disputed bills

Although credit reporting agencies are not required to honor a request to add information to your file, they may do so for a fee. They will, however, verify the information you want added before they will agree to add it.

It is important that you be able to demonstrate your responsible use of credit over time. Therefore, if one of your creditors does not report regularly to a credit bureau and you believe that the missing account information helps demonstrate that you know how to manage your credit, update your credit report periodically by adding the missing information.

CHAPTER 5

Rebuilding Your Credit

As Sam V. sat in my office telling me about the new book he had bought that explained "the secret" of rebuilding credit, I kept thinking how easy it is for people desperate to rebuild their credit to be victimized. Sam's "book" was actually a mere 37 pages long, including copies of standard forms. For that, Sam had paid $49.95! The book discussed a clever way for a consumer to create a new credit identity, including substituting federal identification numbers used for tax purposes for Social Security numbers.

"So what do you think?" Sam asked.

"First of all, some of the things suggested by this book are illegal," I responded. "Plus, I'd be suspicious of any publication that doesn't include the name of the person who wrote it or how to get in touch with the author."

Sam looked at the book as if for the first time. "You're right. Whoever wrote this didn't put their name on it."

"Sam," I said, "this book is suggesting that you participate in a fraud. When it comes to rebuilding credit, the best advice I can give you is that there are no quick fixes despite what that book says. Rebuilding credit requires hard work; it takes time; and it takes diligence. And I might also add that it can take a tough hide to withstand the initial rejections you'll probably get from potential creditors."

I then shared with Sam the same philosophy and practical advice about rebuilding credit that I am going to share with you in this chapter.

A Creditwise Philosophy

A lot changes when you lose your credit. The most noticeable difference is that you have to live on a cash basis, which usually means making difficult choices about how to spend your limited dollars. When you lose your credit, you cannot turn to credit cards when you've used up your paycheck!

Often, people who no longer have credit and who have to rely on themselves begin to reassess their values and priorities. They ask themselves what they really want out of life, how important spending and material possessions are to them, and whether those things are so important that they will use credit to get these possessions. They also begin thinking about sacrificing and saving for things they really need or want.

Reassessing your priorities is an important conversation to have with yourself if your credit history has been seriously damaged and you can now begin to rebuild your credit. From my experience some people who file for bankruptcy or get into serious financial difficulty shared a common pattern: Their desires for things exceeded their ability to pay, and they began using credit to immediately fulfill their every desire. These people failed to distinguish between what they needed and what they wanted and between what they could save for future purchases and what had to be purchased with credit. Many of them tried to get as much credit as possible and then used it, whether they could meet the payments or not.

As a rule, consumers who can distinguish between their needs and their desires, who can delay using credit except when absolutely necessary, and who are willing to sacrifice to get what they want are less apt to develop serious money problems. Credit is not something you use to make all your dreams come true. Credit is a tool you can use to purchase something really important when you have no other practical way of paying for it.

Why Having Credit May Be Necessary

Although there are arguments for living without credit and it can certainly be done, in today's world that's not always practical. Not having credit will make buying a house or another major item more difficult, and it can also mean that you won't be able to obtain a loan to help finance your children's college education. This may not be a problem for those of you who don't consider owning a house or buying a new car a desire or even a necessity. And some of you will no doubt decide that you're going to place most of the financial burden for your children's education on them, not on yourself. But those of you who don't share these views will probably want to be able to obtain new credit at reasonable terms.

A Sound Approach to Credit Rebuilding

To avoid getting into trouble again, strictly limit the amount of credit you apply for, shop for the best deal possible, and get credit only for a specific purpose. In other words, don't get credit just to have credit. That means no more multiple bankcards—one will do—or multiple bank credit lines. You don't need them and having them will only tempt you.

If you want to buy a home, then focus on rebuilding and obtaining credit for that specific purpose. The same holds true for cars and other big-ticket items. The key to successful credit rebuilding is gaining the trust of your creditors, and you'll have to do that the old-fashioned way—earn it. You must prove to potential creditors that despite your past money troubles and regardless of why those troubles developed, in the future you will manage your money wisely and pay all of your debts on time.

I recommend that you begin rebuilding trust at the local level, in your own community. That's where you should focus your efforts to get new credit. You have a better chance of rebuilding if potential creditors can meet you face-to-face, are familiar with where you work, may know your family, or attend your same church. Now let's talk about how to rebuild your credit.

When to Start Rebuilding Your Credit

Once the financial difficulties that contributed to your credit history problems are behind you, you can start rebuilding your credit. Usually, however, if you filed for bankruptcy, you'll have to wait until your bankruptcy has been concluded. Generally, you can start rebuilding 18 to 20 months after its conclusion, although your bankruptcy will remain in your credit record for up to 10 years.

To prepare for getting new credit, the following are some things you need to do first:

- Review your credit record with each of the big three credit bureaus to spot errors, missing positive account information, or accurate negative information that you feel merits an explanation.
- Correct any errors you find and add written statements as necessary.
- Begin saving each month, even if it's only a small amount. Having a financial cushion will help you resist the temptation to use credit in the future.
- Keep trouble-free any credit accounts you may still have.
- Develop good money management skills. Your local Consumer Credit Counseling Service office, a nearby college or university, a county extension service, and the like are all possible sources of help.

The Credit Rebuilding Process

During the rebuilding process you should keep in mind a number of important rules of thumb. First, the credit rebuilding process will take time, so don't get impatient. Be prepared to spend two to three years or longer rebuilding. Second, don't be fooled into thinking that you can speed up the process with the help of a credit repair firm. As Chapter 6 makes clear, you'll be wasting your money when you work with one of these firms because they can't do anything you can't do for yourself for free. Third, keep to a minimum the amount of credit you apply for. One national bankcard is really all you really need as most restaurants, retailers, and other consumer-oriented businesses accept either MasterCard or Visa cards. Having multiple bankcards may be too tempting, and as a result you may take on too much debt. Furthermore, potential creditors will be less inclined to extend you credit if they see that you already have a lot of bankcards. Incidentally, you will probably have to start with a secured national bankcard, described later in this chapter, but once you've established a history of responsible payments on the secured card, apply for an unsecured bankcard.

Most local and regional retailers accept cards issued by Visa, MasterCard, or both, so most charge cards issued by stores are unnecessary and usually have relatively high interest rates.

Set a goal of paying off your bankcard in full each month. If that is sometimes not possible, don't charge more on the card until you've paid off all existing charges.

As I've already suggested, concentrate on building credit in your own community. For example, save money with a local bank. Once you have between $500 and $1,000 in your savings account, apply to the bank for a small loan secured with the funds in your savings account. If the bank where you have your account is unwilling to make you that loan, apply for a cash-secured loan with other banks in your area.

After you've paid off the first bank loan, apply for a second small loan that is not cash secured. You may also want to apply to your bank for a secured national bankcard.

The process I've just described is not the only way to rebuild a damaged credit history, but it is one that has worked well for many of my clients. What is best for you will depend on your previous credit history and your present circumstances. Remember, however, that regardless of how you rebuild your credit, your goal is not to get all the credit you can but to get only the credit you really need.

Getting a Bank Loan

When you are ready to apply to your bank for a loan, call to schedule an appointment with a consumer loan officer. Explain over the phone that you have had money troubles, have damaged your credit, and would like to discuss in person the possibility of getting a cash-secured loan.

If the loan officer tells you over the phone that he or she is not interested in working with you because of your credit history, call another bank in your community. Continue calling banks until you find a loan officer willing to at least meet with you to discuss your needs.

If the bank where you have your savings and/or checking accounts is not willing to work with you, then you should try banks in your community that are actively promoting debt consolidation loans or the bank where your employer banks. If your employer has banked there for a long time and is an important customer, and if you are a valued employee, the bank may be willing to work with you, especially if your employer provides a reference letter. Credit unions are another option.

Banks and Loan Officers

Banks are highly regulated businesses. They are expected to minimize the risks they take lending and investing money to safeguard their depositors' funds. In fact, if a bank makes too many high-risk loans, it may lose its charter and be out of business.

The career of a loan officer is in large part influenced by the success of the loans the officer makes. A loan officer who makes lots of loans that perform well—loans that are paid off on schedule—is much more likely to have a successful career at a bank than one who makes lots of loans that perform poorly. It's understandable therefore that with a damaged credit history, you are not going to be as attractive to a loan officer as someone with an unblemished record. As a result, it may take you a while to locate a loan officer willing to work with you.

If you can't find a loan officer willing to do business with you, recontact those who seemed most sympathetic or with whom you had the best rapport and ask each of them what you should do to get a loan. You may have to save more money as tangible proof of how serious you are about getting your finances back on track; you may have to increase your income; or you may simply have to wait until there is more distance between you and your financial problems.

When You Meet with a Loan Officer

When you find a loan officer willing to meet with you, ask the officer to mail you a loan application. Save time by completing it and bringing it to your initial meeting. Also bring along a copy of your current credit report so you can discuss it, provide explanations as necessary, and demonstrate that you have not had any recent problems with credit.

At the start of this chapter I explained that credit rebuilding is all about building trust. Your meeting with the loan officer provides you an opportunity to begin doing just that. Do whatever you can to assure the officer that your financial problems will not reoccur and that today you're a good candidate for a loan. Explain how your life has changed since you got into financial

HOT TIP

Dress conservatively for your meeting and don't wear a lot of jewelry. Above all, be sure to show up on time!

trouble and/or what you have done to stabilize your financial situation. Remember, loan officers are inherently conservative and risk averse, so you need to convince them that you are a good risk. If your credit problems were the result of poor money management skills, tell the loan officer about the steps you've taken to develop better skills. If your money troubles developed because of problems in your life—your spouse was laid off, you got divorced, you were ill and unable to work—explain how things have changed. Be ready to talk about why you need credit again: You're a businessperson who travels or entertains a lot; your children are approaching college age and you will need to borrow money to help pay for their education; you and your spouse would like to buy a house and start a family.

Should your first meeting go well, the loan officer will probably want to schedule a second meeting after ordering and reviewing another copy of your credit record. The officer will do this to be assured your record does not reflect any reoccurring problems; that you have been forthcoming about all aspects of your financial history; and that you have not begun applying for a lot of new credit. If the officer seems reluctant to make the loan, even on a secured basis, ask what you need to do to get the loan you want.

If the loan officer approves you for a cash-secured loan, the loan will probably be for an amount close to what you have in your savings account. Most likely, you will be asked to put the loan proceeds in a certificate of deposit (CD) at the bank. You will also be expected to begin paying off the loan according to the terms of your loan agreement. Most likely, you'll have a year or so to complete your payments. Be sure to make each payment on time so that you prove to the loan officer you are serious about rebuilding your credit and so that the officer will be open to making you a second loan that is not cash secured. Getting a second loan is important because it usually takes more than a positive payment history on just a single loan to rebuild a damaged credit history.

Getting a Second Loan

After you have paid off your first loan, order a copy of your credit report from each of the big three credit bureaus. Make sure that each of the reports accurately reflects the history of your payments on the cash-secured loan you've just paid off. If one or more do not reflect that history, ask the loan officer if your bank will report your loan payment history to the other credit bureaus. If the bank won't do that, then try to add the information yourself following the directions provided in Chapter 4.

After your first loan has been paid in full, let the loan officer know that you want to apply for a second loan that is not cash secured. If you had no problems paying off your first loan, it should be easy to get this next loan. If you have trouble, however, go to another bank. Once you get a second loan, pay it off just like the first one, and after it's paid off, once again check your credit history with each of the big three.

Shopping for a National Bankcard

Before applying for a national secured bankcard—a Visa or MasterCard card—take some time to understand the terminology and features of bankcards. A lot of offers are out there, and your goal should be to get the best deal. The best deal is not simply the bankcard with the highest credit limit; in fact, the credit limit should be one of your least important considerations. Because the first bankcard you apply for will probably be secured, as explained below, your credit limit will depend on how much money you put up as security. Factors more important to consider when shopping for a bankcard include a card's annual fee, interest rate, late payment fee, and grace period. For a short definition of these and other bankcard terms, refer to Figure 5.1.

Secured or Collateralized Bankcards

Using a secured bankcard responsibly is an excellent way to build creditors' trust in your ability to use new credit so that eventually you can get an unsecured card. Banks that issue secured cards require cardholders to secure or collateralize their credit purchases by opening a savings account with them

FIGURE 5.1 National Bankcard Features

When evaluating the best national bankcard to apply for, the criteria to consider are listed below.

- *Annual fee.* This is the amount you pay each year for use of your national bankcard; although the current average fee is about $20, some bankcard issuers charge their customers as much as $75 for the privilege of using their cards. However, some cards have no annual fee. If you apply for one of these cards, be sure you are not trading no annual fee for a monthly fee, a very high rate of interest, or other charges.

- *Credit limit.* This is the maximum you can charge on your bankcard.

- *Grace period.* This is the amount of time you have to pay your bankcard balance in full each month before you will be assessed interest or finance charges. Not all cards have a grace period, but if you are not going to pay off your account balance each month, the longer the grace period the better.

- *Interest rate.* All bankcard issuers charge interest on an account's unpaid balance. The interest rate you pay will depend on the issuer's terms of credit and the laws of the state where the card issuer is located. If you will not be paying your card balance in full every month, find a card with the lowest possible rate of interest.

- *Late charge.* Some card issuers charge a late fee, which can be as high as $20 if you do not pay your bill on time.

- *Penalty for exceeding your credit limit.* Some card issuers charge users if they charge more on their account than their credit limit allows.

or by purchasing a CD from them. That way, if you don't pay your secured bankcard debt, the bank can get repaid by withdrawing the money you owe from your savings account or by cashing in your CD. On the other hand, if you make your secured bankcard payments in full and on time each month, the bank won't need to tap your collateral and your payment history will gradually improve. Eventually, depending on that payment history, you may be able to obtain a regular bankcard.

HOT TIP

Don't apply for a lot of bankcards. Not only is there no reason for multiple bankcards but every time you apply for another card, the application shows up in your credit history as an inquiry and may make future creditors less interested in working with you.

For a list of banks that offer secured bankcards, write Bankcard Holders of America, 524 Branch Dr., Salem, VA 24153; 540-389-5445. The list costs $4; the organization also publishes lists of national bankcards with low interest rates and no annual fees.

Don't take at face value any bankcard's marketing materials. Remember that they are written to try to sell you something. Read the material's fine print and comparison shop. Shopping for and choosing a bankcard is just as serious as buying a car or a major appliance. It's a very important decision!

Once You Have a Secured Bankcard

Once you have a secured national bankcard, use it to charge only necessities, not something frivolous that you would normally buy with cash. Put aside the cash amount of your charged purchase so that you'll have the money you need to pay your bankcard bill when it arrives. After you have used your card for six months, order a copy of your credit record from each of the big three to make certain your account payments are now a part of your credit history.

Be wary of carrying over your account balance from month to month. Doing so can make it easy to run up a big balance that you may be unable to pay—and carrying a balance from month to month is expensive.

When evaluating secured bankcard offers, one of your primary goals should be to find a bankcard issuer that reports to at least one of the big three. Ideally, however, the bank that issues you a bankcard should report to all of them. If it reports to just one, the credit rebuilding process will take you a lot longer.

HOT TIP

Credit unions tend to offer national bankcards with low annual rates, so you may want to check them out if you're eligible.

You'll have other considerations when you are evaluating different secured bankcard offers. Some of these considerations raise the following questions:

- Do I have to pay an application fee? If I do and fail to qualify, will I get the fee back?
- How much money do I have to deposit as collateral for the bankcard? This is important because you will not have access to that money, which can range from a few hundred dollars to a few thousand.
- What rate of interest will my deposit earn?
- Do I have the option of putting my deposit in a CD or money market account rather than in a lower-yielding savings account?
- What percent of my deposit will my credit line be? It could range from 50 to 100 percent. Obviously, the higher the percent the better.
- May I increase my credit limit without increasing my deposit, assuming that the account has a good payment history?
- How soon after I've had use of the card may I increase my credit limit?
- May I convert a secured card to an unsecured card? If so, under what conditions?
- How soon after an account is past due will the issuer tap into my collateral?
- If I close my account, when can I get my collateral back?
- Are there fees associated with closing the account?

Beware of Bankcard Scams

Some companies deceptively advertise secured and unsecured Visa and MasterCard cards on television, in newspapers, or through postcards. Typically, the ads lead you to believe that all you have to do to obtain a national bankcard is just call an 800 or 900 telephone number. In fact, getting a bankcard is rarely as easy as that and if it is, you can be sure the card will not be a good deal for you. Avoid such ads. If you don't, here are some of the potential problems:

- If you call a 900 number, you'll be charged a per-minute fee and the company you are calling will get a percentage of that fee.
- The ads may not tell you what the cost of the call will be despite the fact that the cost of a 900 call can be high, ranging from 50¢ to $50 or more.
- You may have to pay an application fee for the bankcard.
- The ads may not be clear about the terms of the credit offer, including the amount of the security deposit required, if any, the application cost, processing fees, annual fees, interest rate, and the like.
- The ads may not be clear about all of the requirements, such as age and income, for getting the card.

Alternative Ways to Buy on Credit

As I have already made clear, rebuilding your credit is not going to happen overnight. It will take years for some of you to get a conventional bank loan. Therefore, it's important for those of you with credit problems to be aware of alternative credit sources. Most of these alternatives will cost more than conventional credit, but if you need a car to get to and from work or if owning a house now is really important to you, the following information should be helpful.

Buying a Home

It's unlikely that any bank will grant you a home mortgage until your financial problems have been over for at least two to three years and your bankruptcy is concluded. And when you do get a mortgage, you'll probably need a larger-than-average down payment and may be charged a higher rate of interest than someone without your credit history. With this information in mind, alternative sources of credit for buying a home include the following:

- *HUD (Department of Housing and Urban Development) homes.* These are foreclosed homes originally financed with an insured mortgage from the Federal Housing Administration (FHA). They can be an excellent source of well-priced real estate in your community and can include single-family homes, condominiums, and town houses. Although they are sold "as is," you can get some especially good bargains if you are willing to buy a "fixer upper." To find out about the HUD homes for sale in your area, look in your local paper's real estate classified section or call an area REALTOR®. Real estate brokers who sell HUD homes maintain a complete list of available HUD properties.

- *Owner-financed homes.* Some homesellers are willing to finance the purchase of their home to generate a steady stream of income, perhaps for retirement. Frequently, the seller will have less stringent credit requirements than a lending institution but will probably require a larger down payment than a bank and may charge a relatively high rate of interest.

- *Rent to purchase.* If you've rented a home for a while and the owner likes and trusts you, the owner may be willing to give you a lease agreement with an option to buy.

- *Loan brokers.* Loan brokers make their money by linking people who want to borrow money with investors, including mortgage companies, that will loan them money. Because the money a loan broker may find for you will be considered "high-risk" as a result of your credit problems, it will come with a relatively high rate of interest and you'll have to put up a larger-than-average down payment. The loan broker is paid from the loan he or she arranges for you. Obviously, you would not have to incur this cost if you had a good credit history and could get a loan in the conventional way. Be wary of any loan broker who asks for money up front before a loan has been secured, even if the broker promises that you can have your money refunded if you fail to get a loan. That's not how a reputable loan broker does business: An honest broker gets paid only if you get the loan.

Buying a Car

The biggest and most important purchase many people make is a car. Consider yourself lucky if you live in a community with good public transportation that you can use to commute to work and home because you're in a minority.

What follows are some ways to buy a car when your credit has been damaged.

- *Contact your friendly banker.* If you have already begun cultivating a good relationship with a local banker, schedule an appointment with the banker to find out under what conditions the bank would make you a car loan. The banker will be especially interested in how big a down payment you can afford to pay—the bigger the better—and the age of the car you want to buy. Banks don't like to loan money for old, used cars because of fear they won't be able to get their money back if they have to repossess the car.

  Your banker may also want to know if you can find a cosigner for the car loan. The cosigner would have to be someone with good credit who is willing to sign the loan agreement with you and promise to pay off the debt if you default. Friends, family, and employers are often cosigners. Be aware that if you fail to make timely payments on the loan, you will be damaging your credit record as well as the credit record of your cosigner.

- *Look for "bad credit no problem" ads.* In most major cities, some of the larger car dealerships offer "high-risk" loan programs similar to those loan brokers offer. Typically, these car dealers will sell you a car no matter your past credit history so long as your job is stable, your down payment is big enough, and you don't mind the high interest rate.

- *Used-car dealers.* Many used-car dealers will finance the purchase of a car if you have a stable job and can make an appropriate down payment. Used-car dealers are not going to offer you a bargain, however, and they can be dangerous to deal with. For example, a used-car dealer may know nothing about the history of the car you want to buy or even whether it's mechanically sound. Most sell their cars "as is," which means that you could end up buying someone else's problems.

- *Check out friends and relatives.* Sometimes friends or relatives have cars they don't need anymore. They may be willing to sell a car to you at reasonable terms rather than trading it in or selling it to someone else.

CHAPTER 6

Avoiding Credit Repair Company Rip-Offs

I first met Carlos S. several years ago when he came to my office to file for bankruptcy as a result of a failed business. His business troubles coupled with a divorce had left Carlos's credit history in a shambles. Recently, he returned to see me with his new wife, Michelle.

Michelle had her own financial problems as the result of a divorce. Despite the fact that her former husband had agreed, as part of their divorce settlement, to pay off the debts they had acquired during their marriage, he had not done so. Consequently, Michelle had to pay many of them. Although it had taken a long time, she had finally managed to pay off all of those debts. However, she discovered in reviewing her credit record that it did not reflect her debt payments and showed instead that she still owed on those debts.

Understandably, Carlos and Michelle were concerned that the misinformation in Michelle's credit record, combined with Carlos's bankruptcy, would prevent them from building the life they had envisioned. Michelle especially was feeling frustrated because she had worked very hard and made many sacrifices to pay off the debts from her former marriage.

When Carlos and Michelle arrived for their appointment, they showed me a newspaper advertisement for a company that claimed it could clear a consumer's credit history of all negative information, even a bankruptcy. Carlos and Michelle told me that they were considering hiring it to take care of the problems in Michelle's credit record and asked if I had ever heard of the company.

"It looks pretty good," Carlos told me.

"Too good to be true!" I replied.

I explained to both Michelle and Carlos that the ad was for a credit repair or credit fix-it company. I told them that dealing with such a company could be dangerous because many credit repair firms are rip-offs, and I explained that the FCRA gave them the right to resolve their own credit record problems. I also told them that the FCRA allowed credit bureaus to report certain negative information about a consumer's credit record for up to ten years depending on the nature of the information.

Nearly everyone who has had problems with credit wants to have a clean credit record free of damaging information. However, the desire for a problem-free record can sometimes cause consumers to pay for the assistance of a disreputable credit repair company rather than follow the advice in Chapters 4 and 5.

Many credit repair companies make big promises but rarely give consumers the results they expect and pay for. In this chapter I will explain what credit repair companies are, how they work, and how they can rip off consumers.

What Is a Credit Repair Company?

Although some credit repair firms are legitimate businesses that work within the law to help consumers resolve credit record problems and rebuild their credit, most credit repair firms charge exorbitant fees—anywhere between $50 and $2,000—to "clean up" a consumer's credit record. They claim that they can make bad credit, even bankruptcies, disappear from a consumer's credit record. Some of these firms are little more than floating con artists. They move into a locale, charge unsuspecting consumers a hefty up-front fee for their services, and then skip town, leaving their victims poorer and without the credit record improvements they were promised.

Credit repair companies cannot do anything you can't do yourself for little or no cost under the terms of the FCRA. That law gives you the right to have inaccurate or outdated information deleted from your credit record and to have written statements inserted in your credit record.

Neither you nor a credit repair firm can remove certain types of information from your credit record until the law allows their removal. As indicated in Chapter 1, the FCRA allows most negative information to remain in your credit record for seven years, although bankruptcies may be reported for up to ten years. Credit repair companies can't change the law for their clients. Only time can erase negative information from your credit record unless the negative information is erroneous. In that case you should follow the advice in Chapter 4, not hire a credit repair company. See Figure 6.1 for a summary of those steps.

Figure 6.1 Summary of Steps to Take to Resolve a Credit Record Problem

1. Complete an investigation request form.

2. Attach an explanatory letter and copies of supportive documentation to the investigation request form and mail the materials to the credit bureau.

3. If the credit bureau corrects your problem, ask it to send a copy of your corrected credit report to any employer who reviewed your credit record within the past two years and anyone else who reviewed it within the past six months.

4. Wait a few months and then request another copy of your credit report to make sure that the error has not reappeared.

5. If the credit bureau says that the information you are disputing is not in error, try to locate new documentation that helps you prove it is indeed wrong, or call the consumer protection office of your state's attorney general to see if it can help you.

6. Consider writing a 100-word statement explaining why you think your credit record is in error and asking that the credit bureau you are dealing with makes it a part of your credit file as the FCRA requires.

7. Talk to a lawyer familiar with the FCRA to find out if you have a basis for a lawsuit against the credit bureau.

8. File a formal complaint with the FTC. If the FTC receives enough complaints about a credit bureau or a credit reporting agency practice, it may take legal action. However, it will not take action on your behalf alone.

How to Spot a Fraudulent Credit Repair Company

Some illegitimate credit repair firms are easy to spot; others can be more difficult to identify because they may market themselves as financial counseling and advice companies. To prevent your being duped, the following are some sure signs of a credit repair company that will rip you off:

- The company makes impossibly extravagant promises about what it can do for you, such as: "We can wipe out bankruptcies and other negative information, no matter how bad your credit history."
- The company says it will use "little-known loopholes" in the FCRA to rid your credit record of negative information.
- The company claims that it can get you a major bankcard despite your credit record.

Bogus credit repair firms use a wide variety of techniques to market their services to consumers. These techniques may include distributing fliers in parking lots and posting them on telephone poles, advertising on television, using direct mail, telemarketing, and sending e-mail messages to consumers. Credit repair firms that use direct mail or telemarketing to market their services often develop their target lists of consumers from court records of people who have filed for bankruptcy.

No matter how a fraudulent credit repair firm tries to reach you, its goal is to get you to call a telephone number to learn more about its services or to schedule an appointment with a credit repair firm representative. The firm knows that if you are anxious to get rid of negative information in your credit file, you may fall for the promises of its representative. To help you separate fact from fiction so that you will be less apt to fall for empty promises, I've listed below three of the more common claims that credit repair firms make when they are marketing their services to desperate consumers . . . and the real story behind each claim.

1. **Credit repair company myth:** "If you are bankrupt, you won't be able to get credit for ten years."
   Fact: Although bankruptcies do stay on a consumer's credit record for up to ten years, each creditor has its own standards for granting credit and not all creditors refuse to work with bankrupt consumers. This is especially true for consumers who can demonstrate that their bankruptcy did not result from their misuse of credit but rather from

circumstances beyond their control, such as an unexpected job loss or serious illness, and that they have enjoyed a stable income.

2. **Credit repair company myth:** The credit repair company is affiliated with the federal government in some way.

    Fact: Such claims are simply not true.

3. **Credit repair company myth:** File segregation, a technique used by credit repair firms to create a new, problem-free credit identity for a consumer (explained later in this chapter), is legal.

    Fact: File segregation often requires you to make false statements on a credit or loan application; but you are committing a federal crime if you do. It is also a federal crime to misrepresent your Social Security number and to obtain an employer identification number (EIN) from the IRS under false pretenses, other things the credit repair firm may ask you to do as part of the file segregation process. In addition, if you use the mail or the telephone as part of that process to apply for credit and provide false information, you risk being accused of mail or wire fraud; and in certain states file segregation may constitute civil fraud.

Products and Services of Credit Repair Firms

In addition to their credit repair services, some credit repair firms also offer debt consolidation loans, debt counseling services, and national bankcards. Their loans, however, often come with very high interest rates and substantial up-front fees. Borrowers may also have to post their home as collateral; and sometimes a scamming credit repair firm will misrepresent the terms of the collateralized loan, making consumers vulnerable to the loss of their home.

The debt counseling services of credit repair firms often consist of recommending bankruptcy when bankruptcy is not a consumer's best option. And, typically, their offer for a national bankcard is nothing more than an application for a secured bankcard, something you can obtain on your own, as explained in Chapter 5.

Credit Repair Company Techniques

To fix problems in a credit record, disreputable credit repair companies may use techniques that are illegal or questionable at best. As noted previously, for example, if you make a false statement on a loan or credit application, misrepresent your Social Security number, or obtain an EIN from the IRS under false pretenses—all things that a credit repair firm may ask you to do—you will be committing a federal crime and subject to prosecution. Therefore, it is very important that you understand the kind of fix-it techniques credit repair firms commonly use so that if a company's advertising doesn't tip you off that the company is a credit repair firm, its techniques will.

The Use of Loopholes

The FCRA gives you the right to challenge any information in your credit record that you don't believe is accurate. As explained in Chapter 4, if a credit reporting agency is unable to verify the disputed information within 30 days, it must immediately delete the information from your credit record.

Some credit repair firms try to abuse this provision of the law by inundating credit reporting agencies with numerous and repeated requests to delete negative information in a consumer's credit file. The credit repair firm doesn't care if some of the information it disputes is correct because its strategy is to overwhelm the credit bureau with so many requests that it will be impossible for the credit bureau to verify all of the disputed information by the end of the 30-day deadline and the unverified information will thus have to be deleted, correct or not.

Credit bureaus have a number of defenses to use against this tactic. First, they can dismiss credit record information disputes that they consider to be "frivolous or irrelevant." Second, they have decreased the amount of time it takes them to respond to disputed information by, for example, increasing their use of e-mail to communicate with the provider of the disputed information. Credit repair companies that are determined to victimize consumers, however, continue to figure out ways to manipulate the FCRA at the expense of consumers.

Quick-Fix Methods

A popular credit repair firm technique is to create a new, problem-free credit identity for a consumer. Its objective is to hide the negative information in the consumer's credit file by "tricking" a credit bureau's computer.

One commonly used method for accomplishing such tricking is called *file segregation,* or "skin shedding," an illegal technique, as mentioned earlier, that involves altering a consumer's credit file.

Typically, financially troubled consumers will receive a letter or phone call from a credit repair firm telling them that for a fee the firm can help hide the negatives in their credit records and establish new credit identities for them. The consumers are instructed to use their new identifies when applying for credit in the future. Once consumers pay the fee, the credit repair firm will tell them to apply to the IRS for an EIN and to use it rather than their Social Security number whenever they apply for credit. An EIN resembles a Social Security number and is used by businesses to report information to the IRS and the Social Security Administration. Consumers will also be instructed to use a new mailing address on their credit applications.

Another tactic used by some credit repair firms is to advise their clients to send a check for partial payment of a past-due account and to write on the check that by cashing it the creditor agrees to cease all collection activity and to delete all negative information related to that account from the consumer's credit file. However, creditors are not legally required to honor such terms of payment and, furthermore, if a creditor accepted those terms, the consumer would have to take additional steps to ensure that the terms of payment were actually met. That's because it is unlikely that the credit repair firm would do the necessary follow-up, thereby leaving the consumer poorer from having paid money to both the creditor and the credit repair firm—and with the problem the consumer was trying to erase still in his or her credit file.

As this chapter has already made quite clear, quick-fix credit repair methods are not recommended because they are morally questionable and often illegal as well. Furthermore, if credit repair firms successfully erase bad credit from consumers' files or create a new identity for consumers, they may be helping consumers (whose financial troubles were the result of poor money management skills and overuse of credit) to obtain new credit before the consumers have had an opportunity to put their money problems in perspective, to understand why the problems occurred, and to acquire better money management skills. As a result, those consumers are apt to repeat their mistakes and end up in serious financial trouble again in the future.

The Credit Repair Organizations Act

To help prevent abuses by credit repair firms and to help consumers make more informed decisions if they want help rebuilding their credit, the federal Credit Repair Organizations Act (CROA) was signed into law in 1996 and enforced by the FTC.

Provisions of the CROA include the following:

- A credit repair firm must provide a consumer with a written contract detailing the services it will provide and stating the total cost of its services.
- After signing a contract with a credit repair firm, a consumer may cancel the contract for any reason within three business days of signing by sending the credit repair firm the cancellation form that came with its contract.
- A credit repair firm may not provide the consumer any of the services outlined in its contract until after the three-day cancellation period is up.
- A credit repair firm may not take money from a consumer or charge the consumer in any way until all of the services in the contract have actually been completed.
- Before providing a consumer with a written contract or statement, a credit repair firm must give the consumer a "Consumer Credit File Rights under State and Federal Law" disclosure statement. The statement must be worded exactly as spelled out in the law. Among other things, the statement must inform consumers of their right to dispute inaccurate or out-of-date credit record information without the help of a credit repair firm and the right to obtain a copy of their credit file from a credit bureau. In addition, the disclosure statement must provide consumers with an overview of their rights when working with a credit repair firm, including the right to sue the firm if it violates the CROA.
- A credit repair firm may not make any misleading statements to consumers, provide them with misleading advice, or attempt to deceive them in any way.
- A credit repair firm may not encourage consumers to alter their identification in order to provide them with a new, problem-free credit identity.

HOT TIP

The FTC's Telemarketing Sales Rule forbids telemarketers who sell credit repair services from requiring consumers to pay them until their services have been completed.

Legal Remedies under the CROA

Credit repair firms that violate the CROA face stiff penalties. For example, contracts that don't comply with the requirements of the law are considered void and are unenforceable. Furthermore, consumers can sue any credit repair firm that violates the CROA for actual damages or the amount paid to the firm, whichever is larger; for whatever punitive damages the court allows; and for court costs and attorney fees. Class action lawsuits are also permitted under this law.

State Restrictions

In addition to federal legislation, some 39 states have enacted legislation regulating credit repair firms. A list of these states appears in Figure 6.2.

State laws tend to be similar to the CROA. If you have lost money to a credit repair firm, your state law may be able to help you. In fact, many state laws require that credit repair firms buy insurance (bonding) to help protect consumers who may end up suing them. Call your state attorney general's office of consumer protection for information about the law in your state.

How to Find a Reputable Credit Repair Firm

If you'd like to have a credit repair firm help you deal with problems in your credit record because you lack confidence that you can do it yourself or you don't have the time, you may be concerned about how to tell the good firm from the bad one. But there are things you can do to make it more likely

FIGURE 6.2 States with Legislation Controlling the Actions of Credit Repair Firms

In addition to the District of Columbia, states that have passed legislation to control the activities and business practices of credit repair firms include the following:

Arkansas	Kansas	North Carolina
Arizona	Louisiana	Ohio
California	Maine	Oklahoma
Colorado	Maryland	Oregon
Connecticut	Massachusetts	Pennsylvania
Delaware	Michigan	Tennessee
Florida	Minnesota	Texas
Georgia	Missouri	Utah
Hawaii	Nebraska	Virginia
Idaho	Nevada	Washington
Illinois	New Hampshire	West Virginia
Indiana	New Jersey	Wisconsin
Iowa	New York	

you will get the assistance you want and will be paying for. Those steps include the following:

- Call your state attorney general's office or state office of consumer affairs to find out if there have been any complaints or legal actions taken against the credit repair company you are considering.
- Contact the National Fraud Information Center (NFIC) at 800-876-7060 to find out if it has any complaints on file about the credit repair firm. You can also learn the same information by going to the NFIC Web page at http://www.fraud.org.
- Check out the credit repair firm with your local better business bureau.
- Obtain a written contract from the firm that details exactly what it will do for you and the cost of its services. Ask that the firm's plan of action be based on your credit report specifically and ask the credit firm to state in writing what it can and cannot do to improve your credit record. Remember, a written contract is required by the

CROA. Do not sign the contract until you have read it thoroughly and are sure you understand everything in it.

• Don't give a credit repair company any money up front. As this chapter has already indicated, the CROA bars credit repair firms from charging consumers in any way until they have completed all the services in their contract.

• Avoid companies that promise money-back guarantees, which are usually little more than ploys to get your money and run.

What to Do If You Get Ripped Off by a Credit Repair Company

If you become the victim of a bogus credit repair company, take the following steps right away:

• Contact your state attorney general or state office of consumer affairs. If your state has a law that regulates credit repair companies, you may be able to use it to get back some or all of your money. And states can use the CROA to prosecute a credit repair firm and recover damages for its victims.

• Consider filing a civil lawsuit against the firm. If you win, you can recover actual damages or the amount you actually paid to the credit repair firm, whichever is greater; whatever additional punitive damages are allowed by the court; your legal costs; and your attorney fees.

• Tell your local better business bureau about your problems with the credit repair company.

• Register a complaint with the NFIC. It will forward your complaint to the FTC for entry in that agency's telemarketing fraud database. Again, the number of the NFIC is 800-876-7060.

• File a complaint with the FTC. Although this agency will not take action against a company as a result of an individual complaint, it may do so if it receives enough complaints to establish a pattern of abuse. Filing your complaint could help prevent other consumers from being victimized by the credit repair firm. To contact the FTC about a problem with a credit repair company, write: Federal Trade Commission, Credit Practices Division, Washington, DC 20580.

CHAPTER 7

Women and Credit

The daughter of a long-time client came to me for advice. Sandra C. had just started college and had received several credit card offers through the mail. In talking with her college friends, Sandra had learned how easy it was to get credit, but she was a bright young woman who had seen her parents go through difficult financial times. Therefore, she wanted to do what she could to avoid financial trouble—while she was in college and after she graduated. Sandra's parents had suggested that she get advice from me.

Sandra had many questions. She wanted to know how to build a good credit history for herself and—just as important—how to maintain that history. She also wanted to know whether she would have to make any changes in her credit accounts if she got married. Sandra wanted me to tell her about the mistakes I had seen other women make and how to avoid them. She also asked about the credit-related laws that give women special protection and rights.

Sandra is unique in seeking information about credit during her first days as an adult consumer. Unfortunately, most of my female clients wait too long. As a result, many of them face serious problems with credit if their marital status changes—sometimes very unexpectedly—as the result of divorce or the death of a spouse. To avoid such problems, it is imperative that all women educate themselves about credit and money management and that they establish and maintain their own credit identities separate from their husband's. Single women with established credit histories should continue to maintain their own credit identities if they marry. Similarly, married women who share their husband's credit should build a credit history in their own name with as few ties as possible to their husband's credit.

In this chapter I will discuss the reasons women often have difficulty developing their own credit histories, provide an overview of some of the special credit-related issues commonly faced by women, and talk about how best to deal with those issues. Special issues related to credit and divorce are discussed in Chapter 8.

Why Many Women Have Problems with Credit

Without a credit identity of their own, women who experience changes in their marital status are likely to have problems with credit. Women's credit-related problems tend to be the result of a number of factors that include

- the role women traditionally have played in the American economy, their tendency to take their husband's names and their reliance on their husband to handle such money matters as credit applications and loans;
- women's general lack of knowledge about credit reporting and how credit information is reported to credit bureaus; and
- a lack of understanding on the part of both men and women about why it is important for a woman to have a credit history completely separate from her husband's.

In the past, most women did not work outside the home, and consumer credit was acquired and maintained in their husband's names rather than in their own or in both names. Although many women helped manage their household's finances—and in some cases even helped pay for their family's use of credit—most never developed their own credit identity. These women were financial nonentities in the eyes of creditors and the credit reporting industry.

Today, increasing numbers of women have moved into the workplace, and two-income households are the norm rather than the exception. Many women, however, like consumers in general, remain relatively uninformed about credit, credit bureaus, and the credit reporting process. Furthermore, they tend not to understand the critical importance of having credit in their own name, and consequently many women do not.

In a society in which women often delay marriage to establish their career, wives tend to outlive their husbands, and an estimated 50 percent of all marriages end in divorce, women cannot afford to remain financially naive and vulnerable. They need to know how to manage their own finances whether they are single, married, widowed, or divorced. Married women in particular need to actively participate in the management of their family's finances and maintain or develop their own credit identity.

Learning about Credit and Money Management

You can educate yourself about money matters in a number of ways. For example, you may want to take a money management class at your local community college or university. Your local Consumer Credit Counseling Service office may offer courses in money management and understanding credit. Reading books and magazines on these subjects is also an option.

Another educational resource is the Women's Financial Information Program (WFIP), a seven-week program specifically designed for middle-aged and older women. The WFIP teaches money management skills and helps women develop the confidence to make decisions about money matters; it is offered through local organizations like YMCAs and community colleges. To find out if the WFIP is offered in your area, call your local community college, YMCA, or a local women's professional organization. Other sources of information about the program may include your local chamber of commerce, banker, CPA, or family financial adviser. These resources may also be able to advise you about other ways you can increase your financial savvy.

The Significance of Account-User Status Designations

An important but often overlooked part of credit education is understanding the meaning of common account-user status designations and why some designations are better for building credit than others. This knowledge is invaluable to the woman who wants to build a credit history in her own name.

Account-user status designations indicate to creditors and potential creditors the person or persons who can use a particular account and the degree to which each user is legally responsible for managing and paying on that account. Generally, the person who can use an account and the person who has payment responsibility are established at the time credit is applied for, although often a user can be added at a later date.

Many women do not understand that being listed as an authorized user on their husband's accounts does little to build their own credit identity. Nor do they understand that if all of their accounts are joint accounts—shared with their husband—these women risk losing that credit if they become separated, divorced, or widowed.

Different account designations convey different messages about a user's responsibility for an account. Therefore, various designations will be of greater or lesser help to a woman when she is trying to establish her own credit identity.

The most common account-user designations and their effects on a woman's credit building efforts are summarized below:

- *Authorized-user status.* A woman who is listed as an authorized user on her husband's account has permission to use the account but has no legal responsibility for it. In other words, authorized-user status indicates that a woman is relying on her spouse's earning power to pay. Accounts with this status are of minimal value to women who want to establish their own credit identity.

- *Joint-user status.* If a woman has joint-user status on an account, she and her husband can both use the account and they share equal legal responsibility for account payments. Because there is shared responsibility, joint-user accounts can help women build their own credit history. However, these accounts also link a woman's credit history to her husband's, which means that if a woman's husband abuses a joint credit account, the adverse account information will appear in her credit history as well as his.

- *Individual.* If a woman's accounts are designated as individual, she has sole responsibility for payments and is the only person authorized to use the account. Women with individual accounts qualified for that credit on their own. Individual accounts place women in the strongest financial position if their marital status changes because the accounts do not link a woman's use of credit or her ability to obtain credit to her spouse's income and credit history.

Women Living in Community Property States

It is important for women living in community property states to realize that they will not necessarily enjoy the benefits of individual credit and that they will be less able to insulate themselves from any money troubles that their husbands or former husbands may have. Community property states are:

Arizona	New Mexico
California	Texas
Idaho	Washington
Louisiana	Wisconsin
Nevada	

(The Commonwealth of Puerto Rico also has community property laws.)

In community property states, husbands and wives are viewed as economic partners, and the after-marriage earnings and property of each spouse are considered to be jointly held and controlled. Thus, in a community property state, if your spouse gets credit in his or her own name during your marriage and a creditor wins a lawsuit against your spouse for nonpayment, the creditor has a legal right to collect from any of your marital property no matter who actually bought it or uses it.

When a woman applies for credit in her own name in a community property state, a creditor has the right to ask her about her marital status and to request information about her husband—if her husband will be contractually liable for the debt or if she will be relying on his income to help make the payments. However, if half of the couple's community property and income (in community property states, each spouse owns half of the value of their marital assets) qualifies the woman for the credit she's applying for, her husband will not have to be a coapplicant, although a creditor will still have the right to ask for information about him.

If a woman living in a community property state uses property that is jointly owned by her and her husband as collateral, a creditor may require that her husband cosign the loan even if the woman will be solely responsible for repayment. Her husband cannot be required to be a cosignator on the note unless he will be specifically obligated to help repay the debt.

Women and Credit in Separate Property States

Most states are separate property states in which the credit history of a woman's husband is irrelevant to her request for credit because by law she alone is responsible for making payments on any debt she incurs in her name. In these states, a husband is not required to cosign a credit application, and creditors are barred from asking about a woman's marital status.

Exceptions do apply, however, when property is involved. When a woman wants to finance the purchase of property in her own name and she posts collateral, the creditor may require that her spouse cosign the note. (The same would hold true if the husband purchased property in his own name.) By having the spouse cosign, the creditor is ensuring that the property can be taken back and sold to recover its costs if one spouse defaults. A creditor may also require a spouse to sign a security agreement so that it can repossess the property should the owner spouse default.

For specific information about marital property rights in your state, contact the office of your state's attorney general or your state's office of consumer affairs.

The Advantage of Individual Credit

Having good individual credit provides women several important benefits both in and out of marriage. First, if a woman's husband experiences financial difficulty and has trouble paying his bills or if he is a poor money manager and doesn't make account payments on time, her good credit will remain unblemished even though his is damaged. This would not be the case if the woman and her husband shared the accounts he was not paying on time.

Second, a woman with her own credit is better able to maximize her family's financial options and opportunities—especially important if a woman's spouse gets into financial trouble, loses his job, or becomes seriously ill and has to stop working. In such situations, a woman with her own credit will be able to provide her family with more alternatives for dealing with difficult financial problems.

Third, as discussed earlier, women with their own credit identity will be better positioned to create a positive life for themselves after separation, divorce, or widowhood.

If you are a married woman in the process of building your own credit history, your ultimate goal should be to obtain individual credit in your own name, keeping joint credit to an absolute minimum. Realistically, however, if you have little or no individual credit to start with, you may need to begin by applying for joint credit. Once you've used the joint credit accounts to begin the building process and once you've established a good payment history on those accounts, you can then use that history to get individual credit. A warning: Use this approach only if you feel absolutely confident that your husband will not abuse the credit you share, damaging your credit history and his at the same time. View shared or joint credit only as a means to an end—obtaining individual credit.

 HOT TIP

If, as part of a divorce agreement, your ex-spouse assumes responsibility for paying off your joint accounts but fails to do so, the unpaid creditors have the right to collect from you—another argument for individual, not joint, credit.

How to Build Your Own Credit History

There is no single, surefire way to develop a credit history for yourself, but the approach outlined in this section is an excellent way to begin. It starts with the easiest-to-get types of credit and builds to credit that is more difficult to obtain.

Before you begin the credit building process, make sure that any assets owned by you and your husband—real estate, cars, boats, stocks, and bank accounts, for example—are listed in both of your names. All of these assets should be listed every time you apply for credit.

You should also request a copy of your credit report and your husband's from each of the big three credit bureaus before you begin the credit application process. Doing so will accomplish two things: It will help you determine which, if any, of the major national credit bureaus are maintaining a credit file on you and it will help you find out what is in each credit file. When you receive copies of your credit reports, review them carefully for errors and omissions. If you find any problems, follow the steps outlined in Chapter 4 for dealing with credit record problems.

If all of your credit is in your husband's name, you can request that each of the credit bureaus maintaining a credit file on him establish a file in your name as well. Your file should include any accounts you set up in your own name, accounts in your husband's name that you use, and accounts in your husband's name that you are contractually liable for (applicable only if you live in a community property state). At the same time, ask creditors to begin reporting credit information in your name as well as your husband's.

If you have a credit record in your own name and you need to use joint accounts to help build your history, make sure those accounts are part of your record, assuming they have positive payment histories. Also make sure that any credit you had in your maiden name or in another town is part of your credit record. If you find that certain accounts are missing, write to the appropriate credit bureau and ask that it add the information. Most will, although they may charge a small fee.

Once you have reviewed your credit reports and those of your spouse and dealt with any problems, it's time to initiate the credit building process. If you have little or no credit, the best approach is to obtain a small cash-secured loan from your bank. This is an important first step because if your marital situation changes sometime in the future and you need to borrow money, you will already have a positive relationship established with the bank.

Schedule an appointment with a loan officer and explain what you want to accomplish. If the first bank you talk with is unwilling to work with you, go to another bank. When you find one that is willing to work with you, open a checking account or a savings account in your own name at that bank.

The bank will make you either an unsecured or a secured loan. It may ask that you secure the loan with an asset, or it may want to make a cash-secured loan. If the bank makes you a cash-secured loan, it will probably ask that you put the loan proceeds in a certificate of deposit (CD) at the bank. In other words, you will not have the use of the loan money, which is all right, however, as the purpose of the loan is to build a strong credit history in your own name, not to purchase things. If you default on the loan, the certificate of deposit or the asset you have posted as collateral allows the bank to recover its losses.

 HOT TIP

If the bank requires you to have a cosigner to get a loan, don't ask your husband to cosign; ask a close friend or relative instead.

Once you've paid off your loan, request another copy of your credit report to make sure that it reflects your loan payments. If it doesn't, ask your loan officer to report the payment history.

Depending on your situation, you may now be ready to obtain a credit card in your own name. Or you may need to apply to your bank for a second, this time unsecured, loan or for a loan without a cosignator.

If you apply for a credit card, begin by applying for credit that is relatively easy to obtain, such as retail store charge cards and oil and gas cards. Charge a small amount and make your payments on time.

After you have demonstrated that you can manage this new credit, apply for a national bankcard. Having one can help make other forms of credit more available to you. If your own bank offers a bankcard and if its terms are competitive, apply for it.

Secured Bankcards

If you can't get a national bankcard, apply for a secured bankcard, a card designed for people who want a bankcard but can't qualify for an unsecured MasterCard or Visa credit card. You may be able to use your secured bankcard as a stepping stone to an unsecured bankcard if you demonstrate that you are able to use your secured credit wisely and if you make all account payments on time.

If you are approved for a secured card, you'll be required to collateralize your credit purchases by either opening a savings account with the issuing bank or purchasing a CD from it. Then if you default on your payments, the card issuer can withdraw money from your account—or cash in your CD—to pay your account balance.

When shopping for a secured bankcard, several factors you should consider are the amount of the deposit you will be required to put up and the rate of interest you will be earning on that money; what your credit line will be as a percentage of your deposit; whether you can convert your secured card to an unsecured card, assuming a positive payment history; and the fee for an application or processing.

If you already have some credit in your own name, or if you and your husband have some long-standing, well-performing joint credit accounts, you may be able to shorten the credit building process, especially if you have a well-paying, relatively secure job. In such a situation, credit building may be a matter of simply making sure that you have a bank account, at least one oil

HOT TIP

For an up-to-date list of banks offering secured and unsecured bankcards and the terms of those cards, call Bankcard Holders of America at 540-389-5445.

and gas card, a national bankcard, and a travel and entertainment card in your name.

During the credit building process, be sure to use your full name rather than your husband's name when applying for new credit—for example, Ms. or Mrs. Susan J. Smith and not Mrs. John Smith. Also review the credit cards that you have now to see if any of them are in your husband's name.

If a credit card is not in your name, information for that account is being reported in your husband's name only. In that case you have two options—assuming the account is in good standing. You can ask your husband to contact the creditor and request that you be listed as a joint user on the account and have a new card issued in your own name. Or you can apply for individual credit from the creditor. The option best for you depends on where you are in the credit building process.

Additional Credit Building Advice

As you build your own credit history, be sure to limit the amount of credit you obtain. As this book has already indicated, creditors don't look favorably on consumers who have a lot of credit, even if most of that credit represents inactive accounts. The reason is because creditors have no way of knowing when you might begin using an inactive account, how much additional debt you might assume, and if additional debt will jeopardize your ability to make future payments on already active accounts.

Remember, too, that credit bureaus maintain a record of the number of creditors who make inquiries about your credit history. If creditors feel that you are applying for too much credit and may possibly go beyond your ability to pay, they may view you as a credit risk.

Finally, use your credit to purchase necessities only, not frivolous items, and keep account balances as low as possible. Be sure to make all account payments on time so that the credit history you build will be a positive one.

The Equal Credit Opportunity Act

When building your own credit, you'll want to know about the federal Equal Credit Opportunity Act (ECOA). Enacted in 1974, the ECOA was written to help ensure that, among other things, women are not denied access to credit simply because of their sex. The ECOA also helps married women develop their own credit history.

Before passage of the ECOA, most women, regardless of their marital status, had a difficult time obtaining credit and therefore found it hard, if not impossible, to establish a credit file in their own name because, as indicated earlier in this chapter, men were our society's traditional breadwinners until relatively recently. Therefore, credit and money management were not viewed as subjects that most women needed to be concerned about. Even in cases of women who chose to work after marriage, the credit industry assumed that ultimately marriage, childbirth, and family responsibilities would interrupt their career and affect their ability to pay their bills if they were allowed to have credit of their own. Women, therefore, were considered poor credit risks, and most of the credit they used was in their husband's name. Even if a woman's name was on an account that she actively used, payment history information was reported to credit bureaus in her husband's name only.

To help women develop their own credit history, the ECOA requires creditors to report account payment data in the names of both spouses on any accounts that a married couple both use or are both liable for. Thus, if you are a joint user or an authorized user on an account, that account should appear in both your husband's credit file and your credit file if it was opened after June 1, 1977.

Some creditors may disregard this legal requirement of the ECOA. If you feel that having shared account information—joint-user account information especially—in your credit record will be helpful to you in obtaining individual credit, write to each of the major credit bureaus and ask if it is maintaining a file in your name. If it is, request a copy of your record as well as a copy of your husband's, assuming you have his permission. Then compare both sets of credit reports to determine if there are any creditors who are reporting information on accounts opened after June 1, 1977, in your husband's name only.

If you discover that an account with a positive payment history is being reported in your husband's name only, write to the creditor. Explain that the account is a shared account that was opened after June 1, 1977. Ask that the creditor begin reporting account information in your name as well as your husband's. See the sample letter in Figure 7.1 and ECOA provisions of special interest to women in Figure 7.2.

Attach to the letter a copy of your credit reports and your husband's, and highlight the relevant account name(s) and number(s).

After a few months, request copies of your credit reports again, and check to make certain that the creditor honored your request.

FIGURE 7.1 Sample Letter to Creditor Asking It to Begin Reporting Account Information in Both Spouses' Names

Date

Name and Address of Creditor

Dear *(name of credit manager):*

As of June 1, 1977, according to the provisions of the federal ECOA, creditors were to begin reporting account information on authorized-user and joint accounts in the names of both spouses. In reviewing the credit files maintained on myself and my husband by *(name of the credit bureau),* I noted that you are not reporting information in my name for account # _____ that we have with you. That account was opened after June 1, 1977.

I am writing to ask that you begin reporting account information in my husband's name and in my name. I also ask that you make my file reflect the current status of my husband's file as reported by you.

Thank you for your assistance. If you have any questions, you may call me at *(area code/telephone number).*

Sincerely,

Signature

FIGURE 7.2 Provisions of the ECOA of Special Interest to Women

- Creditors may not discriminate on the basis of race, color, religion, sex, national origin, or marital status.

- A woman may apply for credit under her married name, maiden name, or a combination.

- Creditors must judge the merits of a woman's request for credit based on her earnings and her credit history. Creditors are not allowed to require a husband to cosign an unsecured note. If a woman applies for a secured loan— for a car or a home, for example—the lender is allowed to require the woman's spouse to sign the legal document that describes legal ownership of the property. The lender is not allowed to require the woman's spouse to cosign the bank note if the woman qualifies on her own, an ECOA provivision that does not apply in community property states.

- When a woman applies for credit, the creditor may not ask for information about her husband. An important exception to this provision applies to women who rely on alimony or child support to qualify or to help qualify for credit.

- All of a woman's income—including income from part-time work, public assistance, child support, and alimony—must be considered when a creditor evaluates her application for credit, although the creditor is allowed to consider the reliability of the income.

- Women who are applying for secured credit may be required to indicate whether they are married, separated, or single. A woman's marital status, however, may not be used to deny her credit or limit the amount of credit she may obtain.

- Creditors may not ask a woman to indicate her sex on a credit application unless it is for a home loan. In such instances, gender information is to be used only for government-reporting purposes.

- If a woman is applying for unsecured credit in her own name, a creditor may not ask her to indicate her marital status unless she lives in a community property state.

- Creditors may not ask about a woman's birth control practices or if she plans to have children, nor may creditors make assumptions about such matters.

- Although creditors may ask a woman if she has a phone at home, they may not ask whether the phone is in her name because many home telephones are listed in the man's name.

If you and your husband share accounts that were opened before June 1, 1977, and you would like those accounts reflected in your credit report, write to each creditor and ask that they start doing so. Although creditors are not legally required to, most will probably honor your request.

Because credit bureaus that comply with the ECOA report negative as well as positive account information on authorized-user and joint accounts, the law can harm women whose husbands misused authorized- or joint-user accounts even though one of the goals of the ECOA is to make it easier for women to establish their own credit history.

In such situations, a woman can try to distance herself from her husband's mismanagement by preparing a written statement of no more than 100 words explaining the reason for the negative account information and asking the appropriate credit bureaus to make that statement part of her credit file. She should also attach a copy of this statement to any application for credit she makes in her own name.

Advice for Women Who Have Credit and Are Getting Married

If you are one of countless single working women who have a positive credit history in your own name, it is important to preserve that good history after you marry. When you marry, therefore, do not cancel your credit accounts and do maintain at least one bank account—checking or savings—in your own name. There is no reason to merge your accounts and your money with your husband's; it is far easier to maintain an already-positive credit identity that is separate from your spouse's than it is to lose that identity and then try to reestablish it later. Furthermore, as indicated earlier, having your own credit when married can greatly benefit your family during difficult financial times.

If you change your name at marriage, immediately notify your creditors. Ask them to begin reporting account information to credit bureaus in your married name. A few months later, request a copy of your credit report from each of the credit reporting agencies the creditors report to and make sure that the creditors followed your instructions.

If you marry and have no credit history in your own name, begin immediately to establish one by following the credit building steps outlined earlier in this chapter.

Advice for Women Who Were Married before Enactment of the ECOA

If you were married before the ECOA went into effect, if all of your credit is shared with your husband, and if most of that credit was established before June 1, 1977, it's very likely that the big three credit reporting agencies are not maintaining credit files in your name. As a result, establishing your own credit identity will be somewhat more difficult than for married women who are listed as authorized or joint users on accounts that were opened after June 1977. Nonetheless, it can be done.

Your first step should be to contact each of the big three to confirm that, indeed, none of them is maintaining a file in your name. If you find one that is, request a copy of your credit report so you will know what's in it. If the report contains errors, get them corrected.

Request copies of your husband's reports, too, if your husband says it's okay; you cannot order someone else's credit report without their cooperation. Because you may need to open one or more joint accounts as part of the credit building process, you need to make certain that your husband's record is problem-free.

Talk with your husband about what you are trying to accomplish and why it is important for you to have your own credit. If he doesn't understand why it is important and is reluctant to do what he can to help you get started, suggest that he read this chapter and talk to Consumer Credit Counseling Service, a financial adviser, or a banker.

Once your husband understands the importance of your establishing credit in your own name, suggest that you apply for some new joint credit. Because payment information on this new credit must be reported to credit bureaus in both your names, it will get the credit building process started.

Don't forget that your ultimate goal is to establish credit in your name only; a credit history based on joint accounts is not enough.

Widows and Credit

If your husband is ill with death on the horizon, you must prepare financially for widowhood, preparation that is analogous to preparation for divorce. Build a credit history for yourself; correct problems in your credit file if you already have one (do the same for your husband's credit file); prepare written explanations for any adverse information in your credit record that is the result of events beyond your control—your husband's illness, sudden job loss, or mismanagement of money; and talk with a trusted financial adviser.

 HOT TIP

An excellent book about the financial and psychological issues that widows face is *On Your Own: A Widow's Passage to Emotional and Financial Well-Being,* 2nd edition, by Alexandra Armstrong and Mary Donahue (Dearborn Financial Publishing, Inc.).

If widowhood happens suddenly and you haven't been able to get your credit record in order, you'll face a number of financial obstacles that may impede your ability to build a happy and satisfying life on your own. Without your own credit history, you may find yourself without access to ready credit. You may also find it difficult to obtain adequate insurance or even a job.

If you were an authorized user on your husband's accounts, those accounts may be canceled by his creditors. In addition, creditors can require that you reapply for credit on joint accounts if the accounts were based on your spouse's income. However, if a joint account was based on your income, or if either of you could have qualified by yourselves for the credit at the time of application, you will probably not have to reapply.

To postpone dealing with loss of credit after your spouse's death, you may want to delay reporting the death to his creditors and use the time to get your financial situation in order and begin applying for credit in your own name if possible. Doing so is not always advisable, however, because in some instances if creditors learn about your spouse's death before you tell them, your withholding the information may prejudice them against you in the reapplication process.

Generally, how best to deal with this situation is a judgment call. Many women continue to use their husband's credit cards long after their spouse has died without any problem at all. However, doing so may mean that they delay establishing credit in their own name, which in turn may create problems for them later if they need to borrow money to buy a new car, a smaller home, go back to school, remodel their home, and the like.

HOT TIP

Whatever you do, always tell the truth when asked or when filling out a credit application.

When you apply for credit after your husband's death (and during any credit reapplication process), potential creditors cannot discount or ignore such income as annuities, pensions, and Social Security or disability payments even though they are allowed to evaluate the reliability of these payments when making their credit granting decisions.

If at the time of your husband's death you have little or no credit history of your own, it is essential that you do what you can to build one. As you begin the credit building process, don't forget that the ECOA requires the creditor to consider information in your husband's file when you apply for credit if you can prove that his credit history reflects yours. Although this is a long shot, it may be worth the effort depending upon your particular credit situation.

Other Considerations

Once your husband dies, any bank accounts that you held jointly with a right of survivorship will go directly to you and will not be tied up in the probate process. The same holds true for life insurance benefits. To receive these monies, however, you need to file a claim, and it could take as long as six weeks after filing before you actually see the money that is coming to you. This delay is another reason why it is a good idea to have your own credit and your own bank account—you may need ready and adequate access to cash and possibly credit immediately after your husband's death.

Whether you will have to pay any debt your husband leaves when he dies depends on the type of debt. Most debt you will not have to pay, but you may have to pay off a debt that is a shared or joint obligation with money from the bank accounts, insurance proceeds, or other assets that were not part of the probate process. You are also responsible for any debt owed by your deceased spouse that was secured with property.

HOT TIP

Because the rules governing a widow's obligations for her dead husband's debts are different in community property states than in separate property states, check with your attorney if you live in a community property state.

Once again, the problems just described illustrate why it is important to keep joint credit to an absolute minimum and to avoid it completely if possible. Having at least some individual credit will maximize the options you have for dealing with money matters after your husband's death.

CHAPTER 8

Creating Divorce-Proof Credit

Mary E. was going through a difficult divorce when she came to my office with questions about how the divorce might affect her credit. She had never been concerned about her credit before. She and her husband had been happily married for many years, and she had never anticipated that things would change. Mary had allowed her husband to maintain all the accounts in his name, and whenever they needed new credit, her husband applied for it. An unexpected consequence of the divorce was the failure of her ex-husband's business. As part of their divorce agreement, Mary's husband had agreed to assume responsibility for paying off the debt they had acquired during their marriage. Mary's salary barely covered her basic needs so she was concerned that his financial problems could mean that her husband would not live up to the terms of the agreement and might even file for bankruptcy. She was particularly worried about what would happen to her credit rating if that happened and she wanted to know if she would be responsible for paying off their marital debts if her husband didn't.

As I prepared to give Mary the information and advice she needed, I thought how much better her situation would be if she had planned for the possibility that things might not work out. That information could have been used to help prevent many of her problems.

Because approximately 50 percent of all American marriages now end in divorce, many women face problems like Mary's, especially if they have not planned adequately to minimize the negative financial impact of divorce.

The financial problems that can accompany divorce used to affect women primarily. Now an increasing number of men are facing those problems as well because more women are pursuing successful careers or starting their own business and achieving financial success. In fact, today some women are the major wage earners in their family, and it is their income and not their husband's that qualifies these couples for joint credit.

These changes mean that when couples split up, traditional divorce arrangements may not apply, and it may be the former husband, not the former wife, who experiences postdivorce financial problems. No matter how happy your marital relationship and regardless of your sex, it's a good idea to prepare financially for the possibility that things might not work out.

In this chapter I discuss some of the problems both sexes can face after divorce, how to avoid them, and how to deal with them if they develop. I also provide information about divorce and bankruptcy.

Planning for a Divorce

If you are contemplating divorce, you can minimize any potential financial damage that the change in marital status may cause by taking certain steps before filing. These steps include the following:

- Make sure you have good credit in your own name. If you don't, delay your divorce if possible until you can get some individual credit and open a bank account in your own name. For advice about building individual credit, read Chapter 5.
- Know the status of the accounts you and your husband are currently using. Are they joint, authorized-user, or individual? Is each account current?
- If you already have either joint or individual credit, obtain a copy of your credit report from each of the big three and address any problems you may find in them.

- If some of the accounts in your credit file are joint accounts with negative histories, and if the adverse information is the fault of your soon-to-be former spouse or the result of circumstances beyond your control, prepare a written explanation of the reason(s) for the negative information and ask the credit bureau to make this explanation a permanent part of your credit history. Doing so may help disassociate you from the account's problems. It is also a good idea to attach the same explanation to any credit applications you complete.

- Pay all bills and credit card debts you share with your spouse from your joint funds. Then send a letter to each creditor canceling the cards. If you leave the accounts open, you risk being liable for the balances on the accounts.

- If you have a lawyer or a financial adviser you trust, talk with that person about what you should do to prepare for the change in your marital status.

- If your spouse files for bankruptcy while you are in the process of divorce, it is likely that the divorce proceedings will be stopped until the bankruptcy is completed, or the automatic stay will be lifted so your divorce can proceed. During this time, talk with your lawyer about how to minimize the impact of your spouse's troubles on your financial situation.

Avoiding Trouble with Joint or Shared Accounts

As the previous chapter indicated, creditors consider spouses with joint accounts, including national bankcards, bank loans, debit cards, lines of credit, overdraft checking, and so on, to be equally liable for those accounts. It is critical therefore that you close all joint accounts as soon as possible and reopen new accounts separately in your own name; authorized-user accounts should also be closed. If you don't close those accounts, you risk being liable for any charges your now ex-spouse runs up on them even if your divorce agreement says your former spouse will be 100 percent responsible for the accounts. Because your name is still on the accounts, you are still legally liable from a creditor's perspective. Furthermore, if your ex-spouse is late in making payments on the joint accounts or defaults on them, your credit record, not just your ex-spouse's, will be damaged, possibly hampering your ability to build a life for yourself as a single person.

Close joint accounts by writing to each creditor. If there is an outstanding balance on an account, ask that the balance be transferred to the new individual account of whichever spouse will be responsible for paying off the account according to your divorce agreement. Also ask that the spouse who is not responsible be released from liability for the account. Although the creditor is not obligated to do what you have requested, it is important that both you and your spouse are very clear about exactly who will be responsible for each debt after you are divorced.

HOT TIP

While your joint accounts are still open, keep all account payments up-to-date even if your spouse is no longer helping to pay on them. That way, your credit history will not be damaged.

When you are ready to close your joint accounts, remember that the creditors, if you want individual credit with the same ones, have the right to require you to reapply for credit if the joint accounts were based on your spouse's income. If they were based on your income, however, or if either of you could have qualified for the credit at the time of application, you will probably not be required to reapply.

If at all possible, avoid negotiating a divorce agreement that allows your spouse to maintain your joint accounts in exchange for paying off the outstanding balances on those accounts. As long as those joint accounts remain open—whether you use them or not—you will be legally liable for them regardless of what your divorce agreement provides.

Debts That Your Spouse Agrees to Pay as Part of Your Divorce Settlement

When you and your spouse decide to get divorced, part of your divorce negotiations will involve deciding how to divide your marital debts as well as your assets. Those decisions should be clearly stated in your divorce agreement. Be sure to send a letter to each of the creditors affected by your agreement notifying them of what you and your spouse have decided.

After you are divorced, each of you is expected to pay off the debts for which you assumed responsibility. If, however, your spouse fails to pay a particular creditor, the creditor can seek payment from you if your name was on the account when the debt was first incurred.

HOT TIP

If your former spouse violates the terms of your divorce agreement, consult with your divorce attorney about whether you should take legal action.

Other Credit Problems Created by Divorce

If you get divorced but don't already have credit in your own name, you'll be in a very vulnerable position. For example, as this chapter has already indicated, if you and your ex-spouse agree to keep certain joint accounts open so that you'll have access to credit and if you both use the accounts, you'll both be equally liable for paying on them. This could spell disaster if your former spouse runs up a big account balance and cannot or will not help with the payments. On the other hand, if you and your spouse close all of your joint accounts as part of your divorce, or if you were removed from an authorized-user account, you may be left without ready access to credit after you are divorced at a time when having credit may be important to your ability to establish a new life for yourself as a single person.

As noted in Chapter 7, creditors may not deny a consumer continued use of accounts shared with a former spouse, nor may creditors change the terms of credit simply because of a change in marital status. They may, however, require you to reapply for that credit on your own. In marriages where a significant disparity exists in earnings between spouses and where the spouse with the smaller income shared accounts with the other, the person making less money risks losing the credit.

If you reapply for credit that was once joint or you apply for completely new credit, potential creditors may not discount or refuse to consider nonjob income such as child support and alimony. However, as noted before, they *are* allowed to request that you prove the reliability of these sources of income, and they can deny you credit if they judge them to be unreliable and you need those payments to qualify for credit. Thus, if nonjob income is important to your being viewed by future creditors as creditworthy, it's a good idea to collect and save any documentation you have that supports the reliability of that income, including canceled checks, your divorce agreement, a notarized letter from your ex-spouse, and bank deposit slips.

In evaluating your creditworthiness, creditors must consider the credit history of your former spouse if you can demonstrate that it reflects your history too. If it is a positive history and if you have no credit in your own name and never shared credit with your former spouse, you may want to try using this provision to help you build your own credit record even though there is no guarantee that doing so will be of any real help to you.

To demonstrate that your former spouse's history reflects yours, you may be able to provide copies of checks you wrote to pay on accounts, letters you may have written to creditors regarding the accounts, and so on. If you are on good terms, your former spouse may be willing to write a letter to a potential creditor attesting to the fact that you regularly used the credit and helped manage the accounts.

 HOT TIP

If you decide to take back your maiden name after your divorce, be certain to let your creditors know. Ask them to begin reporting account information to credit bureaus in your new name. Then wait a few months and check your credit record again to make sure your creditors are reporting correctly to credit bureaus.

If Your Former Spouse Files for Bankruptcy

In today's uncertain and credit-oriented economy, it's possible that your former spouse may file for bankruptcy. Even though the bankruptcy may wipe out any debt that your former spouse owes you as part of your divorce agreement, it will not cancel alimony, maintenance, or child support obligations nor will it wipe out most tax debts. In other words, these obligations cannot be discharged through bankruptcy.

If your former spouse files a Chapter 13 bankruptcy (reorganization of debt), he or she will have to pay all of the past due alimony, maintenance, or support payments you are owed while the reorganization plan is in effect. Your former spouse will also be expected to stay up-to-date on all future payments at the same time.

HOT TIP

Alimony, maintenance, and support obligations have priority in a bankruptcy and thus must be paid before tax debts and most unsecured debts.

If your former spouse files a Chapter 7 bankruptcy (liquidation of debt), you may not collect what you are owed until the bankruptcy is over and the automatic stay lifted. The *automatic stay* is a court action that prohibits all creditor collection actions against a debtor once the debtor has filed for bankruptcy. Its protection ends when the bankruptcy is over or when the court lifts it. The automatic stay, however, will have no effect on the obligation of your former spouse to stay current on all support payments he or she must pay you during a Chapter 7 liquidation. That responsibility will remain.

One option available to you if your former spouse files a Chapter 7 is to try to collect what you are owed from the assets that are not part of your ex-spouse's bankruptcy estate while the bankruptcy is ongoing. Such assets are called *exempt assets* and are not affected by the automatic stay. Check with a bankruptcy attorney in your state to find out what property is part of your former spouse's bankruptcy estate because every state is different. You will also need an attorney's help to collect from the exempt assets.

There are two important exceptions to the restriction against your ex-spouse's using bankruptcy to discharge or wipe out the legal obligation to make alimony, maintenance, and support payments according to the terms of your divorce agreement. The first exception exists if your ex-spouse has fallen behind on some or all of those payments and you have voluntarily turned them over to a collection agency or other entity to collect what you are owed. If you have done that, your former spouse's alimony and child support debts to you can be discharged or erased through bankruptcy, although your ex-spouse will still have a legal obligation to make all future payments to you in full and on time.

HOT TIP

If you think that your ex-spouse may be getting ready to file for bankruptcy while paying you alimony, maintenance, or child support, consult with a bankruptcy attorney right away.

The second exception occurs if your former spouse asks the court to rule that a debt classified as child support, alimony, or maintenance is really another type of debt related to his or her change in marital status—a property settlement obligation, for example—and should therefore be discharged. If the court agrees, no matter what kind of bankruptcy your ex-spouse filed, the debt will be wiped out.

Property Settlement and "Hold Harmless" Obligations

Until 1994, if your divorce agreement provided that your ex-spouse would keep a certain asset in exchange for promising to pay you a set amount of money in installments or for promising to pay off certain of your debts, or if it provided that you would accept smaller alimony, maintenance, or support payments in exchange for being "held harmless" (i.e., not liable) for certain debts you incurred during your marriage, your ex-spouse could wipe out those obligations by filing for bankruptcy. If that happened, you could be left with a lot of debt and little or no alimony, support, or maintenance income to help you pay that debt—a situation that could possibly plunge you into bankruptcy.

The 1994 Bankruptcy Code was amended to change the way that divorce-related property settlements and hold harmless agreements are to be treated in a bankruptcy. As a result, bankruptcy now will not necessarily release your former spouse from property settlement and hold harmless obligations if the court believes the resources of your former spouse are sufficient to meet alimony, support, and maintenance obligations as well as his or her own basic living expenses. If your former spouse can prove an inability to meet those obligations and still have money to pay basic living expenses, all or a portion of the property settlement and hold harmless obligations will be discharged. They will also be discharged if your ex-spouse is a business owner and can prove to the court there will not be enough money to continue the business if they remain. But your former spouse's property settlement and hold harmless obligations will not be wiped out if the court believes that erasing them would potentially cause you greater harm than the benefits your former spouse might enjoy.

There is an important catch to these exceptions: To benefit from them, you must file an adversary proceeding—the equivalent of a minilawsuit— against your ex-spouse within 60 days of the date of the first creditor's meeting in your ex-spouse's bankruptcy. For you to be able to meet these criteria, you must be aware that your former spouse has filed for bankruptcy, know the date of the first creditor's meeting, and have sufficient financial resources to hire an attorney who can help you as it's unlikely you'll have the time and the legal know-how to initiate an adversary proceeding yourself.

Other Important Divorce-Related Changes Resulting from the 1994 Bankruptcy Code Reforms

When the Bankruptcy Code was revised in 1994, the reforms included some other changes that affect divorced people. For example, the law now says that a bankruptcy cannot affect any actions necessary to establish the paternity of a child. This means that if you've asked your state attorney general to help you get support for your child and the alleged father subsequently files for bankruptcy, you can continue your efforts to get the support. It also means that if the alleged father is in fact identified as your child's actual father, he must begin making child support payments regardless of his having filed for bankruptcy.

Another change in the Code now allows you to establish or modify an order for alimony, maintenance, or support without getting the bankruptcy court's permission first. In the past, having to get permission first often created expense, delay, and even hardship for the former spouse who was seeking the change.

A final change you should know about relates to judicial liens. Formerly under a division of property agreement in a divorce, one spouse might agree to pay off a certain debt owed by the other spouse. To secure that obligation, the spouse whose debt was to be paid off might place a lien on some of the other spouse's property. In such a situation, an ex-spouse with the obligation to pay off the debt could file for bankruptcy and wipe out that obligation if the lien were on exempt property. The 1994 amendments to the Bankruptcy Code codified a U.S. Supreme Court decision. Now if a lien secures the obligation of one spouse to pay the other under a division of property agreement, that obligation cannot be erased through a subsequent bankruptcy under the amended law.

Special Concerns for Divorced People in Community Property States

Consumers living in community property states face special problems when there is a divorce. Community property states include Arizona, California, Idaho, Louisiana, Nevada, New Mexico, Texas, Washington, and Wisconsin. In these states, both parties in a marriage are jointly liable for *all* debts incurred during the marriage—both individual and joint debts. (In separate property states, this mutual obligation applies only to joint debt.) If a former spouse in a community property state signed a divorce agreement promising to pay off certain individual debts incurred by the other during the marriage but then fails to, the affected creditors have a legal right to try to collect their money from the other former spouse. Otherwise, they can look only to the property accumulated during the marriage to settle their claims.

If your former spouse fails to meet his or her obligations to pay off certain credit accounts and creditors seek you out, you have several options. First, you can pay off the debt to minimize any damage that will be done to your credit history. If you want to pay off the debt but your financial resources are limited, try negotiating new and affordable payment schedules with each creditor.

To negotiate with creditors, contact each one directly—by letter, telephone, or in person. Tell them what your situation is. Explain that you would like to meet your obligations but to do so, you'll need to work out a schedule of monthly payments that you can afford.

If you don't feel comfortable handling these negotiations yourself, call the Consumer Credit Counseling Service (CCCS) office nearest you (800-388-2227) for assistance.

Another option is to file for bankruptcy, but don't pursue this option without giving it a lot of serious thought and speaking first with an experienced bankruptcy attorney. The attorney will help you understand all the ramifications of bankruptcy. For example, bankruptcy will make it more difficult for you to build a financial life for yourself after your divorce because it will remain on your credit record for up to ten years. The attorney should also explore other steps short of bankruptcy that you can take to deal with your money troubles.

 HOT TIP

To learn more about consumer bankruptcy and how the process works, read *The Bankruptcy Kit*, 2nd edition, by John Ventura (Dearborn Financial Publishing, Inc.). The book can help you discover everything you need to know about the new changes in bankruptcy law and relief for your personal finances or small business. It also explains how bankruptcy affects taxes, mortgages, alimony, child support, and more. The book is available through local bookstores nationwide, or call toll-free 800-829-7934.

CHAPTER 9

Protecting Your Financial Privacy

When Susan M. came to see me, she was angry about a phone call she had received from a man trying to sell her financial services. During the conversation, it became clear to Susan that the caller knew a great deal about her personal and financial situation. She became suspicious and asked him how he knew so much about her. He responded evasively and hung up.

Susan wanted to know if I knew how this person could get information about her; she felt the man had invaded her privacy.

Susan also told me that she received a lot of offers from businesses in the mail and solicitations from charities as well. I explained that her name was probably on some mailing lists and that there were things she could do to cut down on the number of solicitations she was receiving.

We talked for a while about the issue of privacy in a high-tech world. I told Susan that sophisticated technology allows companies to amass and store detailed data on consumers in computerized databases. I went on to explain that some of these companies sell their information to other companies such as direct marketers. Susan was disturbed by the realization that in some cases the personal information she had provided to creditors when she applied for credit was being used this way. She was also surprised to learn that she could have contributed to the problem by not being careful to whom she provided financial and personal information about herself.

Susan and I went on to discuss some of the things she could do to help preserve her privacy. I also suggested that she write to her elected representatives in Washington, D.C., to urge that they update and strengthen current laws written to protect the privacy of consumers and consider whether new laws are needed as well.

I hope that after reading this chapter you will become as alarmed as Susan was after our conversation about personal privacy in a high-tech world. I also hope that each of you will write to your elected officials to demand that something be done now to better protect your privacy and to demand that businesses of all kinds be more strictly limited in their access to and use of your credit record data.

In this chapter, I will talk about some of the ways that your privacy is being threatened by increasingly sophisticated computer technology and by the buying and selling of personal information about you, including information about your finances and spending habits. That threat has been increased with the advent of the information superhighway and the prospect of an increasing amount of commerce on the Internet.

I will also discuss the main sources of this threat to our consumer privacy—credit bureaus and other information brokers, creditors, retailers and other businesses that store consumer information in their computers, direct marketers, government agencies, the medical industry, and even unscrupulous individuals. Finally, I will review the major federal privacy laws and offer advice to those of you who want to have more control over who has access to your personal data and how that data are used.

Privacy in the Age of Information

Today, with a mere push of a button or by knowing a special code or account number, personal details about your life can be accessed. In fact, just about anything is available for collection and sale, including information as diverse as your in-store and credit card purchases and general buying habits, your medical history, your employment background, information about any on-the-job injuries you may have suffered, records of your telephone calls, details about your home, your household income, and marital status. For example, Information America, Inc.'s People Finder Data Base includes information on 11 million individuals, 92 million households, and 61 million telephone numbers! The database includes information drawn from telephone directories, post office change-of-address forms, voter registration records, and birth and wedding announcements. Another large information broker, California-based CBD Infotek, maintains thousands of different databases developed from a wide variety of public records, including motor vehicle records, filings at county, state, and federal courts, and tax rolls. Businesses have many uses for this kind of information; for instance, a bank to check out potential borrowers or a personal injury attorney to learn about the assets of the driver who injured his client.

Sometimes the information in one database is combined with information from another to create marketable new information products or to improve existing databases. In other cases, information from one database may be compared with that of another to help identify consumers with particular characteristics or to make an existing database more comprehensive and accurate. Databases are also being linked electronically to create huge information networks.

Consumers' personal information has become a valuable commodity. Yet most of the time we are unaware that information about our finances, personal habits, health, buying patterns, and other such information is being bought, sold, and exchanged, nor are we aware where that information is coming from. And, even worse, there is little we can do to stop what is being done with our personal information.

Unauthorized Access to, and Inappropriate Use of, Credit Record Data

Technology has made unauthorized access to consumer credit files easier, especially now that online electronic access to the files of the big three has become commonplace. Some individuals and businesses are misrepresenting themselves to gain access to credit bureau data; some are circumventing credit bureau security; and in some instances those who have a legitimate reason to access credit record data are using that information for illegal purposes in violation of federal law or are selling it to others for unauthorized uses. An August 1995 article in *Kiplinger's Personal Finance* magazine, entitled "Guarding Your Financial Privacy," pointed out that it is possible for unscrupulous employees at businesses with computer access to credit bureau data—car dealerships, brokerage houses, local banks—to get credit information on consumers and use it for fraudulent purposes. The article referred to a New Jersey car dealership where employees accessed the files of a credit bureau and ran up more than $800,000 of fraudulent credit card charges before they were caught.

The ease with which an unauthorized person can tap into a credit file was also highlighted in 1989 by the now famous incident of the *Business Week* reporter who used his personal computer to access former Vice President Dan Quayle's credit record through a superbureau. Since that time, others have reported using their personal computers to acquire credit record information on famous persons, and there have been instances of private detectives gaining unauthorized access to credit files to secure certain credit information.

Although some of the recent amendments to the FCRA attempt to tighten controls on who has access to credit record data, there is no reason to think that the problem will stop given the potential dollars that businesses and individuals can realize from consumer credit record data. For example, some companies and organizations that do not have a permissible purpose for accessing the information stored in your credit file will continue to obtain that information through intermediaries, and some credit bureaus will not adequately police what their subscribers do with the consumer credit information in their files once they have it. Again, although amendments to the FCRA attempt to address these problems, the potential for abuse remains. At this time, there is no 100 percent guaranteed way to protect against unauthorized access to your credit record or against the possibility that information in your file will be used inappropriately by a credit bureau subscriber. Ultimately, it will take better credit bureau security systems and tougher laws before we can feel more confident about the security of our personal and financial information. And we as consumers need to be more cautious about what we do with that information.

Public Response to Privacy Problems

Privacy groups, consumer watchdogs, and policymakers watching the growing privacy dilemma are alarmed. They believe it's wrong when you provide information about yourself to a company for one purpose, and the company subsequently sells that information for another purpose. They also believe it is wrong for a company or individual to mislead you about why certain information is being requested. Critics are also concerned about the invasive nature of the databases that are being created and their potential for abuse. For example, Congressman Charles Schumer of New York testified as follows before the House Subcommittee on Consumer Affairs and Coinage in June 1991:

> In the modern era, one punch of a computer button can instantly deliver to anyone with a terminal more confidential information about an American consumer than a private detective could unearth in a week. As a result of technology, the privacy of American citizens is imperiled more than at any other time in our history.

There is fear among other policymakers that the era of "Big Brother is watching you" has arrived, created by a combination of forces in both the public and the private sectors.

Consumers are worried too. A 1990 Harris poll commissioned by Equifax, *Equifax Report on Consumers in the Information Age,* revealed that 79 percent of all Americans are concerned about threats to their privacy and 71 percent believe they have lost control over how their personal information is used by companies. Another poll commissioned by *Time* magazine and CNN further reinforces the fact that consumers are concerned. In that poll, conducted by the firm of Yankelovich, Clancy, Shulman, 78 percent of the respondents indicated they are very/somewhat concerned about the amount of computerized information that businesses and the government collect and store about them. Ninety-three percent indicated they felt companies that sell information about consumers should be required by law to ask a consumer's permission before making information available to another individual, company, or organization. Eighty-eight percent believed that these same companies should be required by law to make their information available to consumers so that possible inaccuracies can be corrected.

Although there are ten privacy-related federal laws and some state privacy laws, legislation for the most part does little to check the flow of consumer information.

Federal Privacy Laws

When the Constitution was written, the word *privacy* was not specifically mentioned because a citizen's privacy was considered adequately protected by safeguards against physical searches and seizures. Today, however, searches and seizures of some of the most personal details of your life are being performed by technology rather than by physical means. As a result, most of the federal privacy laws currently on the books, including the FCRA, are woefully inadequate. Not only are these laws outdated, but many are full of exemptions and loopholes that make them easy to circumvent.

In addition to the FCRA, the most important federal privacy laws are the Privacy Act of 1974, the Right to Financial Privacy Act of 1978, the Video Privacy Protection Act, and the Computer Matching and Privacy Protection Act.

The Privacy Act of 1974

The Privacy Act of 1974 applies to federal agencies, prohibiting them from obtaining information for one purpose and then sharing it for another. The exception that the information can be shared when it is for "routine use," however, makes the law essentially useless because nearly any use can be interpreted as "routine."

The Right to Financial Privacy Act

Although the Right to Financial Privacy Act is supposed to govern access of federal agencies to your bank records, exemptions allow the FBI and U.S. attorneys to review bank records. Nor does this law apply to private employers or to local and state governments. Furthermore, new exceptions are added to this law each year, whittling away the power of the law to truly protect your financial privacy.

The Video Privacy Protection Act

The Video Privacy Protection Act forbids retailers from providing—free or for a price—a list of the videos you rent unless you approve the release of that information or unless a court orders its release.

The Computer Matching and Privacy Protection Act

The Computer Matching and Privacy Protection Act regulates the federal government's use of computer-matching techniques that compare data in one computer file to data in another to determine your eligibility for federal benefits. The law also limits the federal government's use of matching techniques to help it collect money, such as back taxes, that you may owe the government. As a result of exemptions written into the law, the act does not apply to many potential matches, including those done for purposes of law enforcement and tax collection.

The Credit Industry and Privacy

Over the years, the larger credit bureaus—the big three and those that buy credit record information from the big three—have developed and marketed a variety of products and services. Critics argue that in offering these products and services, credit bureaus have gone beyond their original mission of helping creditors make credit granting decisions, helping employers make hiring decisions, and aiding insurers in their decisions regarding coverage. Although some of the 1996 amendments to the FCRA are intended to help protect consumer privacy, other provisions will only add to the problem.

Data Mining and Warehousing

Creditors such as retailers and credit card issuers search and analyze their own records or other sources of consumer information, including credit bureau data, for as much detail as possible in order to make better credit granting decisions and formulate better collection strategies. Within the data industry this search of records is euphemistically referred to as "data mining" and the mined information is described as being stored in "data warehouses." Businesses are investing huge amounts of money in this effort.

The big three are getting in on the act by purchasing, merging with, or forming strategic alliances with data mining/warehouse companies. For example, in 1996 Equifax purchased Market Knowledge, and Experian merged with CNN, Inc. As this book was being researched, Trans Union had not yet purchased or merged with a data mining/warehouse company.

How Information Brokers Use Information

Some information brokers sell information that reflects your credit status to direct marketers, including telemarketers—a violation of the FCRA. Some also develop, maintain, and market extensive demographic databases for targeted marketing. Although these databases are separate from those that credit bureaus, including the big three, maintain for credit granting purposes, they may be enhanced with information maintained by credit bureaus and with other data sources. These other sources of data may include phone book information, Census Bureau data, and subscription lists as well as real estate, insurance, and consumer product purchase information. The resulting databases can create very precise profiles of, among other things, your spending habits, lifestyle, hobbies, work, friends, and family. As a result, they can be extremely valuable to direct marketers and telemarketers because the more narrowly these marketers can define their target markets, the more they can sell. As this book has already indicated, whether this practice will be allowed to continue is currently up to the courts to decide.

Special Products and Services

Most of the privacy-related criticism directed at credit bureaus focuses on three very specific products/services: *prescreening, data enhancement,* and *targeted marketing databases.*

Prescreening

Prescreening is a technique by which a credit bureau, using the information in its credit files, creates a list of consumers qualified to receive a preapproved offer of credit or insurance. Prescreening can be accomplished in one of two ways. First, a company may supply a credit bureau with a set of credit granting characteristics that describe its target market. For example, a national bankcard company may want to offer a preapproved card to all consumers who make more than $100,000 a year and have flawless credit records and several unused lines of credit of at least $5,000 each.

The credit bureau doing the prescreening will compare the criteria specified by the bankcard company or insurer with the characteristics of the consumers in its database. From this comparison, it will develop a list of prescreened consumers to whom the company can make its offer.

A company may also provide a credit bureau with a list of consumers and a set of criteria defining the types of consumers to whom it wants to make its offer. The company's list may have been obtained from a list broker or from the credit bureau itself. The credit bureau will then compare the information it has in its database with the criteria the creditor or insurer has specified so as to identify those who should receive the company's offer.

HOT TIP

If you see the letters *prm* or the word *promotional* in the inquiries section of your credit report, it means that your file was prescreened for an offer.

Critics of prescreening object to the practice because it is done without the knowledge of consumers. Although the company that purchases the prescreened list does not actually view the credit files of the consumers on the list, critics are concerned because technology has helped credit bureaus greatly refine the criteria that can be used in the prescreening process. As a result, companies now can learn very specific details about your financial life without ever seeing your credit history. Prescreening has become increasingly intrusive.

Critics also allege that prescreening violates the intent of the FCRA because it doesn't relate to a consumer's solicitation of credit but rather to the company's solicitation of a consumer in order to extend credit to that consumer. On the other hand, supporters say that prescreening reduces the amount of unwanted solicitations a consumer receives by helping businesses better target their solicitations to those consumers most apt to be interested in them.

According to the FCRA, prescreening is legal so long as all those on a prescreened list receive a "firm offer" of credit or insurance. In addition, the amended FCRA provides that a creditor or insurer may establish ahead of time additional criteria for obtaining credit or insurance besides those provided to the credit bureau, and if a consumer does not meet those new criteria, the consumer can be denied the credit or insurance. The amended FCRA also states that you can be denied the credit or insurance if the prescreening criteria have changed by the time you accept the offer.

The amended law requires that the big three establish a joint toll-free phone system that you can use to remove yourself from, or opt out of, prescreened offers. Once you make the call, your name must be removed within five business days and must stay removed for two years, although you can also sign a special form provided by one of the big three asking to opt you out until you tell it otherwise. In turn, that credit bureau must notify the other two major credit bureaus and they must honor your request.

If you opt out, don't expect to see an immediate reduction in the amount of direct mail and telephone solicitations you receive. (See Figure 9.1 later in this chapter for how to opt out.) It may take as long as three months. You will continue to receive some mail and phone offers because the big three are not the only companies that provide information to direct marketers. Furthermore, opting out will have no effect on solicitations from charities, religious organizations, professional and alumni associations, political candidates, and local merchants.

Data Enhancement

The goal of data enhancement is to improve the quality of one database by adding selected information to it from other databases. Some critics argue that data enhancement allows a company to create marketing lists that are as effective as prescreened lists but have broader applications.

An organization may use data enhancement because it wants to learn more about its customer base so that it can do a better job of marketing its products, develop more detailed lists for direct marketing, or sell the lists it develops through data enhancement.

Critics are also upset by the fact that once a consumer's personal data are in another company's files, that person has very little control over how the information will be used. Like prescreening, it's done without your knowledge or permission.

Whether it's legal for a business to procure from a credit bureau consumer identifying information that the business can use to enhance its own database depends on the specific type of information it buys. Furthermore, according to the amended FCRA, if a business procures the information in order to resell it, it must then tell the credit bureau it is working with the identity of the end-user and each permissible purpose for which the information is being furnished to the end-user.

Targeted Marketing Databases

Although the amended FCRA appears to outlaw the development and sale of target marketing lists based on consumer credit record data, the issue has not been settled. Depending on the outcome of an appeals court decision involving Trans Union and target marketing, the practice may be permitted.

Targeted marketing databases are used by marketers of a specific product or service to help them reach narrowly defined audiences. The sales pitch often is delivered through telemarketing or promotional mailings.

Beyond the Big Three

Most privacy-related criticism directed at the credit reporting industry has focused on the big three because of the sheer volume of information they maintain in their databases, the many uses they have for such information, and the fact they are the credit bureaus that consumers interact with most frequently. To focus only on the big three is to ignore a significant part of the problem in the credit reporting industry—information brokers that buy their consumer credit information from the big three and, in turn, sell it and other database information to businesses. Some of these other information brokers are reputed to sell their information to almost anyone willing to buy it, including debt collectors, private detectives, and even a consumer's acquaintances and former spouses. They are able to do this for a number of reasons: They tend to operate less visibly than the big three and receive less public scrutiny; the FTC has a limited ability to "police" the credit reporting industry at all levels and to enforce the FCRA; and they are quite willing to make money by taking advantage of weaknesses in the FCRA.

The *Business Week* editor referred to earlier in this chapter demonstrated just how easily consumer information can be obtained from these information brokers. The editor signed up with two such companies, telling them that he was an editor at McGraw Hill, Inc., and that he might be doing some hiring. He provided both with the names of several individuals he said were potential new hires and indicated he would like to review their credit records. With no more than the most cursory check into the editor's identity, the brokers provided the editor with complete access to the files. One of them even provided the editor with instructions for using his home computer to tap into its database!

It appears that the further consumer credit information travels from the credit bureau that originally collected it, the more opportunities there are for this information to be used inappropriately and for unauthorized persons to acquire that data.

Government and Privacy

The federal government too collects and stores large volumes of information about consumers, thus posing another threat to individual privacy. In fact, it is the nation's largest data gatherer. Numerous federal agencies and departments maintain extensive databases on countless consumers—the FBI, the IRS, the Census Bureau, and the Drug Enforcement Administration (DEA) in particular.

 HOT TIP

Many state motor vehicle departments sell car registration and drivers license records to credit companies.

Despite the Federal Privacy Act, many federal agencies and departments link their databases as they look for consumer matches. Frequently, agencies also match the information in their computers with data purchased from private companies. The IRS, in fact, uses this technique to locate nonfilers.

Profiling

Presently, approximately 16 government agencies use a technique called *profiling* whereby a list of characteristics believed to be common to a particular group of people—tax evaders, drug smugglers, welfare cheaters, for example—is created. Then the government agency compares the individual characteristics of the population at large or of a particular group of persons to identify those who fit the profile.

Although no one can fault the IRS for wanting to crack down on nonfilers or the DEA for trying to reduce the amount of illegal drugs being smuggled into this country, use of profiling by these agencies is disturbing to privacy advocates. First, questions arise about the accuracy of profiling as well as concern because innocent people have been detained or prosecuted for no reason other than that they fit a profile. Second, because there are few restrictions on the use of the technique, there is nothing to stop government agencies from expanding its use.

A New Threat from the Government

Although the recently passed federal Health Care Portability and Account-ability Act (HCPAA) has been much touted, little attention has been paid to a provision of this new law that has the potential to make our health and medical histories an open book. It requires that the medical information doc-tors, hospitals, HMOs, and the like compile about patients be standardized to make it easier for them to share their information with one another electron-ically. The result will be a new national database of medical information about consumers.

Currently, insurers and others cannot obtain your medical records with-out your written permission. Although the HCPAA requires passage of a new federal privacy law to help protect the confidentiality of your medical rec-ords, the difficulty involved in trying to do so in light of today's sophisticated technologies and the number of businesses and organizations that could have legal access to your medical records indicates there is no guarantee that the new law will do an adequate job.

The Private Sector and Privacy

As already reported, many companies other than the big three develop and maintain extensive databases. They include other credit reporting agen-cies, list brokers, credit card companies, and firms in the financial service and direct marketing industries. These companies may augment or improve the data in their files by using a credit bureau's data enhancement service, by purchasing direct marketing lists or Census Bureau information, or by buy-ing information from information brokers. Companies with extensive data-bases may also glean important consumer-specific information from warranty cards, subscriber or user surveys, mail order forms, credit applications, and the like.

Some of these companies not only use the information in their databases for their own purposes but also offer prescreening services similar to those of the larger credit reporting agencies; others may market their data to out-side users. Some credit card companies, for example, sell information detail-ing the types of credit purchases their cardholders have made or market lists of people who have purchased a particular type of product with their card.

The Medical/Insurance Industry and Privacy

The medical industry is another big collector of consumer information. Hospitals, HMOs, doctors' offices, self-insured corporations, and insurance companies all maintain extensive medical information databases on their clients, patients, or employees.

Much of this information ends up with the Medical Information Bureau (MIB), a membership organization of about 680 life insurance companies. Established in 1902 by the medical directors of about 15 insurance companies, the MIB's original purpose was to reduce fraudulent claims. Although it continues to serve this function, the MIB now has a broader potential impact on consumers. According to the FTC, the activities of the MIB are governed by the FCRA; but just as the general public hasn't been aware of the activities of credit bureaus other than the big three, so too has the MIB escaped public knowledge and scrutiny until recently.

The information in the MIB's files can influence your ability to get health, life, or disability insurance, or reimbursement for a claim. It can also affect your employment opportunities if an insurer shares information from your MIB report with your employer or potential employer.

 HOT TIP

Before an MIB member may request a copy of your MIB report in connection with your application for life, health, or disability insurance, it must get your written authorization and it must provide you with information explaining how you can correct any problems in your MIB record.

If you have medical insurance and require medical care, you or your doctor will file a claim with your insurance carrier to get reimbursed. The information on that claim may be shared with the MIB if your insurer is a member. In turn, the MIB will share the claim information with other member companies that provide you insurance or that are assessing you for insurance. Thus, the highly personal information you thought you were telling your doctor in strictest confidence may actually become part of a vast national medical information network. According to the MIB, information about an individual will be sent to it by MIB members "only if an applicant has a condition significant to health or longevity." Such information could include height, weight, blood pressure, EKG readings, and x-ray results. According to the MIB, certain kinds of nonmedical information may also be reported to it, including an adverse driving record or an individual's participation in a hazardous sport.

The FTC has begun holding the MIB and other companies that provide consumer health and medical information to insurers to many of the same standards that apply to credit reporting agencies. For example, the FTC has ruled that if an insurance company denies you health, life, or disability insurance as the result of information in an MIB report, the insurer must tell you where the information came from, including the company's name and address. Usually that company will be the MIB. The insurer must provide you the same information if it raises your insurance premium based on information in a credit bureau report. If you request a copy of your report within 30 days of being denied the insurance, you are entitled to a free report. You may also obtain a free copy of this report if you are charged an extra premium by an insurer and the insurance company provided you with a written notification that identified the MIB as a source of information about you. To qualify for a free MIB report, you will have to send the MIB a copy of the notification along with a completed report request form.

If you have not been denied life, health, or disability insurance but you want to know if the MIB is maintaining a file on you and, if it is, what's in that file, you can obtain an MIB report for $8 (send check or money order only) by writing the Medical Information Bureau, Inc. (PO Box 105, Essex Station, Boston, MA 02112; 617-426-3660).

How Employers Are Using Information about Consumers

Some employers review consumers' credit records when making a hiring, promotion, or other employment-related decision. Critics question the predictive value of credit information for those purposes and are concerned that a job applicant may be denied employment because of misinformation in his or her credit report.

To help protect consumers, the amended FCRA now requires any employer that intends to review a job applicant's credit history as part of its hiring process to obtain the applicant's written permission to do so. The act also states that before denying a job to an applicant due in whole or in part to information in that person's credit record, the employer must provide the applicant with a copy of the record together with information about the applicant's right to dispute any problems in it. In addition, the employer must give the applicant the name and address of the credit bureau that provided the negative information. Critics contend that in light of the past behavior of some employers, there is unfortunately no reason to think that all employers will comply with this requirement.

Private Databases

Private databases now exist that have been expressly designed to provide employers with information that goes beyond that in a traditional employment report provided by a credit bureau. Following are some examples:

- Employer's Information Services in Louisiana has developed a massive national database that contains the names of employees who have claimed on-the-job injuries with details of their claims and lawsuits. This information may be used by employers to screen job applicants. The information—accurate or not and without any consideration given to the circumstances of the injury and claim—may remove a candidate from consideration for a job. Without the candidate's knowledge, the data maintained by Employer's Information Services can wrongfully label workers as troublemakers, effectively blacklisting them from future employment.

- Pinkerton Investigative Services claims that it has access to a worldwide network of databases it uses to perform background checks on prospective employees. The defense industry has traditionally used this kind of check, but today other industries as well are making extensive use of background checks.

- Information Resource Service Company (IRSC) offers employers an opportunity to determine whether a prospective employee has ever been arrested even if the arrest did not result in a conviction. To provide this service, IRSC taps into more than 7,000 databases.

- The National Credit Information Network provides consumer credit information, public record data, and other background information to clients with information needs that include employee screening, in-house background checks, and background investigations. The company obtains its information via electronic links to more than 1,000 local credit bureaus across the country and to other information sources.

What is particularly alarming about these databases is that there is no way for you to know if their information is accurate. And because the FCRA doesn't apply to these database companies, you have no legal right to review their information about you or to have any problem corrected or deleted.

Psychological Testing

Some employers use psychological testing to help screen out "problem" job applicants. Such testing can put applicants in a precarious position—if they don't agree to the testing, they won't get the job, but if they answer, they may have to reveal highly personal information about themselves. Furthermore, if these persons are hired and that personal information is retained in their employer's database, there's no way of knowing who might see the information and where it might end up.

Credit Identity Fraud

Credit identity thieves are yet another threat to your privacy. These crooks steal consumers' credit card numbers, ATM card or personal identification number (PIN), Social Security number, driver's license number, and other identifying information. They may use this information to obtain new and additional credit in your name, which of course they don't repay. Not only will you be legally obligated to pay any charges that result but your credit history may be destroyed as well.

You may not know that your credit identity has been stolen until you are contacted by a debt collector about a debt you are supposed to owe or until you review a copy of your credit report and discover creditors you didn't know about or credit problems you were unaware of. Once you learn about the theft of your credit identity, it can take months and even years to resolve all the problems.

If You Think You've Been a Victim of Credit Fraud

If you think you are the victim of a credit identity thief, here are the steps you should take right away:

- Call your local police.
- Cancel all of your credit cards. The federal Fair Credit Billing Act says that after you report a missing or stolen credit card, you cannot be held liable for more than $50 in unauthorized purchases.
- Call the fraud units of each of the big three credit bureaus. The numbers to call are:
  - Experian: 800-301-7195
  - Equifax: call applicable creditor who in turn will tell you how to contact Equifax
  - Trans Union: 800-680-7289
- Contact your bank. Cancel your existing bank accounts and open new ones.

HOT TIP

You have a right to a free credit report if you think you are the victim of credit fraud.

Online Technology

If you surf the Web, you face a number of new threats to your privacy. Every move you make, every site you visit can be monitored by Web site operators. The result? Operators of Web sites can develop highly detailed portraits of your interests and preferences and customize their products and services or their marketing approach to have special personal appeal. When you provide information about yourself to a Web site, that information may be sold to other companies without your knowledge or, it goes without saying, your permission. Online entrepreneurs are also able to purchase your e-mail address from online companies in the business of compiling and selling such information. One of the consequences is the growing problem of junk e-mail, better known as "spam."

HOT TIP

Using a screen name when you surf the Net or go online does not protect your privacy.

Currently, there are no guidelines or laws to regulate companies and individual entrepreneurs who use the Internet or e-mail to market to consumers, although at the time this book was being researched, the FTC was preparing to hold a series of public hearings on privacy and the Internet. (During the summer of 1996, hearings on the same subject were held.) In addition, a proposal setting out various technological tools and standards has already been drafted by several major Internet software companies. This proposal has the support of other major technology firms such as IBM, media businesses such as the New York Times Company, and advertising agencies such as J. Walter Thompson.

One Way to Protect Yourself When Buying Online

An increasing number of people are shopping for merchandise via Internet news groups, which act as online classified advertising. But when the seller is in another part of the country, you can never be certain that after providing your credit card number or sending a check, money order, or cash, your merchandise will show up or live up to its promise and description. As a result, escrow service companies have sprung up to facilitate online transactions and protect both the buyer and the seller. Typically, you send payment for merchandise to the escrow service company, which in turn gives you a certain number of days to inspect what you're buying. If you're satisfied and want the purchase to go forward, the escrow service company provides the seller with payment for a fee.

Preserving Your Privacy in a High-Tech World

As this chapter has already indicated, it is becoming increasingly difficult for consumers to preserve their privacy in today's high-tech world. New laws must be written and existing laws strengthened to address the dramatic technological changes that have been taking place. No law can protect consumers completely because there will always be companies and individuals figuring out ways to get around the law and getting away with it. Each of you must do what you can to preserve your privacy. Below are some tips on how to do that:

- Monitor your credit record. Request a copy of it from each of the big three once a year and from any independent local or regional credit bureaus maintaining a file on you and check it carefully for problems, including inquiries you do not understand.
- Contact the MIB to find out if it has a record on you. If it does, review it for problems and correct any that you may find.
- Tell the big three that you want to opt out of their prescreening and direct marketing programs. See Figure 9.1 for how to do this.
- Write to the Direct Marketing Association (DMA) to ask to be put on its list of people whose names may not be released to direct marketing firms and telemarketing firms. Doing so will help reduce the number of companies and organizations that can gain access to information about you; it will also reduce the amount of junk mail and unsolicited phone calls that you receive. See Figure 9.1 for DMA addresses.
- Pay cash whenever possible rather than using credit. That way you won't be signing anything, and your transaction will be less likely to become part of a company's data bank. Using cash instead of credit also reduces the possibility that you will develop credit problems.
- Don't carry extra credit cards, your Social Security card, or other identifying information in your wallet or purse unless you absolutely have to.
- Read disclosure statements on any credit forms you sign.
- Check out your credit card billing statements each month to spot any charges you don't understand or didn't make.
- Tear up all credit card receipt carbons.
- Never give your ATM card PIN to anyone and don't write the number on your card or keep it with your card.
- Shield your PIN from others when you're using your ATM card.
- Tear up your ATM and credit card receipts so they can't be read. Don't leave them where strangers can pick them up and don't throw them in the trash without ripping them up.

FIGURE 9.1 How to Opt Out

Here are the addresses to contact if you want your name removed from the prescreening and direct marketing programs of the big three. Don't forget you need only contact one of them. In your letter, include your full name, complete address, and Social Security number.

Equifax Options
Marketing Decisions Systems
PO Box 740123
Atlanta, GA 30374-0123

Trans Union
Name Removal Option
PO Box 7245
Fullerton, CA 92637

Experian Consumer Opt Out
701 Experian Parkway
Allen, TX 75002
You can also call 800-353-0809.

If you want to further reduce the number of solicitations you get via mail as well as phone, you should also contact the Direct Marketing Association, a national organization of direct marketers, including telemarketers. You will remain on the DMA's opt-out lists for five years.

Direct Marketing Association
Mail Preference Service
PO Box 9008
Farmington, NY 11735

Direct Marketing Association
Telephone Preference Service
PO Box 9014
Farmington, NY 11735

- Tear up all preapproved credit offers so they can't be read.
- Don't give out your personal information just because someone asks for it. For example, don't give a caller you don't know your bank account number, your credit card account number, your driver's license number, or your Social Security number; and don't write your Social Security number on your check or on the part of a credit receipt that a business is going to keep. Your Social Security number is a basic identifying number that can be used to call up a variety of information about you, including your credit and bank accounts. No law says you must provide your Social Security number for a credit transaction.
- Don't write your telephone number or address on a merchant's credit slip or receipt. No law requires that you do, and some states actually prohibit merchants from asking consumers to provide such information for their receipts or sales slips.
- Keep your driver's license number to yourself as much as possible. Depending on your state, this number may be the same as your Social Security number.
- Think twice before responding to a telephone or written survey. The information you provide may be used by direct marketers and others.
- Limit the amount of information that you write on a warranty card, product registration form, mail order form, and the like.
- Call your bank, credit card companies, and phone company to tell them you do not want them to give third parties your name or other personal information.
- Recognize that if you respond to a mail or phone offer, then your name, address, and telephone number will probably end up on at least one more list.
- Think twice before including your Social Security number, credit card account numbers, or other personal information in an e-mail message.
- Find out how your Internet service provider protects the consumer credit-related information in its database.
- Recognize the risks involved in buying online.
- Avoid responding to junk e-mail. In addition to representing a new threat to your privacy, spam is often little more than a new marketing vehicle for consumer scams. Steer clear!
- If you subscribe to an online service, avoid obvious passwords.

CHAPTER 10

Now That You Have It

Lois Nelson had been a client of mine more than a decade ago. Back then she was a recent college graduate with an entry-level job in a large public relations firm. Lois had made the mistake many new graduates do—applied for and gotten a lot of credit cards. They had been a huge temptation for her and after just a few years of using credit cards to finance trips to the mall, vacations, and expensive meals out, Lois was unable to pay everything she owed each month. Ultimately, she filed for a Chapter 13 bankruptcy.

Today she sat smiling in my office, something I had not seen her do very often when she was in the midst of her financial crisis. Lois was smiling because she had managed to turn her life around. Not only had she completed her Chapter 13 bankruptcy and begun rebuilding her credit but she had advanced in her career and now made a comfortable living. In addition, she had just gotten married.

Anticipating the life she and her spouse wanted to build together, Lois was anxious to learn all she could about how to avoid future credit problems. She knew that maintaining a sound credit record would be key to achieving the dreams she and her husband shared. Lois also recognized that despite her education and career success, she knew relatively little about how to make wise credit choices and how to manage her money responsibly.

I told Lois that I wished all my former clients would do what she was doing. I explained that many consumers who rebuild their credit after financial difficulty end up in trouble again because of their lack of money management savvy. I then went on to talk with Lois about credit and provided her with a list of books and magazines to read. I also gave her the names and phone numbers of several nonprofit organizations that could offer her solid credit management information at little or no cost.

Avoiding credit problems after you've recovered from money troubles and rebuilt your credit requires that you understand how to evaluate credit offers and manage your use of credit wisely. This chapter will provide you with some of the basic information you need to maintain a solid credit history.

Strategies for Keeping Bad Habits at Bay

After you have rebuilt your credit and the memories of your money troubles have begun to fade, you may be tempted to resume some of the habits that were responsible for getting you into financial trouble and ruining your credit record in the first place. Those habits may include

- applying for and using multiple bankcards;
- running up the balance on your checking account credit line;
- overusing your ATM or debit cards; and
- not putting money in your savings account on a regular basis.

If you find yourself returning to your old bad habits, try to stop and think about the danger of what you are doing. Recovering from serious credit problems, even bankruptcy, is hard enough the first time but can be even more difficult the second time around because most creditors will be much less willing to work with you if they think you didn't learn your lesson the first time.

The secret to keeping your spending under control may be to develop a spending plan, or budget. If your plan is realistic and you stick to it, it will help you allocate your income so that you are able to meet your monthly obligations. It's hoped you'll have money left over each month to put in savings. If you don't, you may want to consider taking a second job or finding a better-paying job. Having money in savings that you can use to purchase big ticket items or something special like a nice vacation will help cut down on your use of credit.

If you need help developing a budget, resources that may be able to help you are listed below:

- Your local CCCS office If you don't find a CCCS listing in your local phone book, the National Foundation For Consumer Credit (800-388-2227) can give you the number of the CCCS office closest to you.
- The nearest cooperative extension service office. To find it, look in the local government listings of your phone book, or call the U.S. Department of Agriculture's Education and Extension Service office at 201-720-3029.
- Your local community college or the adult education program sponsored by your area's public school system or a local college or university.

If you are having trouble controlling your spending, you may have emotional problems with money. For help, consider scheduling an appointment with a psychologist or joining the Debtors Anonymous nearest you. Using many of the same successful techniques developed by Alcoholics Anonymous, Debtors Anonymous helps you understand and overcome your inability to control your spending. If you don't find a phone number for Debtors Anonymous in your local phone book, get in touch with the national organization by writing: Debtors Anonymous, General Service Board, PO Box 400, Grand Central Station, New York, NY 10163-0400.

How Much Credit Is Enough Credit?

Keep to a minimum the number of credit cards you have even if you rarely use some of them. One or two national bankcards, perhaps one travel and entertainment card such as American Express, and a gasoline card are all you need. Avoid retail store charge cards, which tend to carry relatively high rates of interest, and most retailers accept MasterCard and Visa cards.

If you have a lot of credit cards, you may be tempted to use them. Furthermore, your current and potential creditors won't look kindly on you if they know that you have multiple credit cards even if you haven't used some of them in many months and they don't have balances due. As long as you have those accounts, creditors know you can begin using them.

It's a good idea to close all credit accounts except for those you absolutely need even if you still owe money on some of them. Close the accounts with the least advantageous terms of credit.

Cut up each unwanted card and send it along with a letter to the creditor's customer service or customer relations office. You can usually find that address on the back of your credit card statement. Don't send your letter and unwanted card to the address you use when you are paying your bills.

HOT TIP

Be sure that the account you are closing doesn't have an acceleration clause, which allows the card issuer to demand payment in full at any time for any reason. If it does, the company may activate that clause if you close your account.

After you have closed the accounts, wait a few months and then order a copy of your credit report from each of the big three. Make certain that there is a notation for each account indicating that it was closed at your request.

Profile of a Good Credit Manager

Although it is important to keep the number of credit cards you have to a minimum, it is equally important to monitor how much credit you have relative to your monthly income if you want to avoid a reoccurrence of your financial troubles. It's a good idea to do this every six months. Even with just one credit card, you can develop money troubles if you overuse it relative to your income.

When you are applying for important credit, the potential creditor will look at the amount of credit you have relative to your income. If that ratio is too high, even if you make a very comfortable salary, you may have difficulty obtaining the credit you need at reasonable terms.

An easy way to assess if you have too much debt relative to your income is to perform a simple financial self-audit using industry standards for what are considered appropriate or safe debt to income ratios. If your ratios exceed the standards, then you should reduce your debt. To do that you may have to take a second job for a while or do some freelance or consulting work on the side. The ratios you should compare yourself to are as follows:

- Your debt to income ratio for credit cards and loans (don't include your monthly mortgage or rent payment, utility payments, and any monthly tax payments you may make) is your total monthly credit payments divided by your total monthly income (including all regular, guaranteed sources of monthly income).
  - If your debt to income ratio is under 20 percent, you're doing okay although the lower the better; 10 percent or less is ideal.
  - If your ratio is over 20 percent, slow down: Stop using your credit cards and concentrate on paying off your card balances.
  - If your ratio exceeds 35 percent, you are in the danger zone. Although some creditors will still work with you, it's unlikely that you will be eligible for consumer-friendly offers—those that come with favorable terms. You should begin actively reducing the amount of debt you are carrying; an unexpected big expense, the loss of your job, an expensive stay in the hospital, and similar mishaps could be financially disastrous if you don't lower your ratio. Once you get your credit card and loan debt reduced, deposit the money you were putting toward that debt in a savings account.
- Next is the ratio of your mortgage payment (including taxes and insurance) to your monthly gross income. When evaluating a mortgage loan application, banks like to see a ratio in the 28 to 36 percent range, meaning they don't want your monthly house payment to exceed 28 to 36 percent of your gross income. If your ratio is higher than that, you may have to come up with a larger-than-normal down payment and/or pay a higher-than-average interest rate. In such a case, perhaps you should look for a less expensive home or perhaps you may not be able to finance a home at all until you improve your ratio.

What Creditors Look For

When you apply for a bank loan, the bank will assess your creditworthiness using the three C's: capacity, capital, and character.

- *Capacity.* Do you have the ability to repay the credit you want to borrow? To determine this, a creditor will look at the ratios previously described, your employment history, your income, and your payment history on any other debt you already have.

- *Capital.* What assets do you have that you can use to collateralize the credit you are asking for? Creditors are interested in your collateral even if you are applying for unsecured credit because they want to be sure you have assets to cover what you owe if you fail to pay. If you have no significant assets, you may not be able to obtain the credit you want; you may have to settle for less credit; or the credit may come with a very high interest rate or other unfavorable terms of credit.

- *Character.* Are you worthy of a creditor's trust? The creditor will make this assessment based on your payment history with other creditors. It may also look at your history of paying your rent, utilities, and phone bill.

Types of Credit Accounts

When you apply for a credit card or a bank loan, you will be applying for an open-end, a revolving, or an open 30-day account.

Open-End or Revolving Accounts

If your credit account is open-end or revolving, you'll have a fixed amount of credit that you are expected not to exceed. Each month you will have to pay at least the minimum amount due on the account, which will be a percentage of the total amount that you owe. Examples of open-end credit include *Visa and MasterCard cards* and *secured bank cards.*

Closed-End or Installment Accounts

If you have this kind of credit, you'll borrow a set amount of money and be expected to repay it in set amounts over a predetermined period of time. Examples of this kind of credit include the following:

- *Installment bank loans.* Your monthly loan payments will probably include principal plus interest with interest assessed from the date the loan is made. Your loan may or may not be collateralized depending on how much you are borrowing and the health of your credit history.

- *Mortgage loans.* These very large installment loans have long payback periods of up to 30 years. Their monthly payments include principal plus interest and often the cost of the property's insurance and taxes as well. The property you mortgage serves as loan collateral.

Open 30-Day Credit Accounts

With this kind of account you can charge up to a certain credit limit but must pay the full amount of your account balance each month or within 30 days of the billing date. This type of credit includes the following:

- *Travel and entertainment cards.* These cards—American Express is an example—offer a higher credit limit than that offered by most bank cards, but you will be charged a relatively high rate of interest if you don't you pay your balance in full.
- *Oil and gas cards.* These easily attainable, convenient-to-use cards often have very high interest rates. Many oil and gas cards now offer revolving accounts.
- *Retail or store charge cards.* These cards may be open 30-day accounts or revolving accounts. Your state's laws will govern the terms of any retail credit you obtain.

Evaluating Credit Offers

Credit card offers flood our mailboxes these days. Some offers tout their low rates; others encourage us to transfer an existing card balance to the bankcard being marketed. Still other cards lure us with promises of frequent flier miles or other benefits.

To help you evaluate and compare various credit offers, return to Chapter 5, "Rebuilding Your Credit." Figure 5.1 in that chapter defines and explains some of the criteria you should consider.

Once you have refamiliarized yourself with that information, you should think about how you will be using your bankcard, because that should influence your decision making. Listed below are some of the questions to ask yourself:

- Will I be paying my bankcard balance in full each month? If you do, look for a card with no annual fee or a very low fee and with a long grace period—at least 25 days.
- Will I be carrying a balance on my bankcard? If you don't plan on paying off the balance each month, you should opt for a card with a low annual percentage rate, or APR. In addition, you should be aware of how the finance charge will be calculated. Most companies base their APR on a consumer's "average daily balance" with new purchases included, a calculation method that is one of the most expensive for consumers. The method that is most advantageous for consumers is the "adjusted balance method." Next best is "average daily balance not including purchases." There are other APR calculation methods but the most expensive is the "two-cycle average daily balance" because it costs consumers the most in finance charges. You can find out what method is used by reading the fine print in the bankcard solicitation offer. Boring as it may be, read the fine print!! The way your finance charges are calculated can mean a significant difference in your cost of credit.
- What kind of credit limit do I need? Don't opt for a bankcard just because it has a very high credit limit. Using a credit card to finance a major purchase is very expensive; instead, consider applying for a bank loan or saving for the purchase. Furthermore, having a high credit limit may also jeopardize your opportunity to obtain an important future loan.
- Do I want other benefits with my credit card? Some bankcard companies market cards with such added benefits as product rebates or frequent flier miles. The problem with many of these cards is that you have to charge a lot before you can actually take advantage of their added benefits or you may be trading the benefits for a high APR, disadvantageous APR calculation method, a short grace period, or other unfavorable credit terms.

    Some companies offer affinity cards, which typically bear the name or logo of a nonprofit organization. A percentage of each purchase you make with an affinity card, or a portion of your annual fee, goes to the nonprofit organization. Before you opt for an affinity card, be aware that most of them cost more to use than the usual bankcard and that the nonprofit organization you think you will benefit may not get very much from the deal. If you really care about the organization, you'll probably be better off writing it a check.

 HOT TIP

To obtain an up-to-date list of the credit cards with the lowest interest rates, contact CardTrak at 800-344-7714. Card-Track updates its list monthly; the cost of a list is $5.

Credit Card Traps

Credit card solicitations may sound attractive until you read the details of the offer. Many "good" offers are actually bad for consumers and good for the credit card company because they provide the offering businesses a lot of money. Some things to watch for when you're reading the fine print that comes with the offer for a new card include the following:

- High annual fees or annual fees that escalate after a period of time
- Penalties for making your payments on time or not using your card regularly
- Offers that tout an especially low interest rate—a "teaser" rate—to encourage transferring a balance due from one card to another with a lower rate (Often the low rate will last for just a short time to be replaced with a much higher rate.)
- Increases in your annual rate if you exceed your credit limit or don't make a payment on time
- Immediate fees that can be as high as $25 for being late with a payment or exceeding your credit limit (Such fees used to be delayed.)

Take the Offensive

You don't have to wait to be solicited for a bankcard. If you know of one with favorable terms, contact the card offerer and ask to be sent an application. You don't have to limit your bankcard shopping to local banks only; for example, Wachovia Bank in Atlanta (800-842-3262) consistently offers low-rate bankcards.

HOT TIP

The Internet has made it easier to find a bankcard to fit your needs. Get Smart at http://www.getsmart.com and Ram Research Group at http://ramresearch.com are two of the better Web sites that can help you find the right card. Just be aware that some of the Web sites that help you check out credit card offers require you to divulge such personal information as your Social Security number and financial data.

If the terms of the bankcard you already have is not as attractive as some of the offers you've been receiving, consider asking the bankcard company to meet or better the terms of the other cards. If you have a good payment record, the bankcard company may be willing to work with you rather than lose a customer.

If You Receive an Unsolicited Credit Card in the Mail

Although not a common occurrence, occasionally you may receive a card you never applied for. It's usually not a good idea to use it because unsolicited cards tend not to have good credit terms. If you do think about keeping it, however, read all of the enclosed information to make sure the credit terms are reasonable before you use the card.

If you don't want the card, make a copy of it and cut the card in two. Then inform the card issuer in writing that you do not want to accept the card and that you want any card-related information the issuer may have provided to a credit bureau deleted from your credit file. Keep a copy of your letter and store it with the cut-up card and the solicitation offer that came with the card.

Cash Advances—An Expensive Option

If your credit card allows you to obtain a cash advance, the extra money may be tempting for holiday buying, for a vacation, or to help you get through a month when your spending exceeded your income. Think long and hard before you do anything because cash advances are expensive; they come with extremely high interest rates and fees. Typically, the interest rate you pay will be higher than the rate associated with your normal purchases—close to 20 percent in some instances. Another downside to cash advances is that interest usually begins to accrue as soon as the transaction is completed—in other words, there's no grace period. Obviously, if you can't make ends meet, getting a cash advance provides an expensive and very temporary solution to your cash flow problem and you risk making your financial situation worse. And if your finances were under control before getting the cash advance, each advance undermines your financial stability unless you're able to pay off the advance in full right away.

Do You Need Credit Life Insurance?

Credit life insurance ensures that a certain debt—your home mortgage, credit card balance, or auto loan—will be paid off in the event of your death. Although the amount you pay each month to buy this insurance may not seem like very much, credit life insurance is a colossal waste of money and one of the most expensive kinds of insurance you can buy. In fact, two highly respected consumer groups—Consumer Federation of America and the U.S. Public Interest Research Group—have begun a campaign to educate consumers about the problems with credit life insurance.

 HOT TIP

If you want to consider credit life insurance, talk with your insurance broker about your options.

Sometimes the information you receive seems to indicate that credit life insurance is a requirement for getting the credit you're applying for. Such "misinformation" is usually a marketing ploy because credit insurance is rarely mandatory. Some creditors may actually include the cost of this insurance in the loan agreement you're asked to sign. If you don't want the insurance, say so and don't sign the contract until reference to the insurance is deleted and the cost of credit changed accordingly.

HOT TIP

Creditors are allowed to require credit property insurance for loans secured with real estate or other assets that could be destroyed. But, you are allowed to purchase the insurance from a company of your choice to get the best price.

Debit Cards

Debit cards are relatively new but are becoming an increasingly popular way to pay for merchandise. Although they look like a credit card or an ATM card, they function more like a check with a few important differences. In fact, both MasterCard and Visa offer debit cards.

Debit cards can be used in two ways: online and offline. When you use an online debit card, you have to enter your security code before your transaction can be completed, and the cost of your purchase is debited immediately from your checking account. In other words, there is no delay or "float" as there is when you write a check. If you use your debit card at a grocery store, you're probably making an online purchase.

HOT TIP

Some banks have begun sending customers replacement ATM cards that are actually debit cards.

If you use your debit card in an offline transaction, you don't have to enter your security code but instead must sign a receipt to close your transaction. There is a delay between the time that you use the card and the time your checking account is debited for the cost of the purchase. Your debit card functions much like a check when used this way.

Obviously, using a debit card to pay for your purchases is more convenient than carrying a checkbook around and writing out checks. There are, however, some downsides to debit cards, as shown in the following:

- If you don't keep an accurate record of each purchase you make with your debit card, you may quickly spend more money than you have in your checking account.
- Because the cards look so much alike, it's easy to forget you're using a debit card, *not* a credit card, and won't have a month or so to pay off your purchase.
- Depending on the debit card you use, you may pay a significant amount in fees that may include an annual fee, a monthly fee, and a per transaction fee.
- Some businesses will charge you a fee when you use a debit card to pay for your purchase.
- There is no way to stop payment on a purchase.
- You don't get the same legal protections with a debit card that you get when you use a credit card. (Many of the protections you have when you use a credit card are described in the next section of this chapter.) For example, if you realize you have lost your debit card and report within two business days that it was stolen, you are only liable for up to $50 of any charges or withdrawals made with it, according to the federal Electronic Funds Transfer Act. If you don't realize it's missing until you get your statement, you have 60 days after the statement date to report that you lost your debit card or it was stolen, and once again you are only liable for $50 in unauthorized charges and withdrawals. If you report it missing later than this, you may be out of luck and liable for all the unauthorized charges and withdrawals

 HOT TIP

The Electronic Funds Transfer Act also applies to lost or stolen ATM cards.

Federal Laws You Should Know About

Chapter 8 discussed a credit-related federal law important to women, the Equal Credit Opportunity Act. No matter what your sex when applying for or using credit, you should also understand your rights under the Truth in Lending Act and the Fair Credit Billing Act.

The Truth in Lending Act (TLA)

The TLA makes it easier for you to compare the costs of various credit options so that you can make an informed decision. Under the act a creditor must put in writing, using language that most consumers can understand, the full cost of the credit it's offering before you sign a credit agreement. Among other things, you must be told

- the interest rate you will be charged;
- the annual percentage rate, or APR, associated with the credit; and
- any grace period that may be applicable.

Provisions of the TLA that affect lost or stolen credit cards. The TLA limits your liability if you lose one or more credit cards or if they are stolen by providing that once you notify a credit card company about a lost or stolen card, your liability for any unauthorized charges is limited to $50. Even if a stranger "maxes out" your credit card, once you have called the company that issued the card, you won't have to pay more than $50. Obviously, the sooner you notice that a card is missing and notify the card company the better.

Your legal recourse under the TLA. If a creditor fails to comply with the TLA's provisions, the law gives you the right to sue for actual damages and twice the finance charge in the case of certain credit disclosures. If you win your suit, the court may award you no more than $1,000 and no less than $100. You are also able to collect court costs and attorney fees. Class action suits are permitted by the TLA.

The Fair Credit Billing Act (FCBA)

The FCBA can help you resolve billing problems with open-end credit accounts such as bankcards, retail charge cards, and lines of credit. (It does not apply to billing problems with closed-end, or installment, accounts.) Examples of covered billing problems include the following:

- You discover charges on your credit card billing statement that you don't understand or you aren't being properly credited for payments you made.
- Your billing statement shows the wrong dollar amount for a credit purchase you made or the statement for your line of credit is inaccurate; it may show that you accessed more credit than you believe you did or it may not reflect the payment you made.
- Your billing statement reflects charges you don't think you or an authorized user made.
- Your credit line statement shows that you accessed that credit line but you don't believe that you or anyone authorized to do so used your credit line.
- You are charged for goods/services you didn't accept or that you returned.
- You are charged for goods that are different from those you ordered.
- Computational errors were made in your billing statement.

Write—Don't Call!!

If you find one of the problems described in the previous section, you must write—*do not call*—the appropriate creditor about the problem within 60 days of the postmark on the first statement you received that reflected the problem. If you call about the problem, you will not be protected by the FCBA. In your letter, be sure to include your name, account number, the dollar amount you are disputing, and a clearly stated and very specific statement of the problem. Indicate in your letter that you are exercising your legal rights under the FCBA, and be sure to date your letter. Attach a copy of the problem billing statement and make a copy of your letter for your files. Send your letter by certified mail with a return receipt requested to the billing inquiries address listed on your bill. Do not include it in the same envelope as the one you use to mail your payment.

The creditor must acknowledge your letter within 30 days of receiving it unless the problem has already been resolved by the time your letter is received. Within 90 days, the creditor must either provide you with a written explanation of why the statement you received is correct and provide you with proof, if you ask for it, or the creditor must correct the problem.

In the Meantime

While you're waiting to hear from the creditor about its investigation, you don't have to pay the amount in question or any finance charges related to it. Nor can the creditor report your account as delinquent, threaten to damage your credit record, sue you for payment, or close or restrict your account. However, the creditor may apply the amount you are disputing against your total credit limit.

If your creditor claims that your billing statement is correct. If the creditor's investigation finds that your statement is correct, you must be notified in writing. The FCBA also requires that you pay what you owe within ten days of being notified, including applicable finance charges. If you don't pay up, the creditor can begin reporting to credit bureaus that your account is delinquent. If you continue to contend that there is an error on your billing statement and you continue to try to get it corrected, your creditor must report that your account is in dispute when it reports to credit bureaus.

If your creditor says that your billing statement is in error. If the creditor finds that you are right and an error is indeed on your statement, your account must be credited and you won't have to pay any applicable late fees or finance charges.

Resolving Problems with Defective, Damaged, or Inferior Merchandise and Services

If you use your credit card to purchase a product or service that ends up being defective, damaged, or of poor quality, the FCBA allows you to take the same legal action against the credit card issuer that you could against the seller of the product or service under the laws of your state. For example, if your state says that you may withhold payment to the seller or pay and sue for a refund, you might also be able to withhold payment to the card issuer. But you should get the advice of an attorney before you take any action because the FCBA requires that you make a serious effort to resolve your problem directly with the company that sold you the product or service before taking action.

HOT TIP

Unless the business that sold you the good or service is also the card issuer, the FCBA applies to defective, damaged, or inferior goods and services only if your purchase exceeds $50 and was made in your state or within 100 miles of your mailing address. The FCBA therefore will probably not be much help if you do a lot of catalog shopping.

Appendix A

Public Law 91-508
Title VI
The Fair Credit Reporting Act

As amended, including September 30, 1996
Public Law No. 104-208 and
September 23, 1994
Public Law No. 103-325

Enacted October 26, 1970
Effective April 24, 1971

THE FAIR CREDIT REPORTING ACT

As amended by Public Law 104-208 (Sept. 30, 1996)

As a public service, the staff of the Federal Trade Commission (FTC) has prepared the following complete text of the Fair Credit Reporting Act (FCRA), 15 U.S.C. §1681 et seq., as recently amended by Congress. *Most of the amendments go into effect on September 30, 1997,* one year after the President signed them into law. A copy of the FCRA as effective until September 30, 1997 can be obtained by writing to Public Reference Branch, Federal Trade Commission, Washington, D.C. 20580.

In preparing this document, the FTC's staff integrated the amendments set forth in the Consumer Credit Reporting Reform Act of 1996 (Public Law 104-208, the Omnibus Consolidated Appropriations Act for Fiscal Year 1997, Title II, Subtitle D, Chapter 1) into the existing FCRA. Although staff generally followed the format of the U.S. Code as published by the Government Printing Office, the format of this text does differ in minor ways from the Code (and from West's U.S. Code Annotated). For example, this version uses FCRA section numbers (§§ 601–625) in the headings. (The relevant U.S. Code citation is included with each section heading and each reference to the FCRA in the text.)

[This version of the FCRA is complete as of March 17, 1997.]

TABLE OF CONTENTS

§ 601. Short title

This title may be cited as the Fair Credit Reporting Act.

§ 602. Congressional findings and statement of purpose [15 U.S.C. § 1681]

(a) Accuracy and fairness of credit reporting. The Congress makes the following findings:

(1) The banking system is dependent upon fair and accurate credit reporting. Inaccurate credit reports directly impair the efficiency of the banking system, and unfair credit reporting methods undermine the public confidence which is essential to the continued functioning of the banking system.

(2) An elaborate mechanism has been developed for investigating and evaluating the credit worthiness, credit standing, credit capacity, character, and general reputation of consumers.

(3) Consumer reporting agencies have assumed a vital role in assembling and evaluating consumer credit and other information on consumers.

(4) There is a need to insure that consumer reporting agencies exercise their grave responsibilities with fairness, impartiality, and a respect for the consumer's right to privacy.

(b) Reasonable procedures. It is the purpose of this title to require that consumer reporting agencies adopt reasonable procedures for meeting the needs of commerce for consumer credit, personnel, insurance, and other information in a manner which is fair and equitable to the consumer, with regard to the confidentiality, accuracy, relevancy, and proper utilization of such information in accordance with the requirements of this title.

§ 603. Definitions; rules of construction [15 U.S.C. § 1681a]

(a) Definitions and rules of construction set forth in this section are applicable for the purposes of this title.

(b) The term "person" means any individual, partnership, corporation, trust, estate, cooperative, association, government or governmental subdivision or agency, or other entity.

(c) The term "consumer" means an individual.

(d) Consumer report.

(1) In general. The term "consumer report" means any written, oral, or other communication of any information by a consumer reporting agency bearing on a consumer's credit worthiness, credit standing, credit capacity, character, general reputation, personal characteristics, or mode of living which is used or expected to be used or collected in whole or in part for the purpose of serving as a factor in establishing the consumer's eligibility for

(A) credit or insurance to be used primarily for personal, family, or household purposes;

(B) employment purposes; or

(C) any other purpose authorized under section 604 [§ 1681b].

(2) Exclusions. The term "consumer report" does not include

(A) any

(i) report containing information solely as to transactions or experiences between the consumer and the person making the report;

(ii) communication of that information among persons related by common ownership or affiliated by corporate control; or

(iii) any communication of other information among persons related by common ownership or affiliated by corporate control, if it is clearly and conspicuously disclosed to the consumer that the information may be communicated among such persons and the consumer is given the opportunity, before the time that the information is initially communicated, to direct that such information not be communicated among such persons;

(B) any authorization or approval of a specific extension of credit directly or indirectly by the issuer of a credit card or similar device;

(C) any report in which a person who has been requested by a third party to make a specific extension of credit directly or indirectly to a consumer conveys his or her decision with respect to such request, if the third party advises the consumer of the name and address of the person to whom the request was made, and such person makes the disclosures to the consumer required under section 615 [§ 1681m]; or

(D) a communication described in subsection (o).

(e) The term "investigative consumer report" means a consumer report or portion thereof in which information on a consumer's character, general reputation, personal characteristics, or mode of living is obtained through personal interviews with neighbors, friends, or associates of the consumer reported on or with others with whom he is acquainted or who may have knowledge concerning any such items of information. However, such information shall not include specific factual information on a consumer's credit record obtained directly from a creditor of the consumer or from a consumer reporting agency when such information was obtained directly from a creditor of the consumer or from the consumer.

(f) The term "consumer reporting agency" means any person which, for monetary fees, dues, or on a cooperative nonprofit basis, regularly engages in whole or in part in the practice of assembling or evaluating consumer credit information or other information on consumers for the purpose of furnishing consumer reports to third parties, and which uses any means or facility of interstate commerce for the purpose of preparing or furnishing consumer reports.

(g) The term "file," when used in connection with information on any consumer, means all of the information on that consumer recorded and retained by a consumer reporting agency regardless of how the information is stored.

(h) The term "employment purposes" when used in connection with a consumer report means a report used for the purpose of evaluating a consumer for employment, promotion, reassignment or retention as an employee.

(i) The term "medical information" means information or records obtained, with the consent of the individual to whom it relates, from licensed physicians or medical practitioners, hospitals, clinics, or other medical or medically related facilities.

(j) Definitions relating to child support obligations.

(1) Overdue support. The term "overdue support" has the meaning given to such term in section 666(e) of title 42 [Social Security Act, 42 U.S.C. § 666(e)].

(2) State or local child support enforcement agency. The term "State or local child support enforcement agency" means a State or local agency which administers a State or local program for establishing and enforcing child support obligations.

(k) Adverse action.

(1) Actions included. The term "adverse action"

(A) has the same meaning as in section 701(d)(6) of the Equal Credit Opportunity Act; and

(B) means

(i) a denial or cancellation of, an increase in any charge for, or a reduction or other adverse or unfavorable change in the terms of coverage or amount of, any insurance, existing or applied for, in connection with the underwriting of insurance;

(ii) a denial of employment or any other decision for employment purposes that adversely affects any current or prospective employee;

(iii) a denial or cancellation of, an increase in any charge for, or any other adverse or unfavorable change in the terms of, any license or benefit described in section 604(a)(3)(D) [§ 1681b]; and

(iv) an action taken or determination that is

(I) made in connection with an application that was made by, or a transaction that was initiated by, any consumer, or in connection with a review of an account under section 604(a)(3)(F)(ii)[§ 1681b]; and

(II) adverse to the interests of the consumer.

(2) Applicable findings, decisions, commentary, and orders. For purposes of any determination of whether an action is an adverse action under paragraph (1)(A), all appropriate final findings, decisions, commentary, and orders issued under section 701(d)(6) of the Equal Credit Opportunity Act by the Board of Governors of the Federal Reserve System or any court shall apply.

(l) Firm offer of credit or insurance. The term "firm offer of credit or insurance" means any offer of credit or insurance to a consumer that will be honored if the consumer is determined, based on information in a consumer report on the consumer, to meet the specific criteria used to select the consumer for the offer, except that the offer may be further conditioned on one or more of the following:

(1) The consumer being determined, based on information in the consumer's application for the credit or insurance, to meet specific criteria bearing on credit worthiness or insurability, as applicable, that are established

(A) before selection of the consumer for the offer; and

(B) for the purpose of determining whether to extend credit or insurance pursuant to the offer.

(2) Verification

(A) that the consumer continues to meet the specific criteria used to select the consumer for the offer, by using information in a consumer report on the consumer, information in the consumer's application for the credit or insurance, or other information bearing on the credit worthiness or insurability of the consumer; or

(B) of the information in the consumer's application for the credit or insurance, to determine that the consumer meets the specific criteria bearing on credit worthiness or insurability.

(3) The consumer furnishing any collateral that is a requirement for the extension of the credit or insurance that was

(A) established before selection of the consumer for the offer of credit or insurance; and

(B) disclosed to the consumer in the offer of credit or insurance.

(m) Credit or insurance transaction that is not initiated by the consumer. The term "credit or insurance transaction that is not initiated by the consumer" does not include the use of a consumer report by a person with which the consumer has an account or insurance policy, for purposes of

(1) reviewing the account or insurance policy; or

(2) collecting the account.

(n) State. The term "State" means any State, the Commonwealth of Puerto Rico, the District of Columbia, and any territory or possession of the United States.

(o) Excluded communications. A communication is described in this subsection if it is a communication

(1) that, but for subsection (d)(2)(E),[1] would be an investigative consumer report;

(2) that is made to a prospective employer for the purpose of

(A) procuring an employee for the employer; or

(B) procuring an opportunity for a natural person to work for the employer;

(3) that is made by a person who regularly performs such procurement;

(4) that is not used by any person for any purpose other than a purpose described in sub-paragraph (A) or (B) of paragraph (2); or

(5) with respect to which

(A) the consumer who is the subject of the communication

(i) consents orally or in writing to the nature and scope of the communication, before the collection of any information for the purpose of making the communication;

(ii) consents orally or in writing to the making of the communication to a prospective employer, before the making of the communication; and

(iii) in the case of consent under clause (i) or (ii) given orally, is provided written confirmation of that consent by the person making the communication, not later than 3 business days after the receipt of the consent by that person;

(B) the person who makes the communication does not, for the purpose of making the communication, make any inquiry that if made by a prospective employer of the consumer who is the subject of the communication would violate any applicable Federal or State equal employment opportunity law or regulation; and

(C) the person who makes the communication

(i) discloses in writing to the consumer who is the subject of the communication, not later than 5 business days after receiving any request from the consumer for such disclosure, the nature and substance of all information in the consumer's file at the time of the request, except that the sources of any information that is acquired solely for use in making the communication and is actually used for no other purpose, need not be disclosed other than under appropriate discovery procedures in any court of competent jurisdiction in which an action is brought; and

(ii) notifies the consumer who is the subject of the communication, in writing, of the consumer's right to request the information described in clause (i).

(p) Consumer reporting agency that compiles and maintains files on consumers on a nationwide basis. The term "consumer reporting agency that compiles and maintains files on consumers on a nationwide basis" means a consumer reporting agency that regularly engages in the practice of assembling or evaluating, and maintaining, for the purpose of furnishing consumer reports to third parties bearing on a consumer's credit worthiness, credit standing, or credit capacity, each of the following regarding consumers residing nationwide:

(1) Public record information.

(2) Credit account information from persons who furnish that information regularly and in the ordinary course of business

---

1. So in original, however should read (d)(2)(D).

§ 604. Permissible purposes of consumer reports [15 U.S.C. § 1681b]

(a) In general. Subject to subsection (c), any consumer reporting agency may furnish a consumer report under the following circumstances and no other:

(1) In response to the order of a court having jurisdiction to issue such an order, or a subpoena issued in connection with proceedings before a Federal grand jury.

(2) In accordance with the written instructions of the consumer to whom it relates.

(3) To a person which it has reason to believe

(A) intends to use the information in connection with a credit transaction involving the consumer on whom the information is to be furnished and involving the extension of credit to, or review or collection of an account of, the consumer; or

(B) intends to use the information for employment purposes; or

(C) intends to use the information in connection with the underwriting of insurance involving the consumer; or

(D) intends to use the information in connection with a determination of the consumer's eligibility for a license or other benefit granted by a governmental instrumentality required by law to consider an applicant's financial responsibility or status; or

(E) intends to use the information, as a potential investor or servicer, or current insurer, in connection with a valuation of, or an assessment of the credit or prepayment risks associated with, an existing credit obligation; or

(F) otherwise has a legitimate business need for the information

(i) in connection with a business transaction that is initiated by the consumer; or

(ii) to review an account to determine whether the consumer continues to meet the terms of the account.

(4) In response to a request by the head of a State or local child support enforcement agency (or a State or local government official authorized by the head of such an agency), if the person making the request certifies to the consumer reporting agency that

(A) the consumer report is needed for the purpose of establishing an individual's capacity to make child support payments or determining the appropriate level of such payments;

(B) the paternity of the consumer for the child to which the obligation relates has been established or acknowledged by the consumer in accordance with State laws under which the obligation arises (if required by those laws);

(C) the person has provided at least 10 days' prior notice to the consumer whose report is requested, by certified or registered mail to the last known address of the consumer, that the report will be requested; and

(D) the consumer report will be kept confidential, will be used solely for a purpose described in subparagraph (A), and will not be used in connection with any other civil, administrative, or criminal proceeding, or for any other purpose.

(5) To an agency administering a State plan under Section 454 of the Social Security Act (42 U.S.C. § 654) for use to set an initial or modified child support award.

(b) Conditions for furnishing and using consumer reports for employment purposes.

(1) Certification from user. A consumer reporting agency may furnish a consumer report for employment purposes only if

(A) the person who obtains such report from the agency certifies to the agency that

(i) the person has complied with paragraph (2) with respect to the consumer report, and the person will comply with paragraph (3) with respect to the consumer report if paragraph (3) becomes applicable; and

(ii) information from the consumer report will not be used in violation of any applicable Federal or State equal employment opportunity law or regulation; and

(B) the consumer reporting agency provides with the report a summary of the consumer's rights under this title, as prescribed by the Federal Trade Commission under section 609(c)(3) [§ 1681g].

(2) Disclosure to consumer. A person may not procure a consumer report, or cause a consumer report to be procured, for employment purposes with respect to any consumer, unless

(A) a clear and conspicuous disclosure has been made in writing to the consumer at any time before the report is procured or caused to be procured, in a document that consists solely of the disclosure, that a consumer report may be obtained for employment purposes; and

(B) the consumer has authorized in writing the procurement of the report by that person.

(3) Conditions on use for adverse actions. In using a consumer report for employment purposes, before taking any adverse action based in whole or in part on the report, the person intending to take such adverse action shall provide to the consumer to whom the report relates

(A) a copy of the report; and

(B) a description in writing of the rights of the consumer under this title, as prescribed by the Federal Trade Commission under section 609(c)(3) [§ 1681g].

(c) Furnishing reports in connection with credit or insurance transactions that are not initiated by the consumer.

(1) In general. A consumer reporting agency may furnish a consumer report relating to any consumer pursuant to subparagraph (A) or (C) of subsection (a)(3) in connection with any credit or insurance transaction that is not initiated by the consumer only if

(A) the consumer authorizes the agency to provide such report to such person; or

(B) (i) the transaction consists of a firm offer of credit or insurance;

(ii) the consumer reporting agency has complied with subsection (e); and

(iii) there is not in effect an election by the consumer, made in accordance with subsection (e), to have the consumer's name and address excluded from lists of names provided by the agency pursuant to this paragraph.

(2) Limits on information received under paragraph (1)(B). A person may receive pursuant to paragraph (1)(B) only

(A) the name and address of a consumer;

(B) an identifier that is not unique to the consumer and that is used by the person solely for the purpose of verifying the identity of the consumer; and

(C) other information pertaining to a consumer that does not identify the relationship or experience of the consumer with respect to a particular creditor or other entity.

(3) Information regarding inquiries. Except as provided in section 609(a)(5) [§ 1681g], a consumer reporting agency shall not furnish to any person a record of inquiries in connection with a credit or insurance transaction that is not initiated by a consumer.

(d) Reserved.

(e) Election of consumer to be excluded from lists.

(1) In general. A consumer may elect to have the consumer's name and address excluded from any list provided by a consumer reporting agency under subsection (c)(1)(B) in connection with a credit or insurance transaction that is not initiated by the consumer, by notifying the agency in accordance with paragraph (2) that the consumer does not consent to any use of a consumer report relating to the consumer in connection with any credit or insurance transaction that is not initiated by the consumer.

(2) Manner of notification. A consumer shall notify a consumer reporting agency under paragraph (1)

(A) through the notification system maintained by the agency under paragraph (5); or

(B) by submitting to the agency a signed notice of election form issued by the agency for purposes of this subparagraph.

(3) Response of agency after notification through system. Upon receipt of notification of the election of a consumer under paragraph (1) through the notification system maintained by the agency under paragraph (5), a consumer reporting agency shall

(A) inform the consumer that the election is effective only for the 2-year period following the election if the consumer does not submit to the agency a signed notice of election form issued by the agency for purposes of paragraph (2)(B); and

(B) provide to the consumer a notice of election form, if requested by the consumer, not later than 5 business days after receipt of the notification of the election through the system established under paragraph (5), in the case of a request made at the time the consumer provides notification through the system.

(4) Effectiveness of election. An election of a consumer under paragraph (1)

(A) shall be effective with respect to a consumer reporting agency beginning 5 business days after the date on which the consumer notifies the agency in accordance with paragraph (2);

(B) shall be effective with respect to a consumer reporting agency

(i) subject to subparagraph (C), during the 2-year period beginning 5 business days after the date on which the consumer notifies the agency of the election, in the case of an election for which a consumer notifies the agency only in accordance with paragraph (2)(A); or

(ii) until the consumer notifies the agency under subparagraph (C), in the case of an election for which a consumer notifies the agency in accordance with paragraph (2)(B);

(C) shall not be effective after the date on which the consumer notifies the agency, through the notification system established by the agency under paragraph (5), that the election is no longer effective; and

(D) shall be effective with respect to each affiliate of the agency.

(5) Notification system.

(A) In general. Each consumer reporting agency that, under subsection (c)(1)(B), furnishes a consumer report in connection with a credit or insurance transaction that is not initiated by a consumer, shall

(i) establish and maintain a notification system, including a toll-free telephone number, which permits any consumer whose consumer report is maintained by the agency to notify the agency, with appropriate identification, of the consumer's election to have the consumer's name and address excluded from any such list of names and addresses provided by the agency for such a transaction; and

(ii) publish by not later than 365 days after the date of enactment of the Consumer Credit Reporting Reform Act of 1996, and not less than annually thereafter, in a publication of general circulation in the area served by the agency

(I) a notification that information in consumer files maintained by the agency may be used in connection with such transactions; and

(II) the address and toll-free telephone number for consumers to use to notify the agency of the consumer's election under clause (i).

(B) Establishment and maintenance as compliance. Establishment and maintenance of a notification system (including a toll-free telephone number) and publication by a consumer reporting agency on the agency's own behalf and on behalf of any of its affiliates in accordance with this paragraph is deemed to be compliance with this paragraph by each of those affiliates.

(6) Notification system by agencies that operate nationwide. Each consumer reporting agency that compiles and maintains files on consumers on a nationwide basis shall establish and maintain a notification system for purposes of paragraph (5) jointly with other such consumer reporting agencies.

(f) Certain use or obtaining of information prohibited. A person shall not use or obtain a consumer report for any purpose unless

(1) the consumer report is obtained for a purpose for which the consumer report is authorized to be furnished under this section; and

(2) the purpose is certified in accordance with section 607 [§ 1681e] by a prospective user of the report through a general or specific certification.

(g) Furnishing reports containing medical information. A consumer reporting agency shall not furnish for employment purposes, or in connection with a credit or insurance transaction or a direct marketing transaction, a consumer report that contains medical information about a consumer, unless the consumer consents to the furnishing of the report.

§ 605. Requirements relating to information contained in consumer reports [15 U.S.C. § 1681c]

(a) Information excluded from consumer reports. Except as authorized under subsection (b) of this section, no consumer reporting agency may make any consumer report containing any of the following items of information:

(1) Cases[2] under title 11 [United States Code] or under the Bankruptcy Act that, from the date of entry of the order for relief or the date of adjudication, as the case may be, antedate the report by more than 10 years.

(2) Suits and judgments which, from date of entry, antedate the report by more than seven years or until the governing statute of limitations has expired, whichever is the longer period.

(3) Paid tax liens which, from date of payment, antedate the report by more than seven years.

(4) Accounts placed for collection or charged to profit and loss which antedate the report by more than seven years.

(5) Records of arrest, indictment, or conviction of crime which, from date of disposition, release, or parole, antedate the report by more than seven years.

(6) Any other adverse item of information which antedates the report by more than seven years.

(b) Exempted cases. The provisions of subsection (a) of this section are not applicable in the case of any consumer credit report to be used in connection with

(1) a credit transaction involving, or which may reasonably be expected to involve, a principal amount of $150,000 or more;

(2) the underwriting of life insurance involving, or which may reasonably be expected to involve, a face amount of $150,000 or more; or

(3) the employment of any individual at an annual salary which equals, or which may reasonably be expected to equal $75,000, or more.

(c) Running of reporting period.

(1) In general. The 7-year period referred to in paragraphs (4) and (6) of subsection (a) shall begin, with respect to any delinquent account that is placed for collection (inter-

nally or by referral to a third party, whichever is earlier), charged to profit and loss, or subjected to any similar action, upon the expiration of the 180-day period beginning on the date of the commencement of the delinquency which immediately preceded the collection activity, charge to profit and loss, or similar action.

(2) Effective date. Paragraph (1) shall apply only to items of information added to the file of a consumer on or after the date that is 455 days after the date of enactment of the Consumer Credit Reporting Reform Act of 1996.

(d) Information required to be disclosed. Any consumer reporting agency that furnishes a consumer report that contains information regarding any case involving the consumer that arises under title 11, United States Code, shall include in the report an identification of the chapter of such title 11 under which such case arises if provided by the source of the information. If any case arising or filed under title 11, United States Code, is withdrawn by the consumer before a final judgment, the consumer reporting agency shall include in the report that such case or filing was withdrawn upon receipt of documentation certifying such withdrawal.

(e) Indication of closure of account by consumer. If a consumer reporting agency is notified pursuant to section 623(a)(4) [§ 1681s-2] that a credit account of a consumer was voluntarily closed by the consumer, the agency shall indicate that fact in any consumer report that includes information related to the account.

(f) Indication of dispute by consumer. If a consumer reporting agency is notified pursuant to section 623(a)(3) [§ 1681s-2] that information regarding a consumer who was furnished to the agency is disputed by the consumer, the agency shall indicate that fact in each consumer report that includes the disputed information.

------

2. In lower case in original.

§ 606. Disclosure of investigative consumer reports [15 U.S.C. § 1681d]

(a) Disclosure of fact of preparation. A person may not procure or cause to be prepared an investigative consumer report on any consumer unless

(1) it is clearly and accurately disclosed to the consumer that an investigative consumer report including information as to his character, general reputation, personal characteristics and mode of living, whichever are applicable, may be made, and such disclosure

(A) is made in a writing mailed, or otherwise delivered, to the consumer, not later than three days after the date on which the report was first requested, and

(B) includes a statement informing the consumer of his right to request the additional disclosures provided for under subsection (b) of this section and the written summary of the rights of the consumer prepared pursuant to section 609(c) [§ 1681g]; and

(2) the person certifies or has certified to the consumer reporting agency that

(A) the person has made the disclosures to the consumer required by paragraph (1); and

(B) the person will comply with subsection (b).

(b) Disclosure on request of nature and scope of investigation. Any person who procures or causes to be prepared an investigative consumer report on any consumer shall, upon written request made by the consumer within a reasonable period of time after the receipt by him of the disclosure required by subsection (a) (1) of this section, shall[3] make a complete and accurate disclosure of the nature and scope of the investigation requested. This disclosure shall be made in a writing mailed, or otherwise delivered, to the consumer not later than five days after the date on which the request for such disclosure was received from the consumer or such report was first requested, whichever is the later.

(c) Limitation on liability upon showing of reasonable procedures for compliance with provisions. No person may be held liable for any violation of subsection (a) or (b) of this section if he shows by a preponderance of the evidence that at the time of the violation he maintained reasonable procedures to assure compliance with subsection (a) or (b) of this section.

(d) Prohibitions.

(1) Certification. A consumer reporting agency shall not prepare or furnish investigative consumer report unless the agency has received a certification under subsection (a)(2) from the person who requested the report.

(2) Inquiries. A consumer reporting agency shall not make an inquiry for the purpose of preparing an investigative consumer report on a consumer for employment purposes if the making of the inquiry by an employer or prospective employer of the consumer would violate any applicable Federal or State equal employment opportunity law or regulation.

(3) Certain public record information. Except as otherwise provided in section 613 [§ 1681k], a consumer reporting agency shall not furnish an investigative consumer report that includes information that is a matter of public record and that relates to an arrest, indictment, conviction, civil judicial action, tax lien, or outstanding judgment, unless the agency has verified the accuracy of the information during the 30-day period ending on the date on which the report is furnished.

(4) Certain adverse information. A consumer reporting agency shall not prepare or furnish an investigative consumer report on a consumer that contains information that is adverse to the interest of the consumer and that is obtained through a personal interview with a neighbor, friend, or associate of the consumer or with another person with whom the consumer is acquainted or who has knowledge of such item of information, unless

(A) the agency has followed reasonable procedures to obtain confirmation of the information, from an additional source that has independent and direct knowledge of the information; or

(B) the person interviewed is the best possible source of the information.

---

3. So in original. "Shall" probably should not appear.

§ 607. Compliance procedures [15 U.S.C. § 1681e]

(a) Identity and purposes of credit users. Every consumer reporting agency shall maintain reasonable procedures designed to avoid violations of section 605 [§ 1681c] and to limit the furnishing of consumer reports to the purposes listed under section 604 [§ 1681b] of this title. These procedures shall require that prospective users of the information identify themselves, certify the purposes for which the information is sought, and certify that the information will be used for no other purpose. Every consumer reporting agency shall make a reasonable effort to verify the identity of a new prospective user and the uses certified by such prospective user prior to furnishing such user a consumer report. No consumer reporting agency may furnish a consumer report to any person if it has reasonable grounds for believing that the consumer report will not be used for a purpose listed in section 604 [§ 1681b] of this title.

(b) Accuracy of report. Whenever a consumer reporting agency prepares a consumer report it shall follow reasonable procedures to assure maximum possible accuracy of the information concerning the individual about whom the report relates.

(c) Disclosure of consumer reports by users allowed. A consumer reporting agency may not prohibit a user of a consumer report furnished by the agency on a consumer from disclosing the contents of the report to the consumer, if adverse action against the consumer has been taken by the user based in whole or in part on the report.

(d) Notice to users and furnishers of information.

> (1) Notice requirement. A consumer reporting agency shall provide to any person
>
> > (A) who regularly and in the ordinary course of business furnishes information to the agency with respect to any consumer; or
> >
> > (B) to whom a consumer report is provided by the agency; a notice of such person's responsibilities under this title.
>
> (2) Content of notice. The Federal Trade Commission shall prescribe the content of notices under paragraph (1), and a consumer reporting agency shall be in compliance with this subsection if it provides a notice under paragraph (1) that is substantially similar to the Federal Trade Commission prescription under this paragraph.

(e) Procurement of consumer report for resale.

> (1) Disclosure. A person may not procure a consumer report for purposes of reselling the report (or any information in the report) unless the person discloses to the consumer reporting agency that originally furnishes the report
>
> > (A) the identity of the end-user of the report (or information); and

(B) each permissible purpose under section 604 [§ 1681b] for which the report is furnished to the end-user of the report (or information).

(2) Responsibilities of procurers for resale. A person who procures a consumer report for purposes of reselling the report (or any information in the report) shall

(A) establish and comply with reasonable procedures designed to ensure that the report (or information) is resold by the person only for a purpose for which the report may be furnished under section 604 [§ 1681b], including by requiring that each person to which the report (or information) is resold and that resells or provides the report (or information) to any other person

(i) identifies each end user of the resold report (or information);

(ii) certifies each purpose for which the report (or information) will be used; and

(iii) certifies that the report (or information) will be used for no other purpose; and

(B) before reselling the report, make reasonable efforts to verify the identifications and certifications made under subparagraph (A).

§ 608. Disclosures to governmental agencies [15 U.S.C. § 1681f]

Notwithstanding the provisions of section 604 [§ 1681b] of this title, a consumer reporting agency may furnish identifying information respecting any consumer, limited to his name, address, former addresses, places of employment, or former places of employment, to a governmental agency.

§ 609. Disclosures to consumers [15 U.S.C. § 1681g]

(a) Information on file; sources; report recipients. Every consumer reporting agency shall, upon request, and subject to 610(a)(1) [§ 1681h], clearly and accurately disclose to the consumer:

(1) All information in the consumer's file at the time of the request, except that nothing in this paragraph shall be construed to require a consumer reporting agency to disclose to a consumer any information concerning credit scores or any other risk scores or predictors relating to the consumer.

(2) The sources of the information; except that the sources of information acquired solely for use in preparing an investigative consumer report and actually used for no other purpose need not be disclosed: Provided, That in the event an action is brought under this title, such sources shall be available to the plaintiff under appropriate discovery procedures in the court in which the action is brought.

(3) (A) Identification of each person (including each end-user identified under section 607(e)(1) [§ 1681e]) that procured a consumer report

    (i) for employment purposes, during the 2-year period preceding the date on which the request is made; or

    (ii) for any other purpose, during the 1-year period preceding the date on which the request is made.

    (B) An identification of a person under subparagraph (A) shall include

        (i) the name of the person or, if applicable, the trade name (written in full) under which such person conducts business; and

        (ii) upon request of the consumer, the address and telephone number of the person.

(4) The dates, original payees, and amounts of any checks upon which is based any adverse characterization of the consumer, included in the file at the time of the disclosure.

(5) A record of all inquiries received by the agency during the 1-year period preceding the request that identified the consumer in connection with a credit or insurance transaction that was not initiated by the consumer.

(b) Exempt information. The requirements of subsection (a) of this section respecting the disclosure of sources of information and the recipients of consumer reports do not apply to information received or consumer reports furnished prior to the effective date of this title except to the extent that the matter involved is contained in the files of the consumer reporting agency on that date.

(c) Summary of rights required to be included with disclosure.

    (1) Summary of rights. A consumer reporting agency shall provide to a consumer, with each written disclosure by the agency to the consumer under this section

        (A) a written summary of all of the rights that the consumer has under this title; and

        (B) in the case of a consumer reporting agency that compiles and maintains files on consumers on a nationwide basis, a toll-free telephone number established by the agency, at which personnel are accessible to consumers during normal business hours.

    (2) Specific items required to be included. The summary of rights required under paragraph (1) shall include

        (A) a brief description of this title and all rights of consumers under this title;

        (B) an explanation of how the consumer may exercise the rights of the consumer under this title;

(C) a list of all Federal agencies responsible for enforcing any provision of this title and the address and any appropriate phone number of each such agency, in a form that will assist the consumer in selecting the appropriate agency;

(D) a statement that the consumer may have additional rights under State law and that the consumer may wish to contact a State or local consumer protection agency or a State attorney general to learn of those rights; and

(E) a statement that a consumer reporting agency is not required to remove accurate derogatory information from a consumer's file, unless the information is outdated under section 605 [§ 1681c] or cannot be verified.

(3) Form of summary of rights. For purposes of this subsection and any disclosure by a consumer reporting agency required under this title with respect to consumers' rights, the Federal Trade Commission (after consultation with each Federal agency referred to in section 621(b) [§ 1681s]) shall prescribe the form and content of any such disclosure of the rights of consumers required under this title. A consumer reporting agency shall be in compliance with this subsection if it provides disclosures under paragraph (1) that are substantially similar to the Federal Trade Commission prescription under this paragraph.

(4) Effectiveness. No disclosures shall be required under this subsection until the date on which the Federal Trade Commission prescribes the form and content of such disclosures under paragraph (3).

§ 610. Conditions and form of disclosure to consumers [15 U.S.C. § 1681h]

(a) In general.

(1) Proper identification. A consumer reporting agency shall require, as a condition of making the disclosures required under section 609 [§ 1681g], that the consumer furnish proper identification.

(2) Disclosure in writing. Except as provided in subsection (b), the disclosures required to be made under section 609 [§ 1681g] shall be provided under that section in writing.

(b) Other forms of disclosure.

(1) In general. If authorized by a consumer, a consumer reporting agency may make the disclosures required under 609 [§ 1681g]

(A) other than in writing; and

(B) in such form as may be

(i) specified by the consumer in accordance with paragraph (2); and

(ii) available from the agency.

(2) Form. A consumer may specify pursuant to paragraph (1) that disclosures under section 609 [§ 1681g] shall be made

(A) in person, upon the appearance of the consumer at the place of business of the consumer reporting agency where disclosures are regularly provided, during normal business hours, and on reasonable notice;

(B) by telephone, if the consumer has made a written request for disclosure by telephone;

(C) by electronic means, if available from the agency; or

(D) by any other reasonable means that is available from the agency.

(c) Trained personnel. Any consumer reporting agency shall provide trained personnel to explain to the consumer any information furnished to him pursuant to section 609 [§ 1681g] of this title.

(d) Persons accompanying consumer. The consumer shall be permitted to be accompanied by one other person of his choosing, who shall furnish reasonable identification. A consumer reporting agency may require the consumer to furnish a written statement granting permission to the consumer reporting agency to discuss the consumer's file in such person's presence.

(e) Limitation of liability. Except as provided in sections 616 and 617 [§§ 1681n and 1681o] of this title, no consumer may bring any action or proceeding in the nature of defamation, invasion of privacy, or negligence with respect to the reporting of information against any consumer reporting agency, any user of information, or any person who furnishes information to a consumer reporting agency, based on information disclosed pursuant to section 609, 610, or 615 [§§ 1681g, 1681h, or 1681m] of this title or based on information disclosed by a user of a consumer report to or for a consumer against whom the user has taken adverse action, based in whole or in part on the report, except as to false information furnished with malice or willful intent to injure such consumer.

§ 611. Procedure in case of disputed accuracy [15 U.S.C. § 1681i]

(a) Reinvestigations of disputed information.

(1) Reinvestigation required.

(A) In general. If the completeness or accuracy of any item of information contained in a consumer's file at a consumer reporting agency is disputed by the consumer and the consumer notifies the agency directly of such dispute, the agency shall reinvestigate free of charge and record the current status of the disputed information, or delete the item from the file in accordance with paragraph (5), before the end of the 30-day period beginning on the date on which the agency receives the notice of the dispute from the consumer.

(B) Extension of period to reinvestigate. Except as provided in subparagraph (C), the 30-day period described in subparagraph (A) may be extended for not more than 15 additional days if the consumer reporting agency receives information from the consumer during that 30-day period that is relevant to the reinvestigation.

(C) Limitations on extension of period to reinvestigate. Subparagraph (B) shall not apply to any reinvestigation in which, during the 30-day period described in subparagraph (A), the information that is the subject of the reinvestigation is found to be inaccurate or incomplete or the consumer reporting agency determines that the information cannot be verified.

(2) Prompt notice of dispute to furnisher of information.

(A) In general. Before the expiration of the 5-business-day period beginning on the date on which a consumer reporting agency receives notice of a dispute from any consumer in accordance with paragraph (1), the agency shall provide notification of the dispute to any person who provided any item of information in dispute, at the address and in the manner established with the person. The notice shall include all relevant information regarding the dispute that the agency has received from the consumer.

(B) Provision of other information from consumer. The consumer reporting agency shall promptly provide to the person who provided the information in dispute all relevant information regarding the dispute that is received by the agency from the consumer after the period referred to in subparagraph (A) and before the end of the period referred to in paragraph (1)(A).

(3) Determination that dispute is frivolous or irrelevant.

(A) In general. Notwithstanding paragraph (1), a consumer reporting agency may terminate a reinvestigation of information disputed by a consumer under that paragraph if the agency reasonably determines that the dispute by the consumer is frivolous or irrelevant, including by reason of a failure by a consumer to provide sufficient information to investigate the disputed information.

(B) Notice of determination. Upon making any determination in accordance with subparagraph (A) that a dispute is frivolous or irrelevant, a consumer reporting agency shall notify the consumer of such determination not later than 5 business days after making such determination, by mail or, if authorized by the consumer for that purpose, by any other means available to the agency.

(C) Contents of notice. A notice under subparagraph (B) shall include

(i) the reasons for the determination under subparagraph (A); and

(ii) identification of any information required to investigate the disputed information, which may consist of a standardized form describing the general nature of such information.

(4) Consideration of consumer information. In conducting any reinvestigation under paragraph (1) with respect to disputed information in the file of any consumer, the consumer reporting agency shall review and consider all relevant information submitted by the consumer in the period described in paragraph (1)(A) with respect to such disputed information.

(5) Treatment of inaccurate or unverifiable information.

(A) In general. If, after any reinvestigation under paragraph (1) of any information disputed by a consumer, an item of the information is found to be inaccurate or incomplete or cannot be verified, the consumer reporting agency shall promptly delete that item of information from the consumer's file or modify that item of information, as appropriate, based on the results of the reinvestigation.

(B) Requirements relating to reinsertion of previously deleted material.

(i) Certification of accuracy of information. If any information is deleted from a consumer's file pursuant to subparagraph (A), the information may not be reinserted in the file by the consumer reporting agency unless the person who furnishes the information certifies that the information is complete and accurate.

(ii) Notice to consumer. If any information that has been deleted from a consumer's file pursuant to subparagraph (A) is reinserted in the file, the consumer reporting agency shall notify the consumer of the reinsertion in writing not later than 5 business days after the reinsertion or, if authorized by the consumer for that purpose, by any other means available to the agency.

(iii) Additional information. As part of, or in addition to, the notice under clause (ii), a consumer reporting agency shall provide to a consumer in writing not later than 5 business days after the date of the reinsertion

(I) a statement that the disputed information has been reinserted;

(II) the business name and address of any furnisher of information contacted and the telephone number of such furnisher, if reasonably available, or of any furnisher of information that contacted the consumer reporting agency, in connection with the reinsertion of such information; and

(III) a notice that the consumer has the right to add a statement to the consumer's file disputing the accuracy or completeness of the disputed information.

(C) Procedures to prevent reappearance. A consumer reporting agency shall maintain reasonable procedures designed to prevent the reappearance in a consumer's file, and in consumer reports on the consumer, of information that is deleted pursuant to this paragraph (other than information that is reinserted in accordance with subparagraph (B)(i)).

(D) Automated reinvestigation system. Any consumer reporting agency that compiles and maintains files on consumers on a nationwide basis shall implement an automated system through which furnishers of information to that consumer reporting agency may report the results of a reinvestigation that finds incomplete or inaccurate information in a consumer's file to other such consumer reporting agencies.

(6) Notice of results of reinvestigation.

(A) In general. A consumer reporting agency shall provide written notice to a consumer of the results of a reinvestigation under this subsection not later than 5 business days after the completion of the reinvestigation, by mail or, if authorized by the consumer for that purpose, by other means available to the agency.

(B) Contents. As part of, or in addition to, the notice under subparagraph (A), a consumer reporting agency shall provide to a consumer in writing before the expiration of the 5-day period referred to in subparagraph (A)

(i) a statement that the reinvestigation is completed;

(ii) a consumer report that is based upon the consumer's file as that file is revised as a result of the reinvestigation;

(iii) a notice that, if requested by the consumer, a description of the procedure used to determine the accuracy and completeness of the information shall be provided to the consumer by the agency, including the business name and address of any furnisher of information contacted in connection with such information and the telephone number of such furnisher, if reasonably available;

(iv) a notice that the consumer has the right to add a statement to the consumer's file disputing the accuracy or completeness of the information; and

(v) a notice that the consumer has the right to request under subsection (d) that the consumer reporting agency furnish notifications under that subsection.

(7) Description of reinvestigation procedure. A consumer reporting agency shall provide to a consumer a description referred to in paragraph (6)(B)(iv)[4] by not later than 15 days after receiving a request from the consumer for that description.

(8) Expedited dispute resolution. If a dispute regarding an item of information in a consumer's file at a consumer reporting agency is resolved in accordance with paragraph (5)(A) by the deletion of the disputed information by not later than 3 business days after the date on which the agency receives notice of the dispute from the consumer in accordance with paragraph (1)(A), then the agency shall not be required to comply with paragraphs (2), (6), and (7) with respect to that dispute if the agency

(A) provides prompt notice of the deletion to the consumer by telephone;

(B) includes in that notice, or in a written notice that accompanies a confirmation and consumer report provided in accordance with subparagraph (C), a statement of the consumer's right to request under subsection (d) that the agency furnish notifications under that subsection; and

(C) provides written confirmation of the deletion and a copy of a consumer report on the consumer that is based on the consumer's file after the deletion, not later than 5 business days after making the deletion.

(b) Statement of dispute. If the reinvestigation does not resolve the dispute, the consumer may file a brief statement setting forth the nature of the dispute. The consumer reporting agency may limit such statements to not more than one hundred words if it provides the consumer with assistance in writing a clear summary of the dispute.

(c) Notification of consumer dispute in subsequent consumer reports. Whenever a statement of a dispute is filed, unless there is reasonable grounds to believe that it is frivolous or irrelevant, the consumer reporting agency shall, in any subsequent consumer report containing the information in question, clearly note that it is disputed by the consumer and provide either the consumer's statement or a clear and accurate codification or summary thereof.

(d) Notification of deletion of disputed information. Following any deletion of information which is found to be inaccurate or whose accuracy can no longer be verified or any notation as to disputed information, the consumer reporting agency shall, at the request of the consumer, furnish notification that the item has been deleted or the statement, codification or summary pursuant to subsection (b) or (c) of this section to any person specifically designated by the consumer who has within two years prior thereto received a consumer report for employment purposes, or within six months prior thereto received a consumer report for any other purpose, which contained the deleted or disputed information.

---

4. So in original, however should read (6)(B)(iii).

§ 612. Charges for certain disclosures [15 U.S.C. § 1681j]

(a) Reasonable charges allowed for certain disclosures.

(1) In general. Except as provided in subsections (b), (c), and (d), a consumer reporting agency may impose a reasonable charge on a consumer

(A) for making a disclosure to the consumer pursuant to section 609 [§ 1681g], which charge

(i) shall not exceed $8; and

(ii) shall be indicated to the consumer before making the disclosure; and

(B) for furnishing, pursuant to 611(d) [§ 1681i], following a reinvestigation under section 611(a) [§ 1681i], a statement, codification, or summary to a person designated by the consumer under that section after the 30-day period beginning on the date of notification of the consumer under paragraph (6) or (8) of section 611(a) [§ 1681i] with respect to the reinvestigation, which charge

> (i) shall not exceed the charge that the agency would impose on each designated recipient for a consumer report; and

> (ii) shall be indicated to the consumer before furnishing such information.

(2) Modification of amount. The Federal Trade Commission shall increase the amount referred to in paragraph (1)(A)(i) on January 1 of each year, based proportionally on changes in the Consumer Price Index, with fractional changes rounded to the nearest fifty cents.

(b) Free disclosure after adverse notice to consumer. Each consumer reporting agency that maintains a file on a consumer shall make all disclosures pursuant to section 609 [§ 1681g] without charge to the consumer if, not later than 60 days after receipt by such consumer of a notification pursuant to section 615 [§ 1681m], or of a notification from a debt collection agency affiliated with that consumer reporting agency stating that the consumer's credit rating may be or has been adversely affected, the consumer makes a request under section 609 [§ 1681g].

(c) Free disclosure under certain other circumstances. Upon the request of the consumer, a consumer reporting agency shall make all disclosures pursuant to section 609 [§ 1681g] once during any 12-month period without charge to that consumer if the consumer certifies in writing that the consumer

> (1) is unemployed and intends to apply for employment in the 60-day period beginning on the date on which the certification is made;

> (2) is a recipient of public welfare assistance; or

> (3) has reason to believe that the file on the consumer at the agency contains inaccurate information due to fraud.

(d) Other charges prohibited. A consumer reporting agency shall not impose any charge on a consumer for providing any notification required by this title or making any disclosure required by this title, except as authorized by subsection (a).

§ 613. Public record information for employment purposes [15 U.S.C. § 1681k]

A consumer reporting agency which furnishes a consumer report for employment purposes and which for that purpose compiles and reports items of information on consumers which are matters of public record and are likely to have an adverse effect upon a consumer's ability to obtain employment shall

> (1) at the time such public record information is reported to the user of such consumer report, notify the consumer of the fact that public record information is being reported

by the consumer reporting agency, together with the name and address of the person to whom such information is being reported; or

(2) maintain strict procedures designed to insure that whenever public record information which is likely to have an adverse effect on a consumer's ability to obtain employment is reported it is complete and up to date. For purposes of this paragraph, items of public record relating to arrests, indictments, convictions, suits, tax liens, and outstanding judgments shall be considered up to date if the current public record status of the item at the time of the report is reported.

§ 614. Restrictions on investigative consumer reports [15 U.S.C. § 1681l]

Whenever a consumer reporting agency prepares an investigative consumer report, no adverse information in the consumer report (other than information which is a matter of public record) may be included in a subsequent consumer report unless such adverse information has been verified in the process of making such subsequent consumer report, or the adverse information was received within the three-month period preceding the date the subsequent report is furnished.

§ 615. Requirements on users of consumer reports [15 U.S.C. § 1681m]

(a) Duties of users taking adverse actions on the basis of information contained in consumer reports. If any person takes any adverse action with respect to any consumer that is based in whole or in part on any information contained in a consumer report, the person shall

(1) provide oral, written, or electronic notice of the adverse action to the consumer;

(2) provide to the consumer orally, in writing, or electronically

(A) the name, address, and telephone number of the consumer reporting agency (including a toll-free telephone number established by the agency if the agency compiles and maintains files on consumers on a nationwide basis) that furnished the report to the person; and

(B) a statement that the consumer reporting agency did not make the decision to take the adverse action and is unable to provide the consumer the specific reasons why the adverse action was taken; and

(3) provide to the consumer an oral, written, or electronic notice of the consumer's right

(A) to obtain, under section 612 [§ 1681j], a free copy of a consumer report on the consumer from the consumer reporting agency referred to in paragraph (2), which notice shall include an indication of the 60-day period under that section for obtaining such a copy; and

(B) to dispute, under section 611 [§ 1681i], with a consumer reporting agency the accuracy or completeness of any information in a consumer report furnished by the agency.

(b) Adverse action based on information obtained from third parties other than consumer reporting agencies.

(1) In general. Whenever credit for personal, family, or household purposes involving a consumer is denied or the charge for such credit is increased either wholly or partly because of information obtained from a person other than a consumer reporting agency bearing upon the consumer's credit worthiness, credit standing, credit capacity, character, general reputation, personal characteristics, or mode of living, the user of such information shall, within a reasonable period of time, upon the consumer's written request for the reasons for such adverse action received within sixty days after learning of such adverse action, disclose the nature of the information to the consumer. The user of such information shall clearly and accurately disclose to the consumer his right to make such written request at the time such adverse action is communicated to the consumer.

(2) Duties of person taking certain actions based on information provided by affiliate.

(A) Duties, generally. If a person takes an action described in subparagraph (B) with respect to a consumer, based in whole or in part on information described in subparagraph (C), the person shall

(i) notify the consumer of the action, including a statement that the consumer may obtain the information in accordance with clause (ii); and

(ii) upon a written request from the consumer received within 60 days after transmittal of the notice required by clause (i), disclose to the consumer the nature of the information upon which the action is based by not later than 30 days after receipt of the request.

(B) Action described. An action referred to in subparagraph (A) is an adverse action described in section 603(k)(1)(A) [§ 1681a], taken in connection with a transaction initiated by the consumer, or any adverse action described in clause (i) or (ii) of section 603(k)(1)(B) [§ 1681a].

(C) Information described. Information referred to in subparagraph (A)

(i) except as provided in clause (ii), is information that

(I) is furnished to the person taking the action by a person related by common ownership or affiliated by common corporate control to the person taking the action; and

(II) bears on the credit worthiness, credit standing, credit capacity, character, general reputation, personal characteristics, or mode of living of the consumer; and

(ii) does not include

(I) information solely as to transactions or experiences between the consumer and the person furnishing the information; or

(II) information in a consumer report.

(c) Reasonable procedures to assure compliance. No person shall be held liable for any violation of this section if he shows by a preponderance of the evidence that at the time of the alleged violation he maintained reasonable procedures to assure compliance with the provisions of this section.

(d) Duties of users making written credit or insurance solicitations on the basis of information contained in consumer files.

(1) In general. Any person who uses a consumer report on any consumer in connection with any credit or insurance transaction that is not initiated by the consumer, that is provided to that person under section 604(c)(1)(B) [§ 1681b], shall provide with each written solicitation made to the consumer regarding the transaction a clear and conspicuous statement that

(A) information contained in the consumer's consumer report was used in connection with the transaction;

(B) the consumer received the offer of credit or insurance because the consumer satisfied the criteria for credit worthiness or insurability under which the consumer was selected for the offer;

(C) if applicable, the credit or insurance may not be extended if, after the consumer responds to the offer, the consumer does not meet the criteria used to select the consumer for the offer or any applicable criteria bearing on credit worthiness or insurability or does not furnish any required collateral;

(D) the consumer has a right to prohibit information contained in the consumer's file with any consumer reporting agency from being used in connection with any credit or insurance transaction that is not initiated by the consumer; and

(E) the consumer may exercise the right referred to in subparagraph (D) by notifying a notification system established under section 604(e) [§ 1681b].

(2) Disclosure of address and telephone number. A statement under paragraph (1) shall include the address and toll-free telephone number of the appropriate notification system established under section 604(e) [§ 1681b].

(3) Maintaining criteria on file. A person who makes an offer of credit or insurance to a consumer under a credit or insurance transaction described in paragraph (1) shall maintain on file the criteria used to select the consumer to receive the offer, all criteria bearing on credit worthiness or insurability, as applicable, that are the basis for determining

whether or not to extend credit or insurance pursuant to the offer, and any requirement for the furnishing of collateral as a condition of the extension of credit or insurance, until the expiration of the 3-year period beginning on the date on which the offer is made to the consumer.

(4) Authority of federal agencies regarding unfair or deceptive acts or practices not affected. This section is not intended to affect the authority of any Federal or State agency to enforce a prohibition against unfair or deceptive acts or practices, including the making of false or misleading statements in connection with a credit or insurance transaction that is not initiated by the consumer.

§ 616. Civil liability for willful noncompliance [15 U.S.C. § 1681n]

(a) In general. Any person who willfully fails to comply with any requirement imposed under this title with respect to any consumer is liable to that consumer in an amount equal to the sum of

(1) (A) any actual damages sustained by the consumer as a result of the failure or damages of not less than $100 and not more than $1,000; or

(B) in the case of liability of a natural person for obtaining a consumer report under false pretenses or knowingly without a permissible purpose, actual damages sustained by the consumer as a result of the failure or $1,000, whichever is greater;

(2) such amount of punitive damages as the court may allow; and

(3) in the case of any successful action to enforce any liability under this section, the costs of the action together with reasonable attorney's fees as determined by the court.

(b) Civil liability for knowing noncompliance. Any person who obtains a consumer report from a consumer reporting agency under false pretenses or knowingly without a permissible purpose shall be liable to the consumer reporting agency for actual damages sustained by the consumer reporting agency or $1,000, whichever is greater.

(c) Attorney's fees. Upon a finding by the court that an unsuccessful pleading, motion, or other paper filed in connection with an action under this section was filed in bad faith or for purposes of harassment, the court shall award to the prevailing party attorney's fees reasonable in relation to the work expended in responding to the pleading, motion, or other paper.

§ 617. Civil liability for negligent noncompliance [15 U.S.C. § 1681o]

(a) In general. Any person who is negligent in failing to comply with any requirement imposed under this title with respect to any consumer is liable to that consumer in an amount equal to the sum of

(1) any actual damages sustained by the consumer as a result of the failure;

(2) in the case of any successful action to enforce any liability under this section, the costs of the action together with reasonable attorney's fees as determined by the court.

(b) Attorney's fees. On a finding by the court that an unsuccessful pleading, motion, or other paper filed in connection with an action under this section was filed in bad faith or for purposes of harassment, the court shall award to the prevailing party attorney's fees reasonable in relation to the work expended in responding to the pleading, motion, or other paper.

§ 618. Jurisdiction of courts; limitation of actions [15 U.S.C. § 1681p]

An action to enforce any liability created under this title may be brought in any appropriate United States district court without regard to the amount in controversy, or in any other court of competent jurisdiction, within two years from the date on which the liability arises, except that where a defendant has materially and willfully misrepresented any information required under this title to be disclosed to an individual and the information so misrepresented is material to the establishment of the defendant's liability to that individual under this title, the action may be brought at any time within two years after discovery by the individual of the misrepresentation.

§ 619. Obtaining information under false pretenses [15 U.S.C. § 1681q]

Any person who knowingly and willfully obtains information on a consumer from a consumer reporting agency under false pretenses shall be fined under title 18, United States Code, imprisoned for not more than 2 years, or both.

§ 620. Unauthorized disclosures by officers or employees [15 U.S.C. § 1681r]

Any officer or employee of a consumer reporting agency who knowingly and willfully provides information concerning an individual from the agency's files to a person not authorized to receive that information shall be fined under title 18, United States Code, imprisoned for not more than 2 years, or both.

§ 621. Administrative enforcement [15 U.S.C. § 1681s]

(a) (1) Enforcement by Federal Trade Commission. Compliance with the requirements imposed under this title shall be enforced under the Federal Trade Commission Act [15 U.S.C. §§ 41 et seq.] by the Federal Trade Commission with respect to consumer reporting agencies and all other persons subject thereto, except to the extent that enforcement of the requirements imposed under this title is specifically committed to some other government agency under subsection (b) hereof. For the purpose of the exercise by the Federal Trade Commission of its functions and powers under the Federal Trade Commission Act, a violation of any requirement or prohibition imposed under this title shall constitute an unfair or deceptive act or practice in commerce in violation of section 5(a) of the Federal Trade Commission Act [15 U.S.C. § 45(a)] and shall be subject to enforcement by the Federal Trade Commission under section 5(b) thereof [15 U.S.C. § 45(b)] with respect to any consumer reporting agency or person subject to enforcement by the Federal Trade Commission pursuant to this subsection, irrespective of whether that person is engaged in commerce or meets any other jurisdictional tests in the Federal Trade Commission Act. The Federal Trade Commission shall have such procedural, investigative, and enforcement powers, including the power to issue procedural rules in enforcing compliance with the requirements imposed under this title and to require the filing of reports, the production of documents, and the appearance of witnesses as though the applicable terms and conditions of the Federal Trade Commission Act were part of this title. Any person violating any of the provisions of this title shall be subject to the penalties and entitled to the privileges and immunities provided in the Federal Trade Commission Act as though the applicable terms and provisions thereof were part of this title.

(2) (A) In the event of a knowing violation, which constitutes a pattern or practice of violations of this title, the Commission may commence a civil action to recover a civil penalty in a district court of the United States against any person that violates this title. In such action, such person shall be liable for a civil penalty of not more than $2,500 per violation.

(B) In determining the amount of a civil penalty under subparagraph (A), the court shall take into account the degree of culpability, any history of prior such conduct, ability to pay, effect on ability to continue to do business, and such other matters as justice may require.

(3) Notwithstanding paragraph (2), a court may not impose any civil penalty on a person for a violation of section 623(a)(1) [§ 1681s-2] unless the person has been enjoined from committing the violation, or ordered not to commit the violation, in an action or proceeding brought by or on behalf of the Federal Trade Commission, and has violated the injunction or order, and the court may not impose any civil penalty for any violation occurring before the date of the violation of the injunction or order.

(4) Neither the Commission nor any other agency referred to in subsection (b) may prescribe trade regulation rules or other regulations with respect to this title.

(b) Enforcement by other agencies. Compliance with the requirements imposed under this title with respect to consumer reporting agencies, persons who use consumer reports from such agencies, persons who furnish information to such agencies, and users of information that are subject to subsection (d) or (e) of section 615 [§ 1681m] shall be enforced under

(1) section 8 of the Federal Deposit Insurance Act [12 U.S.C. § 1818], in the case of

(A) national banks, and Federal branches and Federal agencies of foreign banks, by the Office of the Comptroller of the Currency;

(B) member banks of the Federal Reserve System (other than national banks), branches and agencies of foreign banks (other than Federal branches, Federal agencies, and insured State branches of foreign banks), commercial lending companies owned or controlled by foreign banks, and organizations operating under section 25 or 25(a) [25A] of the Federal Reserve Act [12 U.S.C. §§ 601 et seq., §§ 611 et seq], by the Board of Governors of the Federal Reserve System; and

(C) banks insured by the Federal Deposit Insurance Corporation (other than members of the Federal Reserve System) and insured State branches of foreign banks, by the Board of Directors of the Federal Deposit Insurance Corporation;

(2) section 8 of the Federal Deposit Insurance Act [12 U.S.C. § 1818], by the Director of the Office of Thrift Supervision, in the case of a savings association the deposits of which are insured by the Federal Deposit Insurance Corporation;

(3) the Federal Credit Union Act [12 U.S.C. §§ 1751 et seq.], by the Administrator of the National Credit Union Administration [National Credit Union Administration Board] with respect to any Federal credit union;

(4) subtitle IV of title 49 [49 U.S.C. §§ 10101 et seq.], by the Secretary of Transportation, with respect to all carriers subject to the jurisdiction of the Surface Transportation Board;

(5) the Federal Aviation Act of 1958 [49 U.S.C. Appx §§ 1301 et seq.], by the Secretary of Transportation with respect to any air carrier or foreign air carrier subject to that Act [49 U.S.C. Appx §§ 1301 et seq.]; and

(6) the Packers and Stockyards Act, 1921 [7 U.S.C. §§ 181 et seq.] (except as provided in section 406 of that Act [7 U.S.C. §§ 226 and 227]), by the Secretary of Agriculture with respect to any activities subject to that Act.

The terms used in paragraph (1) that are not defined in this title or otherwise defined in section 3(s) of the Federal Deposit Insurance Act (12 U.S.C. § 1813(s)) shall have the meaning given to them in section 1(b) of the International Banking Act of 1978 (12 U.S.C. § 3101).

(c) State action for violations.

(1) Authority of states. In addition to such other remedies as are provided under State law, if the chief law enforcement officer of a State, or an official or agency designated by a State, has reason to believe that any person has violated or is violating this title, the State

(A) may bring an action to enjoin such violation in any appropriate United States district court or in any other court of competent jurisdiction;

(B) subject to paragraph (5), may bring an action on behalf of the residents of the State to recover

(i) damages for which the person is liable to such residents under sections 616 and 617 [§§ 1681n and 1681o] as a result of the violation;

(ii) in the case of a violation of section 623(a) [§ 1681s-2], damages for which the person would, but for section 623(c) [§ 1681s-2], be liable to such residents as a result of the violation; or

(iii) damages of not more than $1,000 for each willful or negligent violation; and

(C) in the case of any successful action under subparagraph (A) or (B), shall be awarded the costs of the action and reasonable attorney fees as determined by the court.

(2) Rights of federal regulators. The State shall serve prior written notice of any action under paragraph (1) upon the Federal Trade Commission or the appropriate Federal regulator determined under subsection (b) and provide the Commission or appropriate Federal regulator with a copy of its complaint, except in any case in which such prior notice is not feasible, in which case the State shall serve such notice immediately upon instituting such action. The Federal Trade Commission or appropriate Federal regulator shall have the right

(A) to intervene in the action;

(B) upon so intervening, to be heard on all matters arising therein;

(C) to remove the action to the appropriate United States district court; and

(D) to file petitions for appeal.

(3) Investigatory powers. For purposes of bringing any action under this subsection, nothing in this subsection shall prevent the chief law enforcement officer, or an official or agency designated by a State, from exercising the powers conferred on the chief law enforcement officer or such official by the laws of such State to conduct investigations or to administer oaths or affirmations or to compel the attendance of witnesses or the production of documentary and other evidence.

(4) Limitation on state action while federal action pending. If the Federal Trade Commission or the appropriate Federal regulator has instituted a civil action or an administrative action under section 8 of the Federal Deposit Insurance Act for a violation of this title, no State may, during the pendency of such action, bring an action under this section against any defendant named in the complaint of the Commission or the appropriate Federal regulator for any violation of this title that is alleged in that complaint.

(5) Limitations on state actions for violation of section 623(a)(1) [§ 1681s-2].

(A) Violation of injunction required. A State may not bring an action against a person under paragraph (1)(B) for a violation of section 623(a)(1) [§ 1681s-2], unless

(i) the person has been enjoined from committing the violation, in an action brought by the State under paragraph (1)(A); and

(ii) the person has violated the injunction.

(B) Limitation on damages recoverable. In an action against a person under paragraph (1)(B) for a violation of section 623(a)(1) [§ 1681s-2], a State may not recover any damages incurred before the date of the violation of an injunction on which the action is based.

(d) Enforcement under other authority. For the purpose of the exercise by any agency referred to in subsection (b) of this section of its powers under any Act referred to in that subsection, a violation of any requirement imposed under this title shall be deemed to be a violation of a requirement imposed under that Act. In addition to its powers under any provision of law specifically referred to in subsection (b) of this section, each of the agencies referred to in that subsection may exercise, for the purpose of enforcing compliance with any requirement imposed under this title any other authority conferred on it by law. Notwithstanding the preceding, no agency referred to in subsection (b) may conduct an examination of a bank, savings association, or credit union regarding compliance with the provisions of this title, except in response to a complaint (or if the agency otherwise has knowledge) that the bank, savings association, or credit union has violated a provision of this title, in which case, the agency may conduct an examination as necessary to investigate the complaint. If an agency determines during an investigation in response to a complaint that a violation of this title has occurred, the agency may, during its next 2 regularly scheduled examinations of the bank, savings association, or credit union, examine for compliance with this title.

(e) Interpretive authority. The Board of Governors of the Federal Reserve System may issue interpretations of any provision of this title as such provision may apply to any persons identified under paragraph (1), (2), and (3) of subsection (b), or to the holding companies and affiliates of such persons, in consultation with Federal agencies identified in paragraphs (1), (2), and (3) of subsection (b).

§ 622. Information on overdue child support obligations [15 U.S.C. § 1681s-1]

Notwithstanding any other provision of this title, a consumer reporting agency shall include in any consumer report furnished by the agency in accordance with section 604 [§ 1681b] of this title, any information on the failure of the consumer to pay overdue support which

(1) is provided

(A) to the consumer reporting agency by a State or local child support enforcement agency; or

(B) to the consumer reporting agency and verified by any local, State, or Federal government agency; and

(2) antedates the report by 7 years or less.

§ 623. Responsibilities of furnishers of information to consumer reporting agencies [15 U.S.C. § 1681s-2]

(a) Duty of furnishers of information to provide accurate information.

(1) Prohibition.

(A) Reporting information with actual knowledge of errors. A person shall not furnish any information relating to a consumer to any consumer reporting agency if the person knows or consciously avoids knowing that the information is inaccurate.

(B) Reporting information after notice and confirmation of errors. A person shall not furnish information relating to a consumer to any consumer reporting agency if

(i) the person has been notified by the consumer, at the address specified by the person for such notices, that specific information is inaccurate; and

(ii) the information is, in fact, inaccurate.

(C) No address requirement. A person who clearly and conspicuously specifies to the consumer an address for notices referred to in subparagraph (B) shall not be subject to subparagraph (A); however, nothing in subparagraph (B) shall require a person to specify such an address.

(2) Duty to correct and update information. A person who

(A) regularly and in the ordinary course of business furnishes information to one or more consumer reporting agencies about the person's transactions or experiences with any consumer; and

(B) has furnished to a consumer reporting agency information that the person determines is not complete or accurate, shall promptly notify the consumer reporting agency of that determination and provide to the agency any corrections to that information, or any additional information, that is necessary to make the information provided by the person to the agency complete and accurate, and shall not thereafter furnish to the agency any of the information that remains not complete or accurate.

(3) Duty to provide notice of dispute. If the completeness or accuracy of any information furnished by any person to any consumer reporting agency is disputed to such person by a consumer, the person may not furnish the information to any consumer reporting agency without notice that such information is disputed by the consumer.

(4) Duty to provide notice of closed accounts. A person who regularly and in the ordinary course of business furnishes information to a consumer reporting agency regarding a consumer who has a credit account with that person shall notify the agency of the voluntary closure of the account by the consumer, in information regularly furnished for the period in which the account is closed.

(5) Duty to provide notice of delinquency of accounts. A person who furnishes information to a consumer reporting agency regarding a delinquent account being placed for collection, charged to profit or loss, or subjected to any similar action shall, not later than 90 days after furnishing the information, notify the agency of the month and year of the commencement of the delinquency that immediately preceded the action.

(b) Duties of furnishers of information upon notice of dispute.

(1) In general. After receiving notice pursuant to section 611(a)(2) [§ 1681i] of a dispute with regard to the completeness or accuracy of any information provided by a person to a consumer reporting agency, the person shall

(A) conduct an investigation with respect to the disputed information;

(B) review all relevant information provided by the consumer reporting agency pursuant to section 611(a)(2) [§ 1681i];

(C) report the results of the investigation to the consumer reporting agency; and

(D) if the investigation finds that the information is incomplete or inaccurate, report those results to all other consumer reporting agencies to which the person furnished the information and that compile and maintain files on consumers on a nationwide basis.

(2) Deadline. A person shall complete all investigations, reviews, and reports required under paragraph (1) regarding information provided by the person to a consumer reporting agency, before the expiration of the period under section 611(a)(1) [§ 1681i] within which the consumer reporting agency is required to complete actions required by that section regarding that information.

(c) Limitation on liability. Sections 616 and 617 [§§ 1681n and 1681o] do not apply to any failure to comply with subsection (a), except as provided in section 621(c)(1)(B) [§ 1681s].

(d) Limitation on enforcement. Subsection (a) shall be enforced exclusively under section 621 [§ 1681s] by the Federal agencies and officials and the State officials identified in that section.

§ 624. Relation to State laws [15 U.S.C. § 1681t]

(a) In general. Except as provided in subsections (b) and (c), this title does not annul, alter, affect, or exempt any person subject to the provisions of this title from complying with the laws of any State with respect to the collection, distribution, or use of any information on consumers, except to the extent that those laws are inconsistent with any provision of this title, and then only to the extent of the inconsistency.

(b) General exceptions. No requirement or prohibition may be imposed under the laws of any State

(1) with respect to any subject matter regulated under

(A) subsection (c) or (e) of section 604 [§ 1681b], relating to the prescreening of consumer reports;

(B) section 611 [§ 1681i], relating to the time by which a consumer reporting agency must take any action, including the provision of notification to a consumer or other person, in any procedure related to the disputed accuracy of information in a consumer's file, except that this subparagraph shall not apply to any State law in effect on the date of enactment of the Consumer Credit Reporting Reform Act of 1996;

(C) subsections (a) and (b) of section 615 [§ 1681m], relating to the duties of a person who takes any adverse action with respect to a consumer;

(D) section 615(d) [§ 1681m], relating to the duties of persons who use a consumer report of a consumer in connection with any credit or insurance transaction that is not initiated by the consumer and that consists of a firm offer of credit or insurance;

(E) section 605 [§ 1681c], relating to information contained in consumer reports, except that this subparagraph shall not apply to any State law in effect on the date of enactment of the Consumer Credit Reporting Reform Act of 1996; or

(F) section 623 [§ 1681s-2], relating to the responsibilities of persons who furnish information to consumer reporting agencies, except that this paragraph shall not apply

(i) with respect to section 54A(a) of chapter 93 of the Massachusetts Annotated Laws (as in effect on the date of enactment of the Consumer Credit Reporting Reform Act of 1996); or

(ii) with respect to section 1785.25(a) of the California Civil Code (as in effect on the date of enactment of the Consumer Credit Reporting Reform Act of 1996);

(2) with respect to the exchange of information among persons affiliated by common ownership or common corporate control, except that this paragraph shall not apply with respect to subsection (a) or (c)(1) of section 2480e of title 9, Vermont Statutes Annotated (as in effect on the date of enactment of the Consumer Credit Reporting Reform Act of 1996); or

(3) with respect to the form and content of any disclosure required to be made under section 609(c) [§ 1681g].

(c) Definition of firm offer of credit or insurance. Notwithstanding any definition of the term "firm offer of credit or insurance" (or any equivalent term) under the laws of any State, the definition of that term contained in section 603(l) [§ 1681a] shall be construed to apply in the enforcement and interpretation of the laws of any State governing consumer reports.

(d) Limitations. Subsections (b) and (c)

(1) do not affect any settlement, agreement, or consent judgment between any State Attorney General and any consumer reporting agency in effect on the date of enactment of the Consumer Credit Reporting Reform Act of 1996; and

(2) do not apply to any provision of State law (including any provision of a State constitution) that

(A) is enacted after January 1, 2004;

(B) states explicitly that the provision is intended to supplement this title; and

(C) gives greater protection to consumers than is provided under this title.

§ 625. Disclosures to FBI for counterintelligence purposes [15 U.S.C. § 1681u]

(a) Identity of financial institutions. Notwithstanding section 604 [§ 1681b] or any other provision of this title, a consumer reporting agency shall furnish to the Federal Bureau of Investigation the names and addresses of all financial institutions (as that term is defined in section 1101 of the Right to Financial Privacy Act of 1978 [12 U.S.C. § 3401]) at which a consumer maintains or has maintained an account, to the extent that information is in the files of the agency, when presented with a written request for that information, signed by the Director of the Federal Bureau of Investigation, or the Director's designee, which certifies compliance with this section. The Director or the Director's designee may make such a certification only if the Director or the Director's designee has determined in writing that

(1) such information is necessary for the conduct of an authorized foreign counterintelligence investigation; and

(2) there are specific and articulable facts giving reason to believe that the consumer

(A) is a foreign power (as defined in section 101 of the Foreign Intelligence Surveillance Act of 1978 [50 U.S.C. § 1801]) or a person who is not a United States person (as defined in such section 101) and is an official of a foreign power; or

(B) is an agent of a foreign power and is engaging or has engaged in an act of international terrorism (as that term is defined in section 101(c) of the Foreign Intelligence Surveillance Act of 1978 [50 U.S.C. § 1801(c)]) or clandestine intelligence activities that involve or may involve a violation of criminal statutes of the United States.

(b) Identifying information. Notwithstanding the provisions of section 604 [§ 1681b] or any other provision of this title, a consumer reporting agency shall furnish identifying information respecting a consumer, limited to name, address, former addresses, places of employment, or former places of employment, to the Federal Bureau of Investigation when presented with a written request, signed by the Director or the Director's designee, which certifies compliance with this subsection. The Director or the Director's designee may make such a certification only if the Director or the Director's designee has determined in writing that

(1) such information is necessary to the conduct of an authorized counterintelligence investigation; and

(2) there is information giving reason to believe that the consumer has been, or is about to be, in contact with a foreign power or an agent of a foreign power (as defined in section 101 of the Foreign Intelligence Surveillance Act of 1978 [50 U.S.C. § 1801]).

(c) Court order for disclosure of consumer reports. Notwithstanding section 604 [§ 1681b] or any other provision of this title, if requested in writing by the Director of the Federal Bureau of Investigation, or a designee of the Director, a court may issue an order ex parte directing a consumer reporting agency to furnish a consumer report to the Federal Bureau of Investigation, upon a showing in camera that

(1) the consumer report is necessary for the conduct of an authorized foreign counterintelligence investigation; and

(2) there are specific and articulable facts giving reason to believe that the consumer whose consumer report is sought

(A) is an agent of a foreign power, and

(B) is engaging or has engaged in an act of international terrorism (as that term is defined in section 101(c) of the Foreign Intelligence Surveillance Act of 1978 [50 U.S.C. § 1801(c)]) or clandestine intelligence activities that involve or may involve a violation of criminal statutes of the United States.

The terms of an order issued under this subsection shall not disclose that the order is issued for purposes of a counterintelligence investigation.

(d) Confidentiality. No consumer reporting agency or officer, employee, or agent of a consumer reporting agency shall disclose to any person, other than those officers, employees, or agents of a consumer reporting agency necessary to fulfill the requirement to disclose information to the Federal Bureau of Investigation under this section, that the Federal Bureau of Investigation has sought or obtained the identity of financial institutions or a consumer report respecting any consumer under subsection (a), (b), or (c), and no consumer reporting agency or officer, employee, or agent of a consumer reporting agency shall include in any consumer report any information that would indicate that the Federal Bureau of Investigation has sought or obtained such information or a consumer report.

(e) Payment of fees. The Federal Bureau of Investigation shall, subject to the availability of appropriations, pay to the consumer reporting agency assembling or providing report or information in accordance with procedures established under this section a fee for reimbursement for such costs as are reasonably necessary and which have been directly incurred in searching, reproducing, or transporting books, papers, records, or other data required or requested to be produced under this section.

(f) Limit on dissemination. The Federal Bureau of Investigation may not disseminate information obtained pursuant to this section outside of the Federal Bureau of Investigation, except to other Federal agencies as may be necessary for the approval or conduct of a foreign counterintelligence investigation, or, where the information concerns a person subject to the Uniform Code of Military Justice, to appropriate investigative authorities within the military department concerned as may be necessary for the conduct of a joint foreign counterintelligence investigation.

(g) Rules of construction. Nothing in this section shall be construed to prohibit information from being furnished by the Federal Bureau of Investigation pursuant to a subpoena or court order, in connection with a judicial or administrative proceeding to enforce the provisions of this Act. Nothing in this section shall be construed to authorize or permit the withholding of information from the Congress.

(h) Reports to Congress. On a semiannual basis, the Attorney General shall fully inform the Permanent Select Committee on Intelligence and the Committee on Banking, Finance and Urban Affairs of the House of Representatives, and the Select Committee on Intelligence and the Committee on Banking, Housing, and Urban Affairs of the Senate concerning all requests made pursuant to subsections (a), (b), and (c).

(i) Damages. Any agency or department of the United States obtaining or disclosing any consumer reports, records, or information contained therein in violation of this section is liable to the consumer to whom such consumer reports, records, or information relate in an amount equal to the sum of

> (1) $100, without regard to the volume of consumer reports, records, or information involved;

> (2) any actual damages sustained by the consumer as a result of the disclosure;

> (3) if the violation is found to have been willful or intentional, such punitive damages as a court may allow; and

> (4) in the case of any successful action to enforce liability under this subsection, the costs of the action, together with reasonable attorney fees, as determined by the court.

(j) Disciplinary actions for violations. If a court determines that any agency or department of the United States has violated any provision of this section and the court finds that the circumstances surrounding the violation raise questions of whether or not an officer or employee of the agency or department acted willfully or intentionally with respect to the violation, the agency or department shall promptly initiate a proceeding to determine whether or not disciplinary action is warranted against the officer or employee who was responsible for the violation.

(k) Good-faith exception. Notwithstanding any other provision of this title, any consumer reporting agency or agent or employee thereof making disclosure of consumer reports or identifying information pursuant to this subsection in good-faith reliance upon a certification of the Federal Bureau of Investigation pursuant to provisions of this section shall not be liable to any person for such disclosure under this title, the constitution of any State, or any law or regulation of any State or any political subdivision of any State.

(l) Limitation of remedies. Notwithstanding any other provision of this title, the remedies and sanctions set forth in this section shall be the only judicial remedies and sanctions for violation of this section.

(m) Injunctive relief. In addition to any other remedy contained in this section, injunctive relief shall be available to require compliance with the procedures of this section. In the event of any successful action under this subsection, costs together with reasonable attorney fees, as determined by the court, may be recovered.

LEGISLATIVE HISTORY

House Reports: No. 91-975 (Comm. on Banking and Currency) and No. 91-1587 (Comm. of Conference) Senate Reports: No. 91-1139 accompanying S. 3678 (Comm. on Banking and Currency) Congressional Record, Vol. 116 (1970) May 25, considered and passed House.

Sept. 18, considered and passed Senate, amended.

Oct. 9, Senate agreed to conference report.

Oct. 13, House agreed to conference report.

Enactment: Public Law No. 91-508 (October 26, 1970):

> Amendments: Public Law Nos. 95-473 (October 17, 1978)
> 95-598 (November 6, 1978)
> 98-443 (October 4, 1984)
> 101-73 (August 9, 1989)
> 102-242 (December 19, 1991)
> 102-537 (October 27, 1992)
> 102-550 (October 28, 1992)
> 103-325 (September 23, 1994)
> 104-88 (December 29, 1995)
> 104-93 (January 6, 1996)
> 104-193 (August 22, 1996)
> 104-208 (September 30, 1996)

Appendix B
Federal Trade Commission Offices

FTC Headquarters
  6th & Pennsylvania Ave., N.W.
  Washington, DC 20580
  202-326-2222
  TDD 202-326-2502

FTC Regional Offices
  1718 Peachtree St., N.W., Ste. 1000
  Atlanta, GA 30367
  404-347-4836

10 Causeway St., Ste. 1184
  Boston, MA 02222-1073
  617-565-7240

55 E. Monroe St., Ste. 1437
  Chicago, IL 60603
  312-353-4423

666 Euclid Avenue, Ste. 520-A
  Cleveland, OH 44114
  216-522-4207

100 North Central Expressway, Ste. 500
  Dallas, TX 75201
  214-767-5501

1405 Curtis St., Ste. 2900
  Denver, CO 80202-2393
  303-844-2271

11000 Wilshire Blvd., Ste. 13209
  Los Angeles, CA 90024
  310-575-7575

150 William Street, Suite 1300
  New York, NY 10038
  212-264-1207

901 Market St., Ste. 570
  San Francisco, CA 94103
  415-744-7920

2806 Federal Bldg.
  915 Second Ave.
  Seattle, WA 98174
  206-220-6363

Appendix C
State and Local Consumer Protection Agencies

Usually the government agencies most responsive to our needs are those at the local and state level. These agencies have a better understanding of the needs of the people in their area. Following is a list of state and local government protection agencies that can provide assistance in understanding your rights and helping you enforce them.

Alabama

State Office

Consumer Affairs Division
Office of the Attorney General
11 S. Union St.
Montgomery, AL 36130
334-242-7334
800-392-5658 (toll-free in AL)

Alaska

The Consumer Protection Section in the Office of the Attorney General has been closed. Consumers with complaints are being referred to the better business bureau, small claims court, and private attorneys.

Arizona

State Offices

Consumer Protection
Office of the Attorney General
1275 W. Washington St., Rm. 259
Phoenix, AZ 85007

602-542-3702
602-542-5763 (consumer information and
    complaints)
800-352-8431 (toll-free in AZ)
TDD: 602-542-5002

Assistant Attorney General
Consumer Protection
Office of the Attorney General
402 W. Congress South Building., Ste. 315
Tucson, AZ 85701
602-628-6504

County Offices

Apache County Attorney's Office
PO Box 637
St. Johns, AZ 85936
520-337-4364, ext. 240

Cochise County Attorney's Office
PO Drawer CA
Bisbee, AZ 85603
520-432-9377

Coconino County Attorney's Office
Coconino County Courthouse
100 E. Birch
Flagstaff, AZ 86001
520-779-6518

Gila County Attorney's Office
1400 E. Ash St.
Globe, AZ 85501
520-425-3231

Graham County Attorney's Office
Graham County Courthouse
800 W. Main
Safford, AZ 85546
520-428-3620

Greenlee County Attorney's Office
PO Box 1717
Clifton, AZ 85533
520-865-4108

LaPaz County Attorney's Office
1320 Kofa Ave.
PO Box 709
Parker, AZ 85344
520-669-6118

Mohave County Attorney's Office
315 N. 4th St.
PO Box 7000
Kingman, AZ 86402-7000
520-753-0719

Navajo County Attorney's Office
PO Box 668
Holbrook, AZ 86025
520-524-4026

Pima County Attorney's Office
1400 Great American Tower
32 N. Stone
Tucson, AZ 85701
520-740-5733

Pinal County Attorney's Office
PO Box 887
Florence, AZ 85232
520-868-6271

Santa Cruz County Attorney's Office
2100 N. Congress Dr., Ste. 201
Nogales, AZ 85621
520-287-2468

Yavapai County Attorney's Office
Yavapai County Courthouse
Prescott, AZ 86301
520-771-3344

Yuma County Attorney's Office
168 S. Second Ave.
Yuma, AZ 85364
520-329-2270

City Office

Deputy City Attorney
Consumer Affairs Division
Tucson City Attorney's Office
110 E. Pennington St., 2nd Fl.
PO Box 27210
Tucson, AZ 85726-7210
520-791-4886

Arkansas

State Office

Director, Consumer Protection Division
Office of the Attorney General
200 Catlett Prien
323 Center St.
Little Rock, AR 72201
501-682-2341
TDD: 501-682-2014
800-482-8982 (toll-free voice/TDD in AR)

California

State Offices

Director, California Dept. of Consumer Affairs
400 R St., Ste. 3000
Sacramento, CA 95814
916-445-1254 (consumer information)
916-322-1700 (TDD)
800-952-5200 (toll-free in CA)

Bureau of Automotive Repair
California Dept. of Consumer Affairs
10240 Systems Pkwy.
Sacramento, CA 95827
916-445-1254
TDD: 916-322-1700
800-952-5210 (toll-free in CA, auto repair only)

Office of the Attorney General
Public Inquiry Unit
PO Box 944255
Sacramento, CA 94244-2550
916-322-3360
TDD: 916-324-5564
800-952-5225 (toll-free in CA)

County Offices

Commissioner, Alameda County Consumer Affairs
    Commission
4400 MacArthur Blvd.
Oakland, CA 94619
510-535-6444

District Attorney
Contra Costa County District Attorney's Office
725 Court St., 4th Fl.
PO Box 670
Martinez, CA 94553
510-646-4500

Senior Deputy District Attorney
Business Affairs Unit
Fresno County District Attorney's Office
1250 Van Ness Ave., 2nd Fl.
Fresno, CA 93721
209-488-3156

District Attorney
Criminal Section
Kern County District Attorney's Office
1215 Truxtun Ave., 4th Fl.
Bakersfield, CA 93301
805-861-2421

Director, Los Angeles County Dept. of Consumer
    Affairs
500 W. Temple St., Rm. B-96
Los Angeles, CA 90012
213-974-1452 (public)

Director, Citizens Service Office
Marin County Mediation Services
4 Mount Lassen Dr.
San Rafael, CA 94903
415-499-7454

Deputy District Attorney
Consumer Protection Division
Marin County District Attorney's Office
Hall of Justice, Rm. 183
San Rafael, CA 94903
415-499-6450

District Attorney
Mendocino County District Attorney's Office
PO Box 1000
Ukiah, CA 95482
707-463-4211

Monterey County District Attorney
Consumer Protection Division
PO Box 1369
Salinas, CA 93902
408-755-5073

Deputy District Attorney
Consumer Affairs Division
Napa County District Attorney's Office
931 Parkway Mall
PO Box 720
Napa, CA 94559
707-253-4211

Supervising District Attorney
Consumer/Environmental Protection Unit
Orange County District Attorney's Office
405 West 5th Street, Ste. 606
Santa Ana, CA 92701
714-568-1240

Deputy District Attorney
Economic Crime Division
Riverside County District Attorney's Office
4075 Main St.
Riverside, CA 92501
909-275-5400

Supervising Deputy District Attorney
Consumer and Environmental Protection Division
Sacramento County District Attorney's Office
PO Box 749
Sacramento, CA 95812-0749
916-440-6174

Director, Consumer Fraud Division
San Diego County District Attorney's Office
PO Box X-1011
San Diego, CA 92112-4192
619-531-3507 (fraud complaint line)

Consumer Protection Unit
San Francisco County District Attorney's Office
732 Brannan St.
San Francisco, CA 94103
415-552-6400 (public inquiries)
415-553-1814 (complaints)

Consumer Mediator
San Joaquin County District Attorney's Office
222 E. Weber, Rm. 412
PO Box 990
Stockton, CA 95202
209-468-2481

Director, Economic Crime Unit
Consumer Fraud Dept.
County Government Center
1050 Monterey St., Rm. 235
San Luis Obispo, CA 93408
805-781-5856

Deputy in Charge
Consumer Fraud and Environmental Protection Unit
San Mateo County District Attorney's Office
401 Marshall St.
Hall of Justice and Records
Redwood City, CA 94063
415-363-4656

Deputy District Attorney
Consumer Protection Unit
Santa Barbara County District Attorney's Office
1105 Santa Barbara St.
Santa Barbara, CA 93101
805-568-2300

Deputy District Attorney
Consumer Fraud Unit
Santa Clara County District Attorney's Office
70 W. Hedding St., West Wing
San Jose, CA 95110
408-299-8478

Coordinator, Santa Clara County Consumer
   Protection Unit
70 West Hedding St., West Wing, Lower Level
San Jose, CA 95110-1705
408-299-4211

Coordinator, Division of Consumer Affairs
Santa Cruz County District Attorney's Office
701 Ocean St., Rm. 200
Santa Cruz, CA 95060
408-454-2050

Deputy District Attorney
Consumer Affairs Unit
Solano County District Attorney's Office
600 Union Ave.
Fairfield, CA 94533
707-421-6860

Deputy District Attorney
Consumer Fraud Unit
Stanislaus County District Attorney's Office
PO Box 442
Modesto, CA 95353-0442
209-525-5550

Deputy District Attorney
Consumer Affairs Unit
600 Union Ave.
Fairfield, CA 94533
707-421-6860

Deputy District Attorney
Consumer and Environmental Protection Division
Ventura County District Attorney's Office
800 S. Victoria Ave.
Ventura, CA 93009
805-654-3110

Supervising Deputy District Attorney
Special Services Unit
Consumer/Environmental
Yolo County District Attorney's Office
PO Box 245
Woodland, CA 95776
916-666-8424

City Offices

Chief Deputy District Attorney
Special Services Unit
Consumer/Envirnomental
Yolo County District Attorney's Office
PO Box 245
Woodland, CA 95776
916-666-8424

Supervising Deputy City Attorney
Consumer Protection Division
Los Angeles City Attorney's Office
200 N. Main St.
1600 City Hall East
Los Angeles, CA 90012
213-485-4515

Consumer Affairs Specialist
Consumer Protection, Fair Housing and Public
    Rights Unit
1685 Main St., Rm. 310
Santa Monica, CA 90401
310-458-8336
310-458-8370 (Spainish hotline)

Colorado

State Office

Consumer Protection Unit
Office of the Attorney General
1525 Sherman St., 5th Floor
Denver, CO 80203-1760
303-866-5189

County Offices

District Attorney
Archuleta, LaPlata, and San Juan Counties
District Attorney's Office
PO Drawer 3455
Durango, CO 81302
970-247-8850

District Attorney
Boulder County District Attorney's Office
PO Box 471
Boulder, CO 80306
303-441-3700

Chief
Denver District Attorney's Consumer Economic
    Crimes Division
303 W. Colfax Ave., Ste. 1300
Denver, CO 80204
303-640-5956 (administration)
303-640-3557 (complaints)

Chief Deputy District Attorney
Economic Crime Division
El Paso and Teller Counties District Attorney's Office
105 E. Vermijo, Ste. 205
Colorado Springs, CO 80903-2083
719-520-6002

District Attorney
Pueblo County District Attorney's Office
210 W. 8th Street, Ste. 801
Pueblo, CO 81003
719-583-6030

Chief Investigator
Weld County District Attorney's Consumer Office
PO Box 1167
Greeley, CO 80632
970-356-4010

Connecticut

State Offices

Commissioner, Dept. of Consumer Protection
165 Capitol Ave.
Hartford, CT 06106
860-566-2534
800-842-2649 (toll-free in CT)

Assistant Attorney General
Antitrust/Consumer Protection
Office of Attorney General
110 Sherman St.
Hartford, CT 06015
860-566-5374

City Office

Director, Middletown Office of Consumer Protection
City Hall
245 DeKoven Dr.
PO Box 1300
Middletown, CT 06457
860-344-3491
TDD: 860-344-3521

Delaware

State Offices

Director, Consumer Protection Unit
Department of Justice
820 N. French St.
Wilmington, DE 19801
302-577-3250

Deputy Attorney General
Fraud and Consumer Protection Unit
Office of the Attorney General
820 N. French St.
Wilmington, DE 19801
302-577-2500

District of Columbia

Director, Dept. of Consumer and Regulatory Affairs
614 H St., N.W.
Washington, DC 20001
202-727-7120

Florida

State Offices

Director, Dept. of Agriculture and Consumer
        Services
Division of Consumer Services
407 South Calhoun St.
Mayo Bldg., 2nd Floor
Tallahassee, FL 32399-0800
904-488-2221
800-435-7352 (toll-free in FL)

Chief, Consumer Litigation Section
110 S.E. 6th St.
Fort Lauderdale, FL 33301
954-712-4600

Assistant Deputy Attorney General
Economic Crimes Division
Office of the Attorney General
110 S.E. 6th St.
Fort Lauderdale, FL 33301
954-712-4600

County Offices

Director, Broward County Consumer Affairs Division
115 S. Andrews Ave.
Annex Room A460
Fort Lauderdale, FL 33301
305-765-5355

Consumer Advocate
Metropolitan Dade County
Consumer Protection Division
140 W. Flagler St., Ste. 902
Miami, FL 33130
305-375-4222

Chief, Dade County Economic Crime Unit
Office of the State's Attorney
1350 N.W. 12th Ave., 5th Floor
Graham Building
Miami, FL 33136-2111
305-547-0671

Director, Hillsborough County Commerce Dept.
Consumer Protection Unit
PO Box 1110
Tampa, FL 33601
813-272-6750

Chief, Orange County Consumer Fraud Unit
250 N. Orange Ave.
PO Box 1673
Orlando, FL 32802
407-836-2490

Citizens Intake
Office of the State's Attorney
401 N. Dixie Highway, Ste. 1600
West Palm Beach, FL 33401
407-355-7108

Director, Palm Beach County Division of Consumer
     Affairs
50 S. Military Tr., Ste. 201
West Palm Beach, FL 33415
561-233-4820

Consumer Affairs/Code Compliance Manager
7530 Little Rd., Ste. 140
New Port Richey, FL 34654
813-847-8110

Director, Pinellas County Office of Consumer
     Protection
PO Box 17268
Clearwater, FL 34622-0268
813-464-6219

City Offices

Chief of Consumer Affairs
City of Jacksonville
Division of Consumer Affairs
421 W. Church St., Ste. 404
Jacksonville, FL 32202
904-630-3667

Department Secretary
Lauderhill Consumer Protection Board
1176 N.W. 42nd Way
Lauderhill, FL 33313
954-321-2456

Georgia

State Office

Administrator
Governor's Office of Consumer Affairs
2 Martin Luther King, Jr. Dr., S.E., Ste. 356
Atlanta, GA 30334
404-656-3790
800-869-1123 (toll-free in GA)

Hawaii

State Offices

Executive Director, Office of Consumer Protection
Dept. of Commerce and Consumer Affairs
235 S. Beretania St., Rm. 801
PO Box 3767
Honolulu, HI 96813-3767
808-586-2636

Investigator, Office of Consumer Protection
Dept. of Commerce and Consumer Affairs
75 Aupuni St.
Hilo, HI 96720
808-974-6230

Investigator, Office of Consumer Protection
Dept. of Commerce and Consumer Affairs
54 High St.
P.O. Box 1098
Wailuku, HI 96793
808-984-8244

Idaho

State Office

Deputy Attorney General
Office of the Attorney General
Consumer Protection Unit
650 W. State Street
Boise, ID 83720-0010
208-334-2424
800-432-3545 (toll-free in ID)

Illinois

State Offices

Attorney General
Governor's Office of Citizens Assistance
222 S. College
Springfield, IL 62706
217-782-0244
800-642-3112

Chief, Consumer Protection Division
Office of the Attorney General
100 W. Randolph St., 12th Fl.
Chicago, IL 60601
312-814-3000
TDD: 312-793-2852

Bureau Chief
Consumer Fraud Bureau
100 W. Randolph St., 13th Fl.
Chicago, IL 60601
312-814-3580
TDD: 312-814-3374
800-386-5438 (toll-free in IL)

Regional Offices

Assistant Attorney General
Carbondale Regional Office
Office of the Attorney General
1001 E. Main Professional Park East
Carbondale, IL 62901
618-457-3505
618-457-4421 (TDD)

Assistant Attorney General
Champaign Regional Office
34 E. Main St.
Champaign, IL 61820
217-333-7691 (voice/TDD)
800-243-0618 (toll-free)

Assistant Attorney General and Chief
Consumer Fraud Bureau
Office of the Attorney General
500 S. Second St.

Springfield, IL 62706
217-782-9020
800-252-8666 (toll-free in IL)
800-386-5438 (toll-free in Chicago)

County Offices

Supervisor, Consumer Fraud Division-303
Cook County Office of the State's Attorney
303 Daley Center
Chicago, IL 60602
312-345-2400

State's Attorney
Madison County Office of the State's Attorney
157 N. Main, Ste. 402
Edwardsville, IL 62025
618-692-6280

City Offices

Commissioner, Chicago Dept. of Consumer Services
121 N. LaSalle St., Rm. 808
Chicago, IL 60602
312-744-4006
312-744-9385 (TDD)

Administrator, Des Plaines Consumer Protection
          Commission
1420 Miner St.
Des Plaines, IL 60016
847-391-5378

Indiana

State Office

Chief Counsel and Director
Consumer Protection Division
Office of the Attorney General
Indiana Gov't Center S., 5th Fl.
402 W. Washington St.
Indianapolis, IN 46204
317-232-6330
800-382-5516 (toll-free in IN)

County Office

Marion County Prosecuting Attorney
560 City-County Building
200 E. Washington St.
Indianapolis, IN 46204-3363
317-327-5338

Iowa

State Office

Assistant Attorney General
Consumer Protection Division
Office of the Attorney General
1300 E. Walnut St., 2nd Fl.
Des Moines, IA 50319
515-281-5926

Kansas

State Office

Deputy Attorney General
Consumer Protection Division
Office of the Attorney General
301 W. 10th
Kansas Judicial Center
Topeka, KS 66612-1597
913-296-3751
800-432-2310 (toll-free in KS)

County Office

Head, Consumer Fraud Division
Johnson County District Attorney's Office
Johnson County Courthouse
PO Box 728
Olathe, KS 66051
913-764-8484, ext. 5287

City Office

City Attorney's Office
215 S.E. 7th St.
Topeka, KS 66603
913-368-3885

Kentucky

State Offices

Director, Consumer Protection Division
Office of the Attorney General
1024 Capital Center Dr.
PO Box 2000
Frankfort, KY 40601-2000
502-573-2200

Administrator, Consumer Protection Division
Office of the Attorney General
107 S. 4th St.
Louisville, KY 40202
502-595-3262

Louisiana

State Office

Chief, Consumer Protection Section
Office of the Attorney General
1 America Pl.
PO Box 94095
Baton Rouge, LA 70804-9095
504-342-9638

County Office

Chief, Consumer Protection Division
Jefferson Parish District Attorney's Office
5th Floor, Gretna Courthouse Annex
Gretna, LA 70053
504-364-3644

Maine

State Offices

Director, Office of Consumer Regulation
State House Station
Augusta, ME 04333-0035
207-624-8527
800-332-8529 (toll-free in ME)

Chief, Consumer and Antitrust Division
Office of the Attorney General
State House Station No. 6
Augusta, ME 04333
207-626-8849 (9 AM–1 PM)

Maryland

State Offices

Chief, Consumer Protection Division
Office of the Attorney General
200 St. Paul Pl.
Baltimore, MD 21202-2021
410-528-8662 (9 AM–3 PM)
410-576-6372 (TDD in Baltimore area)

Director, Licensing & Consumer Services
Motor Vehicle Administration
6601 Ritchie Hwy., N.E.
Glen Burnie, MD 21062
301-768-7535

Consumer Affairs Specialist
Eastern Shore Branch Office
Consumer Protection Division
Office of the Attorney General
201 Baptist St., Ste. 30
Salisbury, MD 21801-4976
410-543-6642

Director, Western Maryland Branch Office
Consumer Protection Division
Office of the Attorney General
138 E. Antietam St., Ste. 210
Hagerstown, MD 21740-5684
301-791-4780

County Offices

Administrator, Howard County Office of Consumer
    Affairs
6751 Columbia Gateway Dr.
Columbia, MD 21046
410-313-6420
410-313-6401 (TDD)

Acting Director, Montgomery County Office of
    Consumer Affairs
100 Maryland Ave., 3rd Fl.
Rockville, MD 20850
301-217-7373

Executive Director
Prince George's County Office of Business and
    Regulatory Affairs
County Administration Bldg., Ste. L15
Upper Marlboro, MD 20772
301-952-5323
301-925-5167 (TDD)

Massachusetts

State Offices

Chief, Consumer and Antitrust Division
Dept. of the Attorney General
1 Ashburton Place
Boston, MA 02108
617-727-2200
(information and referral to local consumer offices
    that work in conjunction with the Dept. of
    the Attorney General)

Secretary, Executive Office of Consumer Affairs and
    Business Regulation
One Ashburton Place, Rm. 1411
Boston, MA 02108
617-727-7780 (information and referral only)

Assistant Attorney, Western Massachusetts Consumer
    Protection Division
Dept. of the Attorney General
436 Dwight St.
Springfield, MA 01103
413-784-1240

County Offices

Case Coordinator
Consumer Fraud Prevention
North Western District Attorney's Office
238 Main St.
Greenfield, MA 01301
413-774-5102

Director, Consumer Fraud Prevention
Hampshire County District Attorney's Office
1 Court Square
Northhampton, MA 01060
413-586-9225

Director
Consumer Council of Worcester County
484 Main St., 2nd Floor
Worcester, MA 01608-1690
508-754-1176

City Offices

Commissioner, Mayor's Office of Consumer Affairs
        and Licensing
Boston City Hall, Rm. 817
Boston, MA 02201
617-635-4165

Director, Consumer Information Center
Springfield Action Commission
PO Box 1449 Main Office
Springfield, MA 01101
413-263-6513
(Hampton and Hampshire Counties)

Michigan

State Offices

Assistant in Charge
Consumer Protection Division
Office of the Attorney General
PO Box 30213
Lansing, MI 48909
517-373-1140

Director
Bureau of Automotive Regulation
Michigan Dept. of State
Lansing, MI 48918-1200
517-373-4777
800-292-4204 (toll-free in MI)

County Offices

Chief Investigator
Bay County Consumer Protection Unit
Bay County Building
Bay City, MI 48708-5994
517-895-4139

Director, Consumer Protection Dept.
Macomb County
Office of the Prosecuting Attorney
Macomb Court Building, 6th Fl.
Mt. Clemens, MI 48043
810-469-5350
810-466-8714 (TDD)

City Office

Director, City of Detroit
Dept. of Consumer Affairs
1600 Cadillac Tower
Detroit, MI 48226
313-224-3508

Minnesota

State Office

Director, Consumer Services Division
Office of the Attorney General
1400 NCL Tower, 445 Minnesota St.
St. Paul, MN 55101
612-296-3353

County Office

Citizen Protection Unit
Hennepin County Attorney's Office
C-2000 County Government Center
Minneapolis, MN 55487
612-348-4528

City Office

Director
Minneapolis Dept. of Licenses & Consumer Services
One C City Hall
Minneapolis, MN 55415
612-673-2080

Mississippi

State Offices

Special Assistant Attorney General
Director, Office of Consumer Protection
PO Box 22947
Jackson, MS 39225-2947
601-359-4231
800-281-4418 (toll-free in MS)

Director, Bureau of Regulatory Services
Dept. of Agriculture and Commerce
121 N. Jefferson St.
PO Box 1609
Jackson, MS 39201
601-354-7063

Missouri

State Office

Chief Counsel, Consumer Protection Division
Office of the Attorney General
PO Box 899
Jefferson City, MO 65102
573-751-3321
800-392-8222 (toll-free in MO)

Montana

State Office

Chief Legal Counsel, Consumer Affairs Unit
Dept. of Commerce
1424 Ninth Ave.
Box 200501
Helena, MT 59620-0501
406-444-4312

Nebraska

State Office

Assistant Attorney General
Consumer Protection Division
Dept. of Justice
2115 State Capitol
PO Box 98920
Lincoln, NE 68509
402-471-2682

Nevada

State Offices

Commissioner of Consumer Affairs
Dept. of Business and Industry
1850 E. Sahara, Ste. 101
Las Vegas, NV 89158
702-486-7355
800-326-5202 (toll-free in NV)
702-486-7901 (TDD)

Supervisory Compliance Investigator
Consumer Affairs Division
Dept. of Business and Industry
4600 Kietzke Lane, B-113
Reno, NV 89502
702-688-1800
800-326-5202 (toll-free in NV)
702-486-7901 (TDD)

New Hampshire

State Office

Chief, Consumer Protection and Antitrust Bureau
Office of the Attorney General
33 Capitol St.
Concord, NH 03301
603-271-3641

New Jersey

State Offices

Director, Division of Consumer Affairs
124 Halsey St.
PO Box 45027
Newark, NJ 07101
201-504-6534

Deputy Attorney General
New Jersey Division of Law
PO Box 45029
124 Halsey St., 5th Fl.
Newark, NJ 07101
201-648-7579

County Offices

Director, Atlantic County Consumer Affairs
1333 Atlantic Ave., 8th Fl.
Atlantic City, NJ 08401
609-345-6700

Director, Bergen County Division of Consumer
    Protection
21 Main St., Rm. 101-E
Hackensack, NJ 07601-7000
201-646-2650

Director, Burlington County Office of Consumer
    Affairs
49 Rancocas Rd.
Mount Holly, NJ 08060
609-265-5058

Director, Camden County Office of Consumer
    Protection/Weights and Measures
Jefferson House
Lakeland Road
Blackwood, NJ 08012
609-374-6161

Director, Cape May County Consumer Affairs
4 Moore Road
Cape May Court House, NJ 08210
609-463-6475

Director, Cumberland County Dept. of Consumer
    Affairs and Weights and Measures
788 E. Commerce St.
Bridgeton, NJ 08302
609-453-2203

Sr. Contact Person, Essex County Consumer Services
15 South Munn Ave., 2nd Fl.
E. Orange, NJ 07018
201-678-8071
201-678-8928

Director, Gloucester County Dept. of Consumer
    Protection/Weights & Measures
152 N. Broad. St.
Woodbury, NJ 08096
609-853-3349
609-853-3358
609-848-6616 (TDD)

Director, Hudson County Division of Consumer
    Affairs
595 Newark Ave.
Jersey City, NJ 07306
201-795-6295

Director, Hunterdon County Consumer Affairs
PO Box 283
Lebanon, NJ 08833
908-236-2249

Division Chief
Mercer County Consumer Affairs
640 S. Broad St., Rm. 229
PO Box 8068
Trenton, NJ 08650-0068
609-989-6671

Director, Middlesex County Consumer Affairs
10 Corporate Place South
Piscataway, NJ 08854
908-463-6000
908-463-6008

Director, Monmouth County Consumer Affairs
50 E. Main St.
PO Box 1255
Freehold, NJ 07728-1255
908-431-7900

Director, Ocean County Consumer Affairs
1027 Hooper Ave., Bldg. 2
Toms River, NJ 08754-2191
908-929-2105
908-506-5330

Director, Passaic County Consumer Affairs
401 Grand, Rm. 532
Paterson, NJ 07505
201-881-4547

Somerset County Consumer Affairs
County Administration Building
PO Box 3000
Somerville, NJ 08876-1262
908-231-7000, ext. 7400

Director, Union County Consumer Affairs
300 North Ave. East
PO Box 186
Westfield, NJ 07091
201-654-9840

City Offices

Director, Cinnaminson Consumer Affairs
Municipal Building
PO Box 2100
1621 Riverton Rd.
Cinnaminson, NJ 08077
609-829-6000

Director, Clark Consumer Affairs
430 Westfield Ave.
Clark, NJ 07066
908-388-3600

Director, Elizabeth Consumer Affairs
City Hall
50-60 W. Scott Plaza
Elizabeth, NJ 07201
908-820-4183

Director, Livingston Consumer Affairs
357 S. Livingston Ave.
Livingston, NJ 07039
201-535-7976

Director, Maywood Consumer Affairs
459 Maywood Ave.
Maywood, NJ 07607
201-845-2900
201-845-5749

Director, Middlesex Borough Consumer Affairs
1200 Mountain Ave.
Middlesex, NJ 08846
908-356-8090

Director, Mountainside Consumer Affairs
1455 Coles Ave.
Mountainside, NJ 07092
908-232-6600

Deputy Mayor, Director Consumer Affairs
Municipal Building
4233 Kennedy Blvd.
N. Bergen, NJ 07047
210-392-2157
201-330-7291
201-330-7292

Director, Nutley Consumer Affairs
Public Safety Building
228 Chestnut St.
Nutley, NJ 07110
201-284-4936

Investigator, Perth Amboy Consumer Affairs
City Hall
1 Olive St.
Perth Amboy, NJ 08861
908-826-0290, ext. 72

Director, Plainfield Action Services
510 Watchtung Ave.
Plainfield, NJ 07060
908-753-3519

Director, Secaucus Dept. of Consumer Affairs
Municipal Government Center
Secaucus, NJ 07094
201-330-2019

Director, Union Township Consumer Affairs
Municipal Building
1976 Morris Ave.
Union, NJ 07083
908-688-6763

Director, Wayne Township Consumer Affairs
475 Valley Rd.
Wayne, NJ 07470
201-694-1800, ext. 3290

Director, Weehawken Consumer Affairs
400 Park Ave.
Weehawken, NJ 07087
201-319-6005

Woodbridge Consumer Affairs
Municipal Building
One Main Street
Woodbridge, NJ 07095
908-634-4500, ext. 6058

New Mexico

State Office

Consumer Protection Division
Office of the Attorney General
PO Drawer 1508
Santa Fe, NM 87504
505-827-6060
800-678-1508 (toll-free in NM)

New York

State Offices

Deputy Chief, Bureau of Consumer Fraud and
    Protection
Office of the Attorney General
State Capitol
Albany, NY 12224
518-474-5481
800-771-7755 (toll-free hotline)

Chairperson and Executive Director
New York State Consumer Protection Board
5 Empire State Plaza, Ste. 2101
Albany, NY 12223-1556
518-474-8583

Assistant Attorney General
Bureau of Consumer Fraud and Protection
Office of the Attorney General
120 Broadway
New York, NY 10271
212-416-8345
212-416-8940 (TDD)
800-771-7755 (toll-free)

Regional Offices

Assistant Attorney General in Charge
Central New York Regional Office
44 Hawley St., 17th Fl.
State Office Bldg.
Binghamton, NY 13901
607-721-8779

Assistant Attorney General in Charge
Buffalo Regional Office
Office of the Attorney General
65 Court St.
Buffalo, NY 14202
716-847-7184
800-771-7755 (toll-free)

Assistant Attorney General in Charge
Poughkeepsie Regional Office
Office of the Attorney General
235 Main St.
Poughkeepsie, NY 12601
914-485-3920
800-771-7755 (toll-free)

Assistant Attorney General in Charge
Rochester Regional Office
Office of the Attorney General
144 Exchange Blvd.
Rochester, NY 14614
716-546-7430
716-327-3249 (TDD)
800-771-7755 (toll-free)

Assistant Attorney General in Charge
Suffolk Regional Office
Office of the Attorney General
300 Motor Pkwy.
Hauppauge, NY 11788
516-231-2400

Assistant Attorney General in Charge
Syracuse Regional Office
Office of the Attorney General
615 Erie Blvd. West, Ste. 102
Syracuse, NY 13204-2465
315-448-4848
800-771-7755

Assistant Attorney General in Charge
Utica Regional Office
Office of the Attorney General
207 Genesee St.
Utica, NY 13501
315-793-2225
315-793-2228
800-771-7755 (toll-free)

County Offices

Director, Dutchess County Dept. of Consumer Affairs
38-A Dutchess Turnpike
Poughkeepsie, NY 12603
914-486-2947

Assistant District Attorney
Consumer Fraud Bureau
Erie County District Attorney's Office
25 Delaware Ave.
Buffalo, NY 14202
716-858-2424

Commissioner, Nassau County Office of Consumer
    Affairs
160 Old Country Rd.
Mineola, NY 11501
516-571-2600

Executive Director
New Justice Conflict Resolution Services Inc.
1153 W. Fayette St., Ste. 301
Syracuse, NY 13204
315-471-4676

District Attorney, Orange County District Attorney's
    Office
255 Main St.
County Gov't Center
Goshen, NY 10924
914-294-5471

Commissioner
Rockland County Office of Consumer Protection
County Office Building
18 New Hempstead Rd.
New City, NY 10956
914-638-5280

Director, Steuben County Dept. of Weights,
    Measures and Consumer Affairs
3 E. Pulteney Square
Bath, NY 14810
607-776-9631
607-776-9631, ext. 2406 (voice/TDD)

Commissioner, Suffolk County Executive's Office of
    Consumer Affairs
N. County Complex, Bldg. 340
Veterans Memorial Highway
Hauppauge, NY 11788
516-853-4600

Director, Ulster County Consumer Fraud Bureau
PO Box 1800
Kingston, NY 12402
914-339-5680

Chief, Frauds Bureau
Westchester County
District Attorney's Office
111 Grove St.
White Plains, NY 10601
914-285-3414

Deputy Director, Westchester County Dept. of
    Consumer Protection
112 E. Post Rd., 4th Fl.
White Plains, NY 10601
914-285-3155

City Offices

Citizen Advocate, Office of Citizen Services
Babylon Town Hall
200 E. Sunrise Highway
281 Phelps Lane
Lindenhurst, NY 11757
516-957-7474

Town of Colonie Consumer Protection
Memorial Town Hall
Newtonville, NY 12128
518-783-2790

Commissioner, Mt. Vernon Office of Consumer
    Protection
City Hall
Mt. Vernon, NY 10550
914-665-2433

Commissioner, New York City Dept. of Consumer
    Affairs
42 Broadway
New York, NY 10004
212-487-4401
212-487-4465 (TDD)

Director, Queens Neighborhood Office
New York City Dept. of Consumer Affairs
120-55 Queens Blvd., Rm. 301A
Kew Gardens, NY 11424
718-261-2990

Schenectady Bureau of Consumer Protection
City Hall, Rm. 204
Jay St.
Schenectady, NY 12305
518-382-5061

Director, Yonkers Office of Consumer Protection,
    Weights and Measures
201 Palisade Ave.
Yonkers, NY 10703
914-377-6807

North Carolina

State Office

Special Deputy Attorney General Consumer
    Protection Section
Office of the Attorney General
Raney Building
PO Box 629
Raleigh, NC 27602
919-733-7741

North Dakota

State Offices

Office of the Attorney General
600 E. Blvd. Ave.
Bismarck, ND 58505
701-224-2210
800-472-2600 (toll-free in ND)

Director, Consumer Fraud Section
Office of the Attorney General
600 E. Blvd. Ave.
Bismarck, ND 58505
701-224-3404
800-472-2600 (toll-free in ND)

County Office

Executive Director
Community Action Agency
1013 N. 5th St.
Grand Forks, ND 58201
701-746-5431

Ohio

State Offices

Consumer Frauds and Crimes Section
Office of the Attorney General
30 E. Broad. St.
State Office Tower, 25th Fl.
Columbus, OH 43266-0410
614-466-4986 (complaints)
614-466-1393 (TDD)
800-282-0515 (toll-free in OH)

Office of Consumers' Counsel
77 S. High St., 15th Fl.
Columbus, OH 43266-0550
614-466-9605 (voice/TDD)
800-282-9448 (toll-free in OH)

County Offices

Director, Corrupt Activities Protection Unit
Franklin County Office of Prosecuting Attorney
369 S. High St.
Columbus, OH 43215
614-462-3555

Assistant Prosecuting Attorney
Montgomery County Fraud and Economic Crimes
    Division
301 W. 3rd St.
Dayton Montgomery County Courts Building
Dayton, OH 45402
513-225-4747

Prosecuting Attorney
Portage County Office of the Prosecuting Attorney
466 S. Chestnut St.
Ravenna, OH 44266-3000
216-296-4593

Prosecuting Attorney
Summit County Office of the Prosecuting Attorney
53 University Ave.
Akron, OH 44308-1680
330-643-2800

City Offices

Department of Neighborhood Services
Division of Human Services
City Hall, Rm. 126
801 Plum St.
Cincinnati, OH 45202
513-352-3971

Director, Youngstown Office of Consumer Affairs
    and Weights and Measures
26 S. Phelps St.
City Hall
Youngstown, OH 44503-1318
216-742-8884

Oklahoma

State Offices

Assistant Attorney General
Office of the Attorney General
4545 Lincoln Blvd., Ste. 260
Oklahoma City, OK 73105
405-521-4274
405-521-2029 (consumer hotline)

Administrator, Dept. of Consumer Credit
4545 Lincoln Blvd., Ste. 104
Oklahoma City, OK 73105-3408
405-521-3653

Oregon

State Office

Attorney in Charge
Financial Fraud Section
Dept. of Justice
1162 Court St. N.E.
Salem, OR 97310
503-378-4732

Pennsylvania

State Offices

Director, Bureau of Consumer Protection
Office of the Attorney General
Strawberry Square, 14th Fl.
Harrisburg, PA 17120
717-787-9707
800-441-2555 (toll-free in PA)

Consumer Advocate
Office of Consumer Advocate–Utilities
Office of the Attorney General
1425 Strawberry Square
Harrisburg, PA 17120
717-783-5048 (utilities only)

Deputy Attorney General
Bureau of Consumer Protection
Office of the Attorney General
1251 S. Cedar Crest Blvd., Ste. 309
Allentown, PA 18103
215-821-6690

Director, Bureau of Consumer Services
Pennsylvania Public Utility Commission
PO Box 3265
203 N. Office Building
Harrisburg, PA 17105-3265
717-787-1740
800-782-1110 (toll-free in PA)

Deputy Attorney General
Bureau of Consumer Protection
Office of the Attorney General
919 State St., Rm. 203
Erie, PA 16501
814-871-4371

Sr. Deputy Attorney General
Bureau of Consumer Protection
Office of the Attorney General
171 Lovell Ave., Ste. 202
Ebensburg, PA 15931
814-949-7900
800-4412555 (toll-free in PA)

Deputy Attorney General
Bureau of Consumer Protection
Office of the Attorney General
21 S. 12th St., 2nd Fl.
Philadelphia, PA 19107
215-560-2414
800-441-2555 (toll-free in PA)

Deputy Attorney General
Bureau of Consumer Protection
Office of the Attorney General
Manor Complex, 6th Fl.
564 Forbes Ave.
Pittsburgh, PA 15219
412-565-5394
800-441-2555 (toll-free in PA)

Deputy Attorney General
Bureau of Consumer Protection
Office of the Attorney General
214 Samters Bldg.
101 Penn Ave.
Scranton, PA 18503-2025
717-963-4913

Regional Office
Office of the Attorney General
Bureau of Consumer Protection
132 Kline Village
Harrisburg, PA 17104
717-787-7109

County Offices

Director, Beaver County Alliance for Consumer
    Protection
699 Fifth St.
Beaver, PA 15009-1997
412-728-7267

Director/Chief Sealer, Bucks County Consumer
    Protection, Weights and Measures
50 N. Main
Doylestown, PA 18901
215-348-7442

Director, Chester County Bureau of Consumer
    Protection, Weights and Measures
Government Services Center, Ste. 390
601 Westtown Rd.
West Chester, PA 19382-4547
610-344-6150
800-692-1100 (toll-free in PA)

Consumer Mediator, Cumberland County Consumer
    Affairs
One Courthouse Square
Carlisle, PA 17013-3330
717-240-6180

Director, Delaware County Office of Consumer
    Affairs, Weights and Measures
Government Center Building
Second and Olive Sts.
Media, PA 19063
610-891-4865

Director, Montgomery County Consumer Affairs
    Dept.
County Courthouse
Norristown, PA 19404
610-278-3565

City Office

Chief, Economic Crime Unit
Philadelphia District Attorney's Office
1421 Arch St.
Philadelphia, PA 19102
215-686-8750

Puerto Rico

Secretary, Dept. of Consumer Affairs (DACO)
Minillas Station, PO Box 41059
Santurce, PR 00940-1059
787-721-0940
787-726-6570

Secretary, Dept. of Justice
PO Box 192
San Juan, PR 00902
787-721-2900

Rhode Island

State Offices

President, Consumer Credit Counseling Service
535 Centerville Rd., Ste. 103
Warwick, RI 02886
401-732-1800
800-781-2227 (toll-free in RI)

Director, Consumer Protection Division
Dept. of the Attorney General
72 Pine St.
Providence, RI 02903
401-274-4400
401-453-0410 (TDD)
800-852-7776 (toll-free in RI)

South Carolina

State Offices

Sr. Assistant Attorney General
Consumer Fraud and Antitrust Section
Office of the Attorney General
PO Box 11549
Columbia, SC 29211
803-734-3970

Administrator, Consumer Advocate
Dept. of Consumer Affairs
PO Box 5757
Columbia, SC 29250-5757
803-734-9452
803-734-9455 (TDD)
800-922-1594 (toll-free in SC)

State Ombudsman
Office of Executive Policy and Program
1205 Pendleton St., Rm. 308
Columbia, SC 29201
803-734-0457
803-734-1147 (TDD)

South Dakota

State Office

Assistant Attorney General
Division of Consumer Affairs
Office of the Attorney General
500 E. Capitol
State Capitol Building
Pierre, SD 57501-5070
605-773-4400

Tennessee

State Offices

Deputy Attorney General
Antitrust and Consumer Protection Division
Office of the Attorney General
450 James Robertson Pkwy.
Nashville, TN 37243-0485
615-741-2672

Director, Division of Consumer Affairs
Dept. of Commerce and Insurance
500 James Robertson Pkwy., 5th Fl.
Nashville, TN 37243-0600
615-741-4737
800-342-8385 (toll-free in TN)
800-422-CLUB (toll-free health club hotline in TN)

Texas

State Offices

Assistant Attorney General and Chief, Consumer
  Protection Division
Office of the Attorney General
Supreme Court Building
PO Box 12548
Austin, TX 78711
512-463-2070

Assistant Attorney General
Consumer Protection Division
Office of the Attorney General
714 Jackson St., Ste. 700
Dallas, TX 75202-4506
214-742-8944

Assistant Attorney General
Consumer Protection Division
Office of the Attorney General
6090 Surety Dr., Rm. 260
El Paso, TX 79905
915-772-9476

Assistant Attorney General
Consumer Protection Division
Office of the Attorney General
1019 Congress St., Ste. 1550
Houston, TX 77002-1702
713-223-5886

Assistant Attorney General
Consumer Protection Division
Office of the Attorney General
1208 14th St., Ste. 900
Lubbock, TX 79401-3997
806-747-5238

Assistant Attorney General
Consumer Protection Division
Office of the Attorney General
3600 N. 23rd St., Ste. 305
McAllen, TX 78501-1685
512-682-4547

Assistant Attorney General
Consumer Protection Division
Office of the Attorney General
115 E. Travis St., Ste. 925
San Antonio, TX 78205-1607
512-225-4191

Office of Consumer Protection
State Board of Insurance
816 Congress Ave., Ste. 1400
Austin, TX 78701-2430
512-322-4143

County Office

Assistant District Attorney and Chief of Dallas
        County District Attorney's Office
Specialized Crime Division
133 N. Industrial Blvd., LB 19
Dallas, TX 75207-4313
214-653-3820

Assistant District Attorney and Chief Harris County
        Consumer Fraud Division
Office of the District Attorney
201 Fannin, Ste. 200
Houston, TX 77002-1901
713-221-5836

City Office

Director, Dallas Consumer Protection Division
Health and Human Services Dept.
320 E. Jefferson Blvd., Ste. 312
Dallas, TX 75203
214-948-4400

Utah

State Offices

Director, Division of Consumer Protection
Dept. of Commerce
160 E. 3rd S.
PO Box 45802
Salt Lake City, UT 84145-0802
801-530-6601

Assistant Attorney General for Consumer Affairs
Office of the Attorney General
115 State Capitol
Salt Lake City, UT 84114
801-538-1331

Vermont

State Offices

Assistant Attorney General and Chief, Public
        Protection Division
Office of the Attorney General
109 State St.
Montpelier, VT 05609-1001
802-828-3171

Supervisor, Consumer Assurance Section
Dept. of Agriculture, Food and Market
120 State St.
Montpelier, VT 05620-2901
802-828-2436

Virgin Islands

Commissioner, Dept. of Licensing and Consumer
        Affairs
Consumer Affairs
Property and Procurement Building
Subbase #1, Rm. 205
St. Thomas, VI 00802
809-774-3130

Virginia

State Offices

Chief, Antitrust and Consumer Litigation Section
Office of the Attorney General
Supreme Court Building
101 N. Eighth St.
Richmond, VA 23219
804-786-2116
800-451-1525 (toll-free in VA)

Director, Division of Consumer Affairs
Dept. of Agriculture and Consumer Services
Rm. 101, Washington Building
1100 Bank St.
PO Box 1163
Richmond, VA 23219
804-786-2042

Investigator, Northern Virginia Branch
Office of Consumer Affairs
Dept. of Agriculture and Consumer Services
100 N. Washington St., Ste. 412
Falls Church, VA 22046
703-532-1613

County Offices

Section Chief, Office of Citizen and Consumer Affairs
#1 Court House Plaza, Ste. 314
2100 Clarendon Blvd.
Arlington, VA 22201
703-358-3260

Director, Fairfax County Dept. of Consumer Affairs
3959 Pender Dr., Ste. 200
Fairfax, VA 22030-6093
703-246-5949
703-591-3260 (TDD)

Administrator, Prince William County Office of
    Consumer Affairs
4370 Ridgewood Center Dr.
Prince William, VA 22192-9201
703-792-7370

City Offices

Director, Alexandria Office of Citizens' Assistance
City Hall
PO Box 178
Alexandria, VA 22313
703-838-4350
703-838-5056 (TDD)

Coordinator, Division of Consumer Affairs
City Hall
Norfolk, VA 23501
804-441-2821
804-441-2000 (TDD)

Assistant to the City Manager
Roanoke Consumer Protection Division
364 Municipal Building
215 Church Ave., S.W.
Roanoke, VA 24011
703-981-2583

Director, Consumer Affairs Division
Office of the Commonwealth's Attorney
3500 Virginia Beach Blvd., Ste. 304
Virginia Beach, VA 23452
804-431-4610

Washington

State Offices

Investigator, Consumer and Business Fair Practices
    Division
Office of the Attorney General
111 Olympia Ave., N.E.
Olympia, WA 98501
206-753-6210

Director of Consumer Services
Consumer and Business Fair Practices Division
Office of the Attorney General
900 Fourth Ave., Ste. 2000
Seattle, WA 98164
206-464-6431
800-551-4636 (toll-free in WA)

Chief, Consumer and Business Fair Practices Division
Office of the Attorney General
W. 1116 Riverside Ave.
Spokane, WA 99201
509-456-3123

Contact Person, Consumer and Business Fair
    Practices Division
Office of the Attorney General
1019 Pacific Ave., 3rd Fl.
Tacoma, WA 98402-4411
206-593-2904

City Offices

Director, Dept. of Weights and Measures
3200 Cedar St.
Everett, WA 98201
206-259-8810

Chief Deputy Prosecuting Attorney
Fraud Division
1002 Bank of California
900 4th Ave.
Seattle, WA 98164
206-296-9010

Director, Seattle Dept. of Licenses and Consumer
    Affairs
102 Municipal Building
600 4th Ave.
Seattle, WA 98104-1893
206-684-8484

West Virginia

State Offices

Director, Consumer Protection Division
Office of the Attorney General
812 Quarrier St., 6th Fl.
Charleston, WV 25301
304-348-8986
800-368-8808 (toll-free in WV)

Director, Division of Weights and Measures
Dept. of Labor
1800 Washington St., East
Building #3, Rm. 319
Charleston, WV 25305
304-348-7890

City Office

Director, Dept. of Consumer Protection
PO Box 2749
Charleston, WV 25330
304-348-8172

Wisconsin

State Offices

Administrator, Division of Trade and Consumer
    Protection
Dept. of Agriculture, Trade and Consumer
    Protection
801 W. Badger Rd.
PO Box 8911
Madison, WI 53708
608-266-9836
800-422-7128 (toll-free in WI)

Regional Supervisor, Division of Trade and
    Consumer Protection
Dept. of Agriculture, Trade and Consumer
    Protection
927 Loring St.
Altoona, WI 54720
715-839-3848
800-422-7218 (toll-free in WI)

Regional Supervisor, Division of Trade and
    Consumer Protection
Dept. of Agriculture, Trade and Consumer
    Protection
200 N. Jefferson St., Ste. 146A
Green Bay, WI 54301
414-448-5111
800-422-7128 (toll-free in WI)

Regional Supervisor, Consumer Protection Regional
    Office
Dept. of Agriculture, Trade and Consumer
    Protection
3333 N. Mayfair Rd., Ste. 114
Milwaukee, WI 53222-3288
414-257-8956

Assistant Attorney General
Office of Consumer Protection and Citizen Advocacy
Dept. of Justice
PO Box 7856
Madison, WI 53707-7856
608-266-1852
800-362-8189 (toll-free)

Assistant Attorney General
Office of Consumer Protection
Dept. of Justice
Milwaukee State Office Building
819 N. 6th St., Rm. 520
Milwaukee, WI 53203-1678
414-227-4948
800-362-8189 (toll-free)

County Offices

District Attorney
Marathon County District Attorney's Office
Marathon County Courthouse
Wausau, WI 54401
715-847-5555

Assistant District Attorney
Milwaukee County District Attorney's Office
Consumer Fraud Unit
821 W. State St., Rm. 412
Milwaukee, WI 53233-1485
414-278-4792

Consumer Fraud Investigator
Racine County Sheriff's Dept.
717 Wisconsin Ave.
Racine, WI 53403
414-636-3125

Wyoming

State Office

Assistant Attorney General
Office of the Attorney General
123 State Capitol Building
Cheyenne, WY 82002
307-777-7874

Information in this section was taken from the
Consumers' Resource Handbook, 1992 edition,
U.S. Office of Consumer Affairs.

Index

"Spam," 166
Spending plan, 172–73
State motor vehicle departments,
160
Stolen credit cards, 184
Store charge cards, 177
Subscribers, to credit bureaus, 3, 20
products and services for,
15–16
reporting patterns of, 29, 30

T

Taxing entities, negotiating with,
88–89
Tax liens, 4, 16
"Teaser" interest rates, 179
Telemarketers, 155
Tennessee consumer protection
agencies, 253
Texas consumer protection
agencies, 253–54
Trans Union, 3, 7, 23, 24, 155
credit report, 38–50
sample, 39–47
name removal option, 169
target marketing and, 158
Travel and entertainment cards,
173, 177
Truth in Lending Act, 184

TRW. *See* Experian
Two-cycle average daily balance, 178

U

Used cars, 106
Utah consumer protection agencies,
254
Utility bills, 30

V

Ventura, John, 147
Vermont consumer protection
agencies, 254
Video Privacy Protection Act, 154
Virginia consumer protection
agencies, 254–55
Virgin Islands consumer protection
agency, 254
Visa, 96, 173, 176, 182

W

Wachovia Bank (Atlanta), 179
Washington consumer protection
agencies, 255–56
Web sites, 166, 180

West Virginia consumer protection
agencies, 256
Widows, and credit, 133–36. *See
also* Women, and credit
Willful noncompliance, 217
Wisconsin consumer protection
agencies, 256–57
Women, and credit, 119–36
account-user status
designations, 121–24
advantage of individual credit,
124–25
advice for about-to-be-married
women, 132
advice for women married
before ECOA, 133
building a credit history,
125–32
credit-related problems,
120–21
education and, 121
widows and credit, 133–36
Women's Financial Information
Program, 121
Wyoming consumer protection
agency, 257

Y

Yankelovich, Clancy, Shulman, 153